THE PLAIN OF ESDRAELON

THE HISTORY AND RELIGION OF ISRAEL

BY

W. L. WARDLE

M.A., D.D.

Reader in Old Testament
Manchester University

GREENWOOD PRESS, PUBLISHERS
WESTPORT, CONNECTICUT

Library of Congress Cataloging in Publication Data

Wardle, William Lansdell.
   The history and religion of Israel.

   Reprint of the 1942 ed. published at the Clarendon
Press, Oxford, which was issued as v. 1 of the
Clarendon Bible, Old Testament.
   Includes index.
   1. Jews--History--To 70 A.D. 2. Judaism--
History--To 70 A.D. 3. Bible. O.T.--Chronology.
I. Title. II. Series: The Clarendon Bible ;
v. 1.
DS117.W36   1979   933   78-11741
ISBN 0-313-21016-0

© Oxford University Press 1963.

First published 1936.

This reprint has been authorized by the Oxford University Press.

Reprinted in 1979 by Greenwood Press, Inc.
51 Riverside Avenue, Westport, CT 06880

Printed in the United States of America

10 9 8 7 6 5 4 3 2 1

EDITORS' PREFACE

THE problem of the teaching of Holy Scripture at the present time presents many difficulties. There is a large and growing class of persons who feel bound to recognize that the progress of archaeological and critical studies has made it impossible for them to read, and still more to teach, it precisely in the old way. However strongly they may believe in inspiration, they cannot any longer set before their pupils, or take as the basis of their interpretation, the doctrine of the verbal inspiration of Holy Scripture. It is with the object of meeting the requirements not only of the elder pupils in public schools, their teachers, students in training colleges, and others engaged in education, but also of the clergy and the growing class of the general public, which, we believe, takes an interest in Biblical studies, that the present series has been projected.

The writers will be responsible each for his own contribution only, and their interpretation is based upon the belief that the books of the Bible require to be placed in their historical context, so that, as far as possible, we may recover the sense which they bore when written. Any application of them must rest upon this ground. It is not the writers' intention to set out the latest notions of radical scholars—English or foreign—or even to describe the exact position at which the discussion of the various problems has arrived. The aim of the series is rather to put forward a constructive view of the books and their teaching, taking into consideration and welcoming results as to which there is a large measure of agreement among scholars.

In regard to form, subjects requiring comprehensive treatment are dealt with in Essays, whether forming part of the introduction or interspersed among the notes. The notes themselves are mainly concerned with the subject-matter of the books and the points of interest (historical, doctrinal, &c.) therein presented; they deal with the elucidation of words, allusions, and the like only so far as seems necessary to a proper comprehension of the author's meaning.

THOMAS STRONG
HERBERT WILD *General Editors*
GEORGE H. BOX

AUTHOR'S PREFACE

THIS volume is intended to provide an account first of the history of Israel, and secondly of Israel's religion. The two are, of course, very closely connected, and the treatment of them separately has involved a slight amount of repetition; but it is easier to understand either subject when it is treated as a unity. The planning of the sections is essentially that suggested by the late Canon G. H. Box. A continuation of the history from the point reached in this volume will be found in the volume which he has contributed to the series.

I have given special attention to the earlier periods both of the history and the religion, so that these have been allotted a disproportionate amount of the space. For this there are two reasons. In the first place this volume is part of a series, in the several volumes of which the later periods of the history and religion have been treated with attention to detail, and it seemed advisable to avoid repetition, save in so far as it was necessary to make the treatment of each subject a unity. In the second place the earlier phases of the history and religion are less familiar to most readers, and while, particularly in the case of the religion, they may be of less importance, an understanding of them is necessary to any ordered view of the Old Testament. I hope that the outlines furnished may be filled in by more detailed study of the subject.

Except in small matters I have not presented any original views, and am debtor throughout to the long succession of Old Testament scholars who have brought our knowledge to its present state. I must express my special indebtedness to the late Canon Box, to the General Editors for valuable suggestions, and to the authorities of the Clarendon Press for their patience and courtesy not less than for the valuable contribution they have made in providing the maps and illustrations. My thanks are due also to the Rev. E. C. Barton, of the Epworth Press, for permitting me to make use of material from my Hartley Lecture, *Israel and Babylon*, now out of print. And finally I am grateful to the Rev. Dr. H. G. Meecham, who has read the proofs with great care.

W. L. WARDLE

CONTENTS

THE HISTORY OF ISRAEL

Chapter I. INTRODUCTORY

The new perspective in ancient history	1
Its bearing on the history of Israel	2
The geography of Palestine	2
Palestine a bridge between the great empires	4
Internal features	4
Climate	8
Fertility	10
Effect of geography on politics and religion	11
Early inhabitants of Palestine	12
The great empires and their relation to Palestine	16
Egypt	16
Babylonia	20
The Hittites and Assyria	26

Chapter II. ISRAEL'S ORIGINS

The stories of the patriarchs	29
The migration from Ur	30
The Habiru	31
The Egyptian 'bondage'	32
The Exodus	33
The sojourn at Kadesh	37
The 'Conquest'	38
The Philistines	43

Chapter III. THE PERIOD OF THE JUDGES

What were the 'judges'?	45
Othniel	46
Ehud	47
Shamgar	47
Barak and Deborah	47
Gideon	49
Abimelech	50
Jephthah	51
Samson	51

Chapter IV. THE RISE OF THE KINGDOM

The situation at the end of the 'judges' era	53
Nature of *Samuel* and *Kings*	53
Comparison with situation at the time of Deborah	53
The struggle against the Philistines	54
The idealized portrait of Samuel	56

Contents

Saul	57
David	60
Solomon	70

Chapter V. THE DIVIDED KINGDOMS

Rehoboam	76
The relative importance of the kingdoms	76
The impact of foreign nations on the history	77
History of Ephraim	77
Jeroboam I	77
Nadab; Baasha; Elah; Zimri	78
Omri	79
Ahab	80
The Mesha Stone	82
Ahaziah; Jehoram; (Elisha)	84
Jehu	85
Jehoahaz	90
Jehoash	90
Jeroboam II	90
Zechariah; Shallum; Menahem	91
Pekahiah; Pekah	92
Hoshea	92
The fall of Samaria	93
History of Judah	93
Rehoboam	94
Abijah; Asa	96
Jehoshaphat	97
Jehoram; Ahaziah	97
Athaliah	97
Joash	98
Amaziah	98
Azariah	99
Jotham	100
Ahaz	100
Hezekiah	101
Manasseh	104
Amon; Josiah	104
Jehoahaz	107
Jehoiakim	107
Jehoiachin	108
Zedekiah	110
The fall of Jerusalem	110

Chapter VI. THE EXILE AND THE PERSIAN PERIOD

Number of exiles in Babylonia	113
Condition of exiles in Babylonia	114
Condition of Jews in Judaea	114
Decay of Babylon's power	115
Cyrus and the Return	115
Situation in Jerusalem as revealed by	
Haggai and Zechariah	118
Nehemiah and Ezra	120

Contents

THE RELIGION OF ISRAEL

Chapter VII. THE BACKGROUND OF THE RELIGION

- The religions of Israel 127
- Totemism 128
- Sacred trees 129
- Sacred stones 129
- Sacred streams 129
- 'Holiness' 133
- The ban 135
- Magic 136
- Life after death 139

Chapter VIII. MOSES AND YAHWEH

- Ethical monotheism 141
- Moses the founder 142
- Moses and the Decalogue 142
- Yahweh, the God of Israel 147
- Monotheism outside Israel? 150

Chapter IX. THE INFLUENCE OF CANAANITE RELIGION ON THE RELIGION OF ISRAEL

- Local shrines 152
- Human sacrifice 154
- The Festivals 155
- Teraphim; Ephod; Urim and Thummim . . 156
- The Ark 157
- The local Baal 158
- Reformation under Josiah 160
- The Tyrian Baal in Ephraim and Judah . . 160
- Rechabites; Nazirites 162

Chapter X. LAW

- Israel a covenant people 164
- Development of law from case decisions . . 164
- Decalogue of Exodus 34 166
- Book of the Covenant 167
- Deuteronomic Code 169
- Ezekiel's Code 171
- The Holiness Code 171
- The Priestly Code 172

Chapter XI. THE DEVELOPMENT OF PROPHECY

- The function of a prophet 174
- Early prophecy 174
- Ecstasy in the writing prophets 176
- Use of symbolism by the prophets . . . 177
- Who were the 'false prophets'? 178
- The prophets as statesmen 179
- Attitude of the prophets to the cult . . . 180
- Hebrew prophecy unique? 181

Contents

Chapter XII. THE WRITING PROPHETS

Amos	182
Hosea	184
Isaiah	187
Micah	189
Zephaniah	189
Jeremiah	190
Nahum; Habakkuk	192
Ezekiel	193
Deutero-Isaiah	197
Haggai; Zechariah	199
Trito-Isaiah	200
Malachi	201
Joel	201

Chapter XIII. THE LATER LITERATURE

Proverbs	202
Ecclesiastes	203
Job	203
Daniel	204
The Psalms	205

Chapter XIV. ISRAEL'S DEBT TO OTHER NATIONS

Babylon	208
Egypt	218
Persia	222
Our debt to Israel	223

INDEX　　　225

CHRONOLOGICAL TABLE　　　*at end*

LIST OF ILLUSTRATIONS

Physical Map of Palestine . . . . *Front end-paper*
The Plain of Esdraelon. Photograph, American Colony, Jerusalem.
Frontispiece
Tell Jemmeh, the Mound of Gerar, near Gaza. Photograph by Sir Flinders Petrie 3
Palestine (photographed from the air). Photograph, *The Times*, and Imperial Airways 7
An air-view of the rolling uplands of Moab, in Trans-Jordania. Royal Air Force Official—Crown Copyright reserved . . 9
A cave shelter in northern Galilee. Photograph, *Antiquity* . . 15
The great river Euphrates, from the air. Photograph, *The Times* . 21
The Hittites. A sculptured slab at the Hittite city of Carchemish. Photograph by Dr. D. G. Hogarth 27
An Oasis in the desert. Photograph, London Electrotype Agency . 39
The Philistines. Reliefs from the Temple of Ramses III at Medinet Habu. By courtesy of Dr. H. R. Hall 60
A stone altar found at Gezer with protuberances at each corner. From Macalister, *The Excavation of Gezer*, vol. ii (Palestine Exploration Fund) 71
The Assyrians. A sculptured slab found at Nineveh, representing a camp scene. Staatliche Museen, Berlin 83
The Black Obelisk of Shalmaneser. British Museum . . . 89
Shishak's inscription on the Temple of Amun at Karnak. Photograph, American Colony, Jerusalem 95
The Scythians. A relief showing two Scythian horsemen. From Ebert, *Reallexikon*, vol. ii 106
The Site of Nineveh to-day. Photograph by Dr. R. Campbell Thompson 109
A model of the Ishtar Gate and procession-way at Babylon. Staatliche Museen, Berlin 117
Samaritan Country. Photograph by Miss I. Allen . . . 123
Tree Worship. British Museum 131
Two Babylonian Devils. British Museum 137
A coin of south Palestine showing Yahu as a solar Zeus. From *Zeus*, vol. i, by Dr. A. B. Cook (Cambridge University Press) . . 149
Bas-relief of a Semitic Baal found at Amrith in Phoenicia. From *Catalogue méthodique et raisonné*, by de Clercq and Menant (Librairie Ernest Leroux) 159
The Stele of Hammurabi. British Museum . . . 209
A Babylonian relief, possibly representing the combat of Marduk with Tiamat 213
An Egyptian procession-scene, showing King Amen-Hetep III burning incense before the ark of Amen-Ra' 219
Physical Map of the Near East . . . . *Back end-paper*

CHAPTER I

INTRODUCTORY

The new perspective in ancient history

IN Queen Victoria's reign when people spoke of 'ancient history' they usually meant the history of ancient Greece and Rome, and their view into the past extended to only a few centuries before Christ. It was thought that nothing could be known about the earlier times except what is found in the pages of the Old Testament. Most people supposed that the stories at the beginning of the Bible were to be understood as matter-of-fact history, and some even constructed chronologies of world history based upon them. So in many Bibles dates are given on every page, beginning with 4004 B.C. for the creation—a system which goes back to Archbishop Usher. In this way it was easy to think of the Hebrews as the most important folk in ancient times, and to regard the other nations mentioned in the records as important only for the part they played in connexion with the Hebrews.

During the last fifty years the fields of space and time open to the eye of man have been wonderfully extended. The astronomers with their improved instruments have searched the heavens and shown us that what was once supposed to be the universe is but a small part of the celestial system—or, perhaps, we should more correctly say, one amid many universes. And what astronomers have done in the realm of space has been done to a large extent in the realm of time by the geologists and excavators. The geologists have shown us that the world has been in existence for millions of years, and that men have lived on its surface for scores of thousands of years. The work of the excavators has revealed to us much of the history of men who lived as far back as four thousand years before Christ. This is especially true in the case of the great nations that dwelt in the valleys of the Nile and the Tigris and Euphrates. The digging in Palestine itself has uncovered for us the civilization that existed there before the Hebrews were a nation. If the dark curtain which hid the past from us has not been removed it has at least been pierced so that we can see, in some places distinctly, in others but dimly, what lies behind it.

The History of Israel

Its bearing on the history of Israel

All this new knowledge has made it necessary for us to reshape our ideas about the history of Israel. We may still believe that from the view-point of religion the Hebrews are the most important people of antiquity. But we have to admit that, so far from being the oldest nation in the world, they are comparatively young, and as regards world politics comparatively unimportant. If by some unhappy chance *Hamlet* had been lost to us save for a few fragments containing parts of the speeches of Polonius we might have supposed that Polonius was the most important character in the lost play. If later the whole of the text had been recovered we should have been compelled to revise our opinions and to recognize that Polonius is quite a subordinate figure in the drama. So has it been with the drama of oriental history in which Israel plays a part. For a long time the only considerable fragments that we could read concerned Israel, and we looked on Israel as the hero of the piece. Now we are able to read great sections of the drama that have been buried for long centuries, and we learn that the leading characters are the great empires—Egypt, Babylon, Assyria—and that Israel's part is a comparatively minor one.

The geography of Palestine

The political history of a land is always influenced by its geography, and this is very true of Palestine. The commonest name for it in the Old Testament is 'the land of Canaan'; 'Palestine', a Greek word which means 'Philistine-land', is used for the whole country first by Herodotus. We may deduce from this last name that the importance of the Philistines, who descended upon the south-east coast of the country at a comparatively late date, is greater than our records would have led us to suppose.

The limits of Palestine on the north are difficult to determine, because national boundaries there were vague and fluctuating. On the south are the desert lands of the Arabian peninsula. Desert country borders its eastern frontier too. Its western limit is the Mediterranean Sea. Roughly reckoned, its extent from north to south is about a hundred and fifty miles, and its average width between the Mediterranean Sea and the desert country on the east may be little more than a third of its length.

DIGGING IN PALESTINE. Tell Jemmeh, the mound of Gerar, near Gaza. The figures of excavators can be seen on the skyline.

Palestine a bridge between the great empires.

But though the country was small its situation was one of very great strategic importance. Close by on the south-west was Egypt, through centuries one of the great world-powers. And, because the desert on the east of Palestine could not be traversed, the only road from Egypt to the great empires of Babylon and Assyria, those equally important centres of civilization on the Tigris and Euphrates, lay along the western seaboard of Palestine, and thence through her northern territory. So Palestine was the bridge over which flowed all the traffic between these great commercial powers. Another stream of traffic, less considerable, crossed the country in another direction, from Arabia to the Phoenician ports. But not all the traffic that passed over the bridge was peaceful. The rivalry between Egypt and the empires of Babylonia was inveterate, like the rivalry between France and Germany in Europe. Whenever their armies advanced to attack one another the route led necessarily through Palestine; and for these rivals it was of the utmost importance to control this road. So, just as Belgium has been the historical battle-ground of the European rivals, Palestine became the battle-ground of the ancient empires, and a pawn in the great game of war.

We find from the Tell-el-Amarna letters that about 1500 B.C. Egypt had sought to make good her hold on Palestine, and secure the road against invaders from the north, by maintaining fortified cities in the country. Such fortified cities served also another purpose. From time to time the populations of the deserts on the east and south became too great for their territory, which afforded but a limited amount of food to sustain them. When this happened the fertile country of Palestine was an irresistible lure, and the dwellers in the desert would throng over the border and seek to supplant the existing inhabitants. It will be seen, then, that Palestine was likely again and again to resound with the tramp of great armies, bringing devastation in their train, and was subject to constant pressure from the desert-dwellers.

Internal features.

The internal features of the geography are also of very great importance for a clear understanding of the history of Judah and

Israel. By the side of the Mediterranean Sea runs the maritime plain. From the 'brook of Egypt', now known as the Wady el-Arish, which formed the traditional boundary of Palestine on the south-west, to approximately as far as Joppa, the modern Jaffa, this plain averages about fifteen miles in breadth, and is best known as the Plain of Philistia, for here were the famous five cities, Gaza, Askelon, Ashdod, Ekron, and Gath—taking them from south to north, though the site of Gath is a matter of conjecture—which were the strongholds of the Philistine invaders who descended upon the coast some twelve centuries before the Christian era. Although this district is rather sandy it is reasonably fertile, and much corn was grown in it.

North of Joppa the maritime plain is known as the Plain of Sharon. This narrows towards its northern end, and when it reaches its terminus at Mt. Carmel its width has shrunk to less than a mile. This district was perhaps the most fertile part of the country, and well cultivated. One of its characteristic flowers, the rose of Sharon, became a symbol of beauty in the Old Testament. On the north of the Carmel range, which runs, stretching right across the breadth of Palestine, from the sea to the Jordan valley, almost from north-west to south-east, lies the Plain of Esdraelon. Along the coast the maritime plain continues, narrowing from a breadth of about ten miles at Carmel to a mere three miles or so where it joins the Plain of Tyre.

On the opposite side from the sea the plains of Philistia and Sharon are bounded by low rolling hills, only a few hundred feet high, known in the Old Testament as the Shephelah. They are a sort of outwork of the great central mountain range which runs like a backbone through the land from north to south, broken only by the Plain of Esdraelon. North of Esdraelon this range runs up to the mountains of Lebanon, of which, indeed, it is the southern extension. In the north of Galilee its peaks reach a height of nearly 4,000 feet, but from that point they diminish towards the south until near Esdraelon they are more like downs, with much open ground that can be cultivated. South of Esdraelon the range becomes wilder, the peaks higher, the level places suitable for cultivation few and small; it is very much broken by steep ravines, which in the rainy season run with torrents. Its general characteristics are the same until it reaches the Negeb, or 'South country' of the Old Testament, the district south of Hebron, where the range subsides gradually into the desert which forms the southern boundary of Palestine. There is no well-defined break in it which might have served as a natural boundary between the kingdoms of Israel and Judah, with the result that it is hard to fix exactly where that boundary—never far north of Jerusalem—lay. At times the border-line was pushed north or south a little, according as Judah or Israel happened to be the stronger power.

East of the central range, almost due north and south, runs the Jordan valley, a deep fault in the earth's crust. From the small lake Huleh, just above sea-level, north of Galilee, the river Jordan runs in a narrow valley dipping so steeply that by the time the Sea of Galilee is reached it is almost 700 feet below sea-level. Between the Sea of Galilee and the Dead Sea, a distance of some sixty-five miles, the valley of the Jordan widens, varying in breadth from five to fifteen miles. The descent continues, but not so steeply. The river sometimes meanders through the valley, sometimes dashes down steep rapids, and contrives in its wanderings to travel about three times the actual distance between the two seas. The Dead Sea is nearly 1,300 feet below sea-level. It is easy to understand how the Jordan got its name, which means 'The Down-goer'. South of the Dead Sea the Jordan valley continues, though the river loses itself in the Dead Sea, through the desert, to the head of the Gulf of Akaba. This continuation is known as the Wadi Arabah.

The country to the east of the Jordan has always been so separated from the main part of Palestine as hardly to form a unity with it. Even to-day this natural division is recognized by the fact that the Palestine of the British mandate lies entirely west of the Jordan, the territory on the east side being under Arab rule, and known as Trans-Jordania. Down Trans-Jordania runs another mountain range, comparable with that which forms the central part of Palestine. Leaving Mt. Hermon in the north at a height of about 2,000 feet, it maintains that average until the river Yarmuk, a tributary running into the Jordan just south of the Sea of Galilee, is reached. This territory is known as the Hauran,

PALESTINE (*photographed from the air*)

An infra-red panorama, looking west. In the foreground are the city of Jericho and the Jordan valley. In the middle distance, to the left, are the mountains of Judah, and farther away, to the right, is the hill country of Ephraim. In the far distance, fifty miles away, is the Mediterranean Sea.

and is bounded on the east by the Hauran mountain range, now the home of the Druzes. The southern part of this Hauran territory, which is well watered, probably coincides with the district known in the Old Testament as Bashan. This was regarded by the Hebrews as an especially fertile area. Isaiah (2^{13}) compares its oaks with the cedars of Lebanon. Ezekiel in his description (27) of Tyre as a ship made of the most splendid materials says that the cedars of Lebanon form its masts, while its oars are from Bashan oaks, and in Zechariah 11^2 the same comparison is implied. The pastures of Bashan were far-famed, the bulls that fed on them lusty—the Psalmist (22^{12}) compares his foes to 'strong bulls of Bashan'—the cows so fat that when Amos taunts the luxurious women of Samaria he calls them (4^1) 'Ye kine of Bashan', or in other words 'Ye fat old cows'.

From the Yarmuk to the Dead Sea this range is known as Gilead. The territory about it is still very fertile, if less so than Bashan. It is almost bisected by another tributary of the Jordan, the Jabbok. From the Dead Sea southwards it becomes more mountainous and more arid, rising into the higher mountain country of Moab. On the east this whole range merges almost imperceptibly into the desert.

Climate.

The climate of Palestine is usually described as sub-tropical. Even in the winter the temperature only exceptionally falls below freezing-point. In the summer the heat of the day is sultry. One of the features of the happy future painted in the prophetic writings is that in those days every man will dwell beneath the shade of his own vine and fig-tree, for shade was in Palestine a boon almost as much desired as water. As evening comes the temperature falls rapidly, so that even in the summer time the nights are cool. Morning mists occur not infrequently, but are soon dispersed by the sun's heat. Thus Hosea (6^4) likens the transient goodness of the people to the 'morning cloud'. Heavy dews that—as Hosea says in the same passage—'go away early' moisten the land during the summer nights. While the moist sea breezes from the Mediterranean help to make the climate on the western side of the central mountain range more tolerable, the hot winds from the desert,

Royal Air Force Official. Crown copyright reserved.

An air-view of the rolling uplands of Moab, in Trans-Jordania. The view is taken near Amman (Rabboth Ammon), the capital of modern Trans-Jordania.

laden with sand, scorch up the vegetation on the eastern side. The Jordan valley, cut off from the sea breezes, becomes intensely hot. This heat causes rapid evaporation from the Sea of Galilee and the Dead Sea, and explains how it is that despite the millions of tons of water which the latter receives from the Jordan daily its level does not rise.

The winter is a season of rain, which falls heavily, sometimes for several days in succession, from late September onwards. In March and April the rainfall diminishes, and the rains of these months, which are most important for the growing crops, are distinguished in the Old Testament as 'the latter rains'. Hail and thunder are common. The country is of volcanic formation, and therefore subject to shocks of earthquake, the phenomena of which are frequently referred to by the prophets. One sufficiently important to reckon dates from is mentioned in Amos 1^1. Josephus records one in 31 B.C. which caused great loss of life, and in 1837 another very disastrous one occurred. As recently as 1930 shocks were felt at Hebron, which the superstitious Arabs interpreted as a punishment for their butchery of the Jewish inhabitants in the preceding year.

Fertility.

In Old Testament times the land was evidently very fertile. Palestine is again and again described as a land 'flowing with milk and honey'. Soil that received insufficient rain was made fertile by means of irrigation. Grain—wheat, barley, rye, sesame—was regularly grown, and fruit trees were abundant. Of these the olive, fig, and vine were the most useful. Fruit palms were found on the coastal plains and in the Jordan valley. Generally the land could not be described as well-wooded, though the cedar forests on the slopes of Carmel and Lebanon were famous, and the kings of Babylon, Assyria, and Egypt all record how they cut down the cedars of Palestine for use as building material. Sheep and goats were kept in large numbers, their milk furnishing a large part of the people's food, as their wool provided most of their clothing. Cattle were not reared to so great an extent except on the east side of the Jordan. Apart from agriculture industries were almost negligible, except in so far as they supplied the wants of the

Introductory

people themselves in such simple things as pottery and weapons, though salt-making of a crude kind has always been carried out on the shores of the Dead Sea.

Effect of geography on politics and religion.

From this general picture it will be seen that the land is divided by its natural features into comparatively small sections, plain, valley, and hill, in which the natural conditions were very different. This fact had a very considerable influence on the course of Hebrew history. The people lived for the most part in small groups, often cut off by natural boundaries from regular intercourse with their neighbours. Their interests in life varied largely with their conditions. The same type of mistrust that we find existing between the Highlander and the Lowlander in Scotland was likely to develop between these small communities. This would have been the case even if the various small groups, with their diverse interests, had belonged to the same stock. But when we realize—as we shall see later—that the inhabitants of the country were drawn from many different races, it is clear that there can have been little unity among the people.

The segregation of the inhabitants into small groups, each living within its own boundaries and governed by its own interests, led to important consequences both for religion and politics. Each community would have its own special gods, so that there would be no unifying religion. And it was wellnigh impossible to weld all these diverse groups into a single nation ruled from a central seat of authority. The physical nature of the country in itself would have made this a difficult problem, apart altogether from divergences of race, interest, and custom. Never before the time of David and Solomon did there exist a single kingdom embracing the greater part of the country. That those kings, building upon the foundation laid by Saul, did achieve a large measure of success in unifying the country was a remarkable piece of statesmanship. The difficulties of their task are made clear in the subsequent history, for the kingdom endured no longer than the strong personalities who made it, and after the death of Solomon the forces which inevitably made for division reasserted themselves. At no later time was there a Hebrew or Jewish kingdom in effective control of Palestine.

Early inhabitants of Palestine

Our historical information as to the people who inhabited Palestine before the time of the Hebrews is very sparse: indeed the history of Palestine in the ordinary sense does not go back further than the sixteenth century B.C. Such information as we can gather about the earlier times is derived almost exclusively from the discoveries of the excavators. Unfortunately excavation in Palestine has only in the last generation been undertaken in any systematic way. The very reason that makes excavation so desirable, the fact that Palestine is the land of most importance in the eyes of the adherents of three great religions, Judaism, Christianity, and Mohammedanism, accounts for the delay. The feeling that the soil of the country is sacred ground long prevented its disturbance by the spade of the excavator.

The Palestine Exploration Fund, founded in London in 1865, initiated the movement for systematic and scientific work in this field. Credit is due also to the German Oriental Society and the French Biblical School at Jerusalem. By this time numerous sites have been systematically explored. Among the most important excavations may be mentioned those of Petrie at Tell-el-Hesy, the Lachish of the Old Testament, 1891–2, Macalister at Gezer, 1901–8, Sellin at Taanach, 1902–3, and Jericho, 1909–10, Schumacher at Megiddo, 1903–4, and those at Samaria under the auspices of Harvard University, 1908–10. Since the War fresh impetus has been given to this work, and Garstang, who excavated at Askelon, 1920–2, is now engaged in a thorough excavation of the site of Jericho. These excavations have produced but little in the way of artistic treasures, or inscriptions, but they have enabled us to understand much about the life and religion of the early times. In many cases the excavators find that six or seven cities have succeeded one another on the same site. An exception to this rule is Samaria, where the digging has made it clear that the Old Testament is correct in its statement (1 Kings 16[24]) that Omri of Israel built his royal city on virgin soil.

From the excavations we learn that the oldest inhabitants of

Introductory

the country were a primitive race who dwelt in caves and lived by hunting and fishing; they did not cultivate the ground or keep cattle and sheep; they did not know the arts of making pottery or weaving; their tools and weapons were of unworked flint. Later this people learned to work and polish their flint implements. Nor did they belong to the Semitic race, of which the Hebrews form part. The evidence goes to show that they cremated their dead—a practice abhorrent to Semitic feeling—and practised cannibalism. Many people think that these cave-dwellers are the Horites mentioned in Deuteronomy $2^{12,\ 22}$, because the name Horite may mean 'cave-dweller'. Early Egyptian records refer to the inhabitants of Palestine by the name Charu, which is certainly the Hebrew name in a different form. On the other hand the references to the Horites in Genesis $36^{20f.,\ 29}$ would imply that they were a Semitic people, so the identification of the Horites with the cave-dwellers is uncertain.

These early inhabitants left behind them numerous monuments of stone, menhirs—tall standing stones—dolmens, consisting of two standing stones with a horizontal stone lying upon them, such as we are familiar with at Stonehenge, and cromlechs, or stones arranged in a circle upon the ground, like the 'Druid circles' found in our own country. It is probable that the Old Testament name Gilgal means a cromlech. Dolmens are very common on the east side of the Jordan, and not rare in Palestine proper. One group contains almost a thousand of them. Exactly what these dolmens were for we do not know. It has often been said that they are altars. But some were certainly too tall for such a use, and it is not easy to see why there should be so many in one group if they were really altars. On the whole it is more probable that they are connected with the cult of the dead, though in this case cremation can hardly have been universal. In some cases they might later come to be used as altars. Rock altars are found very frequently, the most famous of them being the one now enclosed in the Dome of the Rock, or Mosque of Omar, at Jerusalem.

We have already noticed that the dolmen and cromlech can be paralleled in our own country, and as a matter of fact such stone monuments are found over a wide area which includes India and North Africa. It is thought that the prehistoric people of Palestine may have been a part of the race known as the Indo-Germanic, to whom the erection of such monuments over the wider area is attributed. At any rate it seems clear that they did not belong to the Semitic race, for, in addition to the difference in their method of disposing of the dead there is the fact that the place-names which they have handed down cannot be explained by Semitic etymologies.

Whatever may be the case with the earliest inhabitants of Palestine the population in Old Testament times was Semitic. This race—named after Shem, the son of Noah, Genesis 10^{21-31}—included the Assyrians and Babylonians, the Arameans (or Syrians), the Arabs, the Phoenicians, Moabites, Ammonites, Edomites, as well as the Hebrews. It is generally agreed that the original stock from which these various nations came had its home in the Arabian peninsula. The countries occupied by the Semitic peoples, apart from the desert-dwelling Arabs, form roughly a crescent, and in contrast with the Arab desert the area they cover has been happily named 'The Fertile Crescent'. It may not be out of place at this point, perhaps, to warn the reader that in the Old Testament the word *desert* rarely means an absolutely arid tract of country; it is the description of country which could be grazed, though it was unsuited to the processes of agriculture. And further it should be said that the Arabian peninsula was much better watered and far more fertile 4,000 years ago than it is to-day.

The Fertile Crescent has played a grat part in the story of the Nearer East. Its history has been well described by Breasted as 'an age-long struggle between the mountain peoples of the north and the desert-wanderers of the grass-lands—a struggle which is still going on—for the possession of the Fertile Crescent'. Again and again when the population of the desert has become too great to be sustained by its produce, or when the ability of the desert to feed its inhabitants has been reduced by abnormally dry periods, the desert-dwellers have swarmed over the borders into the cultivated lands. One such emigration occurred in the fourth millennium B.C., when the tide flowed over Mesopotamia and Syraia. A second on a large scale about the middle of the following millennium filled Canaan with a Semitic population. The people concerned in this movement are known in the ancient records as

A cave shelter in northern Galilee, in which remains of prehistoric man were found.

Amurru, from which is derived the Old Testament word *Amorite*. About a thousand years later still came another great wave, in which the Hebrews and their kinsmen and neighbours the Edomites, Ammonites, and Moabites reached the lands on either side of the Jordan.

Palestine and Egypt.

But before we come to the question of the Hebrew occupation of Canaan we will look at the relations which existed between Palestine and the great civilized empires on the south-west and the north-east, because these had a great deal to do with the shaping of the conditions in which the Hebrew nation grew up. Indeed, only when we regard Palestine as part of a large area embracing the great empires of Egypt, Babylon, and Assyria, to whose civilization and religion Palestine was heavily indebted, can we get a true perspective for the development of Hebrew civilization and religion.

Southern Palestine was inevitably in close touch with Egypt, and relations between the two can be traced back to at least the third millennium B.C. The excavations at Byblus have revealed numerous objects showing intercourse with Egypt, and it seems clear that both at this city and at Gezer there were Egyptian colonies during the Middle Empire (2000–1800 B.C.). Snefru of Egypt as early as *c.* 3100 B.C. sent a fleet of forty ships to Byblus to bring cargoes of Syrian cedar-wood. Kittel points out that even as far back as this Byblus is known by the Semitic name Gebal, which shows that the port had been for some time in the possession of Semitic inhabitants. The goddess 'Hathor of Byblus' is mentioned on an Egyptian tomb inscription of the Middle Empire.

The earliest military expeditions of Egypt against Palestine that can be definitely dated are recorded in an inscription found in the tomb of Weni, now in the Cairo Museum. Weni tells how the king, Pepy I, *c.* 2795, assembled a vast host and placed them under his command. The expedition returned in triumph after having ravaged the land of the 'Sand-dwellers', destroying cities and hewing down orchards. This shows that the name 'Sand-dwellers' must have been given to these inhabitants of Palestine, not from the nature of the land in which they were then living, but because of the characteristics of an earlier home, and suggests that they must have been originally nomads in the Arabian deserts. Weni records other similar expeditions, and also one in which he conveyed his troops not over land, but on ships, landing at the end of the mountain range on the north of the land of the Sand-dwellers, by which he may mean Carmel. This inscription is evidence that by this time Egypt exercised a more or less effective control over Palestine.

In the succeeding centuries the power of Egypt decayed, and Palestine was freed from the fear of subjugation until the rulers of the Twelfth Dynasty took up the task begun by Pepy I. Amenemhet I, *c.* 2212, appears to have sent troops against Palestine, and also—though this is not quite so certain—Sesostris I, *c.* 2192. The romance of Sinuhe, a favourite Egyptian adventure story relating to this period, represents the conditions in Palestine as very similar to those revealed five centuries later by the Tell-el-Amarna letters. The country is divided into numerous small kingdoms with no central controlling power. There is intercourse between these and Egypt, but the latter exercises no effective suzerainty over them. So far from this being the case, an exile from Egypt may find in one of them a safe refuge from the Pharaoh.

Sesostris III, *c.* 2099, invaded Palestine, overthrowing a city called Sekmem. The likeness of this name to the Shechem of the Bible is obvious, and some scholars, though not all, assume that the same place is meant. It may be observed that in one of the Tell-el-Amarna letters written by Abdihiba of Jerusalem a place Shakmi is mentioned as in the neighbourhood of Betsani, which would seem to be the Biblical Bethshan. We may deduce that many Old Testament names are inherited from the predecessors of the Hebrews.

Subsequent Pharaohs proudly describe themselves as 'Rulers of the Asiatics', but it is probable that this was a description rather of their ambitions than of their achievements. Before long it was the fate of Egypt herself to fall under the domination of the invading Hyksos, and it was only after Amosis I, *c.* 1580, succeeded in driving them out that Egypt was able to resume the invasion of Palestine. Her efforts became more persistent, and

The History of Israel

Thothmes I, c. 1540, asserted his suzerainty over all territory up to the Euphrates, and made Palestine and Syria tributary to Egypt.

Thothmes III made many important expeditions, in the course of which he fought a famous battle at Megiddo, c. 1479. He strengthened his hold over Palestine, and received tribute even from the Hittites and the Babylonians. Garrisons of Egyptian soldiers were established in the fortified towns of Palestine and Syria. This was the highwater mark of Egypt's power over Palestine, and afterwards the tide began to ebb. The decline of Egypt's power was slow at first, but under Akhenaten, c. 1375-1357, it proceeded rapidly towards complete collapse. The pressure exercised by Hittites from the north and Amorites from the west largely accounted for the ousting of Egypt from effective control of the country.

Much light has been thrown upon conditions in Palestine during Akhenaten's reign by the letters found in 1887 at Tell-el-Amarna, the site of Akhenaten's capital, about 170 miles south of Cairo. These are written in the Babylonian cuneiform script on tablets like those that have been found in such large numbers in Babylonia. Most of them are diplomatic communications from Egyptian vassal kings in Palestine and Syria to their lord the Pharaoh. A few are letters from Akhenaten to these vassals and other kings; these, presumably, are duplicates of the originals actually sent.

From the tablets we learn that Palestine was in a state of confusion and turmoil. Abdi-ashirta, prince of Amurru, whose domain corresponded roughly with the Lebanon district, had allied himself with the Hittites, and—though he was all the time pretending to be a loyal subject to Akhenaten—was attacking the Phoenician cities which were faithful to Egypt. He writes protesting that he is diligently defending the Pharaoh's interests against hostile powers, and even appeals for Egyptian troops to be sent to his assistance! But his duplicity is revealed in the letters of Rib-addi, the loyal governor of Gebal, who pathetically pleads with Akhenaten to send him help against the attacks of Abdi-ashirta, concerning whom he asks 'What is Abdi-ashirta, the slave, the dog, that he should take the king's land for himself?'

In southern Palestine similar conditions prevailed. The petty princes of the city-states were quarrelling among themselves, some

Introductory

busy with intrigues against Egypt while pretending to be loyal, and accusing others who really were so of disloyalty. Like Ribaddi of Gebal, the king of Jerusalem, Abdi-hiba, seems himself to have been faithful to Egypt. It is true that another petty king—Shuwardata—accuses Abdi-hiba of taking his city from him, and appeals for Egyptian assistance against him. But the six letters of Abdi-hiba himself make the impression of sincerity. He repeatedly complains that his enemies have slandered him to the Pharaoh, and on his part appeals for aid. It must have been far from easy for Akhenaten to distil the truth from these letters of accusation and counter-accusation.

The letters of Abdi-hiba are especially important for the history of the Hebrews because he mentions no fewer than eight times a people whom he describes as plundering the king's country, and who are known as the Habiru. We shall see later that there is good ground for the view that a close connexion exists between the Habiru and the Hebrews. What with the hostile incursions on the north and east, and the civil wars within Palestine itself, the Egyptian empire in Palestine crumbled to pieces, while Akhenaten seems to have taken no decisive step to prevent its decay.

Not until the reign of Sety I, c. 1310–1290, did Egypt recover her hold upon Palestine. An inscription commemorating his successful campaigns relates that the Bedouins, by whom the successors to the Habiru of the Tell-el-Amarna period are meant, were in a state of confusion and revolt, and that Sety, 'who loved an hour of battle more than a day of joy', completely subdued them. He defeated the Hittites and recovered Syria for his empire. Revolts in Palestine were put down by his successors, Ramses II and Merenptah, c. 1225–1215. Then once more Egypt's grasp became slack, though recent excavations appear to show that Bethshan remained in the possession of Egypt during the years 1313–1167. Ramses III at the beginning of the twelfth century once more recovered Palestine for Egypt, but after his death the Philistines seized the south-west of Palestine. From this time, although Egypt made one or two campaigns in the country and was responsible for incessant political intrigue with its kingdoms, she was never in effective control of Palestine during the period with which the Old Testament is concerned.

Palestine and Babylonia.

Turning now towards the great alluvial plain lying about the great rivers Tigris and Euphrates, conveniently known as Babylonia, we find the seat of another ancient civilization that exercised a decisive influence upon Palestine during the centuries before the birth of the Hebrew nation. In the earliest records this territory was divided into a northern district, known as Akkad, and a southern district, called Sumer. The inhabitants of the latter, known as Sumerians, were not of Semitic race, whereas the Akkadians of the north were predominantly Semitic. The kings who claimed to rule over the whole area describe themselves as kings of 'Sumer and Akkad'—always in that order. From this we may reasonably conclude that in the earliest period the former was the more important. Some historians suppose that the Akkadians were the original inhabitants of Sumer, driven northward by invaders. But it is more likely that they came into Babylonia later than the Sumerians. It is commonly asserted that they came from Arabia, but of this there is no proof. The geographical situation would suggest rather that they entered from Syria.

The early history of Sumer is known only in fragments. Each city was a separate state, and these petty kingdoms lived in a state of constant strife for overlordship. The earliest king to establish a united kingdom embracing Sumer and Akkad was Sargon of Agade, whose date may be *c.* 2872. He also defeated the Elamites and subdued the territory which was later the seat of the Assyrian empire. He boasts also that he was overlord of Amurru, which would include Syria. A romantic story of his origin tells us that he was born in concealment, and placed by his mother in a reed basket which she cast adrift on the Euphrates. The resemblance between this legend and the story of Moses in the 'ark of bulrushes' leaps to the eye. In his records Sargon asserts that he passed over 'the sea in the East', and conquered the 'Western land to its furthest extremity'.

The claims of Sargon are so far-reaching that when they were first discovered the tendency of scholars was to regard them as legendary; but sufficient evidence is now available to prove that —allowing for the customary exaggeration—they are well founded. It now seems certain that his activities extended to the Mediter-

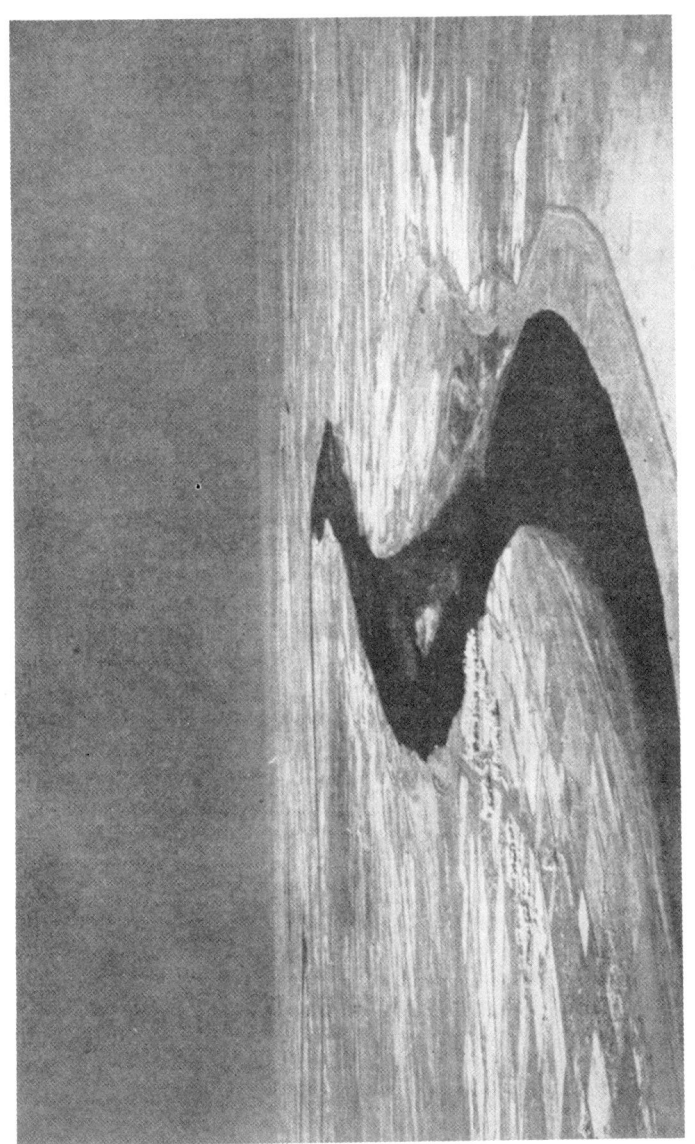

THE GREAT RIVER EUPHRATES photographed from the air.

ranean coast and that he must have exercised some control over the country between that coast and Babylonia. It has been asserted that he invaded Cyprus, though the evidence for this is disputed: Winckler even held that he conquered Crete, and that the Minoan civilization derives ultimately from this event. We can, however, be reasonably sure that Syria and Palestine were influenced by Babylonian civilization during his reign. But, brilliant as Sargon's exploits were, his career ended in misfortune, with his whole empire in revolt. Sumer once more became the political centre, and its several city-states held supreme power in turn. It was during this period of Sumerian revival that the dynasty of Ur, whose civilization has recently been revealed to us by the excavations under Sir Leonard Woolley's supervision, flourished.

At last the city of Babylon came to the front, its first dynasty being founded by Sumu-abu towards the beginning of the last quarter of the third millennium B.C. This dynasty was of foreign origin. Older writers asserted that it was the product of a wave of immigration from Arabia, but Clay's view that the dynasty and the forces that enthroned it came from Amurru seems more plausible. Some even of the historians who hold the theory that Semitic populations derive from Arabia make an exception in this case and concede that this particular wave of immigration is West-Semitic. In passing it may be observed that the old dispute between those who regard all the ancient civilizations of the Nearer East as of Egyptian origin, and those who would trace their beginnings to Babylonia, may be solved by an alternative theory, which regards Syria 'as the possible seat of an early culture that inspired both Egypt and Mesopotamia in certain respects'.[1]

Sumu-abu and the four kings of the dynasty who succeeded him during a period of about a century gradually extended the authority of Babylon. But the sixth king of the dynasty, the famous Hammurabi, achieved even more brilliant results, and left an impress which endured for many centuries. He is by fairly general consent, though in the writer's opinion on most inadequate grounds, identified with the king Amraphel mentioned in Genesis 14. There is, unfortunately, still very considerable uncertainty as

[1] *Cambridge Ancient History*, i, p. 582.

Introductory

to the exact dating of this great king. The Oxford astronomer, Dr. Fotheringham, on the basis of astronomical data furnished by a tablet containing observations made in the reign of Ammizaduga, the fourth king in succession to Hammurabi, would make the latter's reign begin *c.* 2068 B.C. Kugler puts it more than a century later, and the *Cambridge Ancient History* inclines to make it half a century earlier.

In any case there is no doubt as to the great achievements of Hammurabi. His long reign of forty-two years was marked by brilliant success, hard won by persistent effort. After thirty years he succeeded in breaking the formidable power of Elam, and then, by subduing the ruler of Larsa, Rim-sin, united Sumer and Akkad under his own authority. Later he brought Assyria under his control and extended his dominion far into the territory of the Hittites. But, magnificent as were his military achievements, which entitle him to a place beside Alexander and Napoleon, his fame is even more securely based on the great work he did as administrator of his realm, his crowning glory being, of course, the famous code of laws that bears his name. His reign marks the culminating point of Babylon's splendour, and after his death a period of steady decline followed.

Samsu-iluma, his son and successor, was troubled by the raids of Kassite tribes from western Elam, and the diversion of his attention in this direction afforded his father's old antagonist Rim-sin the opportunity to raise once more the standard of revolt in the south. Samsu-iluma succeeded both in repelling the raiders and repressing the revolt. But his exertions left him somewhat exhausted and less able to encounter a new foe. The extreme south of Babylonia, bordering on the Persian Gulf, was full of marshes, and in general characteristics resembled the fenlands of the Isle of Ely, where Hereward the Wake made the last stand of the English against the Norman conquerors. In this district Iluma-ilum raised a revolt, and made such good use of the difficulties which the fenland presented to the movements of Samsu-iluma's forces that the king, despite desperate efforts, was unable to subdue him, and the empire was shorn of its southern province.

Further trouble came in the shape of an Amurrite attack, and though the king managed to beat it off the bounds of his authority were withdrawn on several sides. His successors occupied themselves largely with commerce, content to hold, as far as they could, what territory they inherited. They were busy, too, in elaborating the splendour of the national temples and ritual, and particularly interested in developing a cult of divine worship paid to themselves. The dynasty lasted in all about three centuries, and Samsuditana, its last king, seems to have been crushed by a Hittite invasion.

During this time the Kassites had become more and more powerful, and finally they brought Babylon under their own domination. They managed to subdue even the difficult marsh territory of the south, whose rulers had up to this point been able to maintain their independence, and once more a dynasty was established at Babylon in control of a united Babylonia. But the Kassite conquerors formed only a minority of the population, and the old social and religious traditions of the Hammurabi dynasty survived.

Our knowledge of the Kassite dynasty's history, which covered a period of nearly six hundred years, is but fragmentary, though the Tell-el-Amarna letters enable us to penetrate its obscurity to some extent. Five of these letters are part of a correspondence between Amenhotep III of Egypt and Kadashmanharbe I, who was the Kassite king of Babylon at the beginning of the fourteenth century. The first of the five, from Amenhotep, shows that Kadashmanharbe had written to the Egyptian king complaining that envoys whom he had sent to Egypt had failed to find any trace of a sister of the Kassite ruler, who had been added to the Egyptian harem, and about whose fate he was concerned. Amenhotep in his reply suggests that Kadashmanharbe had not sent envoys who could recognize the princess, and complains that the envoys had in other respects deceived their master. Three of the letters, from Kadashmanharbe, are concerned largely with the interchange of gifts between the two courts, and in particular with a supply of gold sent from Egypt to Babylon. Egypt was the chief source of gold at this time, and the Kassite monarch seems to have been a persistent applicant for supplies. His dignity, too, had been offended because of Amenhotep's failure to return his compliment by sending an Egyptian princess for the harem of Babylon. The

Introductory

last of the five letters, written by the Egyptian Pharaoh, contains an interesting catalogue of furniture with gold decorations which he is transmitting to Babylon. There seems to be reason for supposing that some of the art treasures found by Mr. Howard Carter in the tomb of Tutankhamen, a Pharaoh of slightly later date, were of Babylonian origin. If this is the case we should have evidence of a regular interchange of gifts between Babylon and Egypt. The point which we are particularly concerned to notice is the implication of constant traffic between Egypt and Babylon by way of Palestine.

Other illuminating letters in the Tell-el-Amarna find are six from Burraburriash of Babylon, who was slightly later than Kadashmanharbe, to Amenhotep III and Amenhotep IV, the latter of whom is better known as Akhenaten. Two of these are of special value for our purpose. One of them complains that certain envoys of the Babylonian king have been killed on a journey through Canaan 'thy land', and the other recalls that the Canaanites had previously sought the aid of Burraburriash's father to free them from Egypt's power, though the Babylonian king had refused to grant their request. Other letters deal with lists of presents passing between the royal correspondents, one list alone running to several pages in translation.

Among the Tell-el-Amarna letters are also found two from the Assyrian king Ashur-uballit to Amenhotep IV, in which he speaks of sending horses to Egypt, and begs for a supply of gold, 'which in thy land is as dust', in order that he may beautify a new palace with which he is busy. A slightly earlier one, from Amenhotep III, addressed to Tarhundaraba of Arzawa, an independent kingdom under the influence of the Hittite empire, deals with matrimonial alliances and presents similar to those mentioned earlier.

A study of these letters enables us to draw the main outlines of a picture portraying the international relationships in the Nearer East at this period, immediately preceding the rise of the Hebrew nation. The most important power of all is Egypt, and the land of Canaan is generally recognized to be a province of the Egyptian empire. The Canaanites are uneasy under Egyptian control, and would welcome an alliance with Babylon if by contracting one they could throw off the Egyptian yoke. This is the situation which recurs again and again during the history of the Hebrew kingdoms when efforts are made to play off Egypt against Babylon or Assyria, and vice versa. But during this period Babylon stands too much in awe of Egypt to provoke a quarrel. She is constantly demanding supplies of gold, and these are sent, we may imagine, to keep the northern powers quiet. But in spite of the immense quantities of gold derived from Nubia by Egypt the demands of these persistent beggars are insatiable. We have evidence here, also, of a very considerable and well-organized traffic between Mesopotamia and Egypt by the caravan roads through Palestine. Diplomatic relations are regular, and organized as well as were such relations in Europe before the days of rapid communication. We note also the emergence of the Assyrian and Hittite empires as forces exercising some influence over the whole of this territory.

That the Hittite empire indeed played a part of importance in the political drama which centred round Palestine is proved by the tablets excavated at Boghaz-keui, which occupies the site of the old Hittite capital. Kadashmanharbe II, who occupied the throne of Babylon about a century later than his namesake whose letters were found at Tell-el-Amarna, was anxious about a treaty that Egypt had made with the Hittite king Khattusil, and wrote to the latter making inquiries as to the exact purport of the treaty, quite in the manner of a modern European Foreign Office. In his letter he also complains, just as his namesake had done a century before, that certain Babylonian merchants had been murdered when travelling through northern Phoenicia. As he holds Khattusil responsible for this we may deduce that by this time the suzerainty of northern Palestine had passed from Egypt to the Hittites. Among the tablets recovered is also Khattusil's reply to this letter. In it he attempts to lull Kadashmanharbe's suspicions about the purport of the treaty, and pleads with him to join forces against a common foe. King is probably right in identifying this foe with Assyria, which, under Shalmaneser I, was at this time pursuing an aggressive policy. A noteworthy feature of the Hittite correspondence with Egypt is the absence of requests for gold such as were insistently made by the rulers of Babylon. This may be interpreted as evidence of the greater virility and self-confidence of the Hittite empire.

THE HITTITES. A sculptured slab at the Hittite city of Carchemish on the upper Euphrates, showing the king and queen, and his family, moving in procession.

The vigorous power of Assyria soon began to affect the Babylonian empire adversely. Relationships between the two powers were at first friendly. The Ashur-uballit of the Amarna period married his daughter to Burraburriash of Babylon. But as the strength of Assyria increased friction between the two states developed into open conflict, and eventually Tukulti-ninib I of Assyria completely subdued Babylon, and the latter became no more than an Assyrian province. The later Kassite rulers of Babylon managed to free themselves for a few decades from Assyria's grasp, but Ashur-dan I again brought Babylon under Assyrian control.

CHAPTER II

ISRAEL'S ORIGINS

The stories of the patriarchs.

IN the preceding account we have tried to describe the land which was the cradle of Israel, and to give some idea of its political conditions in the era before the origin of the nation. We have now to consider whence the Hebrew people came, and how they established themselves. Our task would be very much easier if only we could assume that the stories related of the patriarchs in Genesis and the narratives of the Exodus are even approximately historical.

The Old Testament story of the birth of the nation is given in a condensed form in Deuteronomy 26$^{5-9}$, which puts into the mouth of the nation these words:

A Syrian ready to perish (mg. *wandering* or *lost*) was my father, and he went down into Egypt, and sojourned there, few in number; and he became there a nation, great, mighty, and populous: and the Egyptians evil entreated us, and afflicted us, and laid upon us hard bondage: and we cried unto Yahweh, the God of our fathers, and Yahweh heard our voice, and saw our affliction, and our toil, and our oppression: and Yahweh brought us out of Egypt with a mighty hand, and with an outstretched arm, and with great terribleness, and with signs, and with wonders: and he hath brought us to this place, and hath given us this land.

But unfortunately the matter is not as simple as this. The stories of Genesis and Exodus, while they undoubtedly contain elements of very old tradition, in their present form are products of the post-exilic period. Moreover, the stories contain tales and *motifs* that are familiar in the folk-lore of other peoples. The same story is told of different persons, and different accounts are given of the same thing. Indeed many scholars would deny that the patriarchs are in any real sense of the word historical characters.

How the stories should be interpreted is a matter of dispute. A favourite contention is that the names of the patriarchs are really names not of individuals but of tribes or clans. In this view there is undoubtedly an element of truth. It is very probable, for example, that in some of the matrimonial alliances recorded of individuals we have a symbolic way of putting relationships between two clans. Marriage will mean the amalgamation of the two clans. Brotherhood signifies a close relationship between clans that do not actually merge. But any attempt to explain the whole of the patriarchal history by the application of this theory soon breaks down.

Another line of explanation finds in the patriarchs 'faded deities'. That is to say, the names of the patriarchs were originally the names of gods and in the course of time were transferred to the clans or tribes that worshipped them. It is pointed out, for example, that Gad is the name of an old god of 'Fortune', and inferred that Gad was originally not the human ancestor but the deity of the tribe known by that name. But very little can be found in the stories themselves to support this theory, and any attempt to work it out in detail is so difficult as to become absurd. Comparison with the legends of other peoples shows that while men are often raised by tradition to the rank of gods the reverse process is rare, if it can be shown to exist at all. A theory even more precarious is that which finds in the patriarchal stories astral myths, Abraham, for instance, being a manifestation of the moon-god.

While accepting without hesitation the conclusion of scholars that the stories of the patriarchs are not history the present writer believes that Abraham represents an historical person, and that the story of an immigration to Palestine from Ur of the Chaldees by way of Haran is founded upon sound tradition. On this basis we find one source from which the Hebrew nation sprang. When this migration took place we cannot determine within narrow limits. Of course if the superficially attractive, but far from proved, theory that Amraphel of Genesis 14 is to be identified with the great Hammurabi of Babylon be accepted, Abraham must have been his contemporary, and the migration would be dated c. 2000 B.C. But even if we accept this extremely hazardous identification we should still be faced with the difficulty of showing that the story in Genesis 14 is itself of historical worth. We must be content to say that the oldest strain of the Hebrew nation is to be found in an immigration from Mesopotamia into Palestine which may have taken place anywhere between 2050 and 1650 B.C.

The Habiru.

A very interesting problem is that which deals with the relation between the Habiru, who according to the Tell-el-Amarna letters were invading Palestine in the time of Akhenaten, and the Hebrews. The likeness of the names is obvious, and it is agreed that there is no philological difficulty in equating them: the identification is accepted by many scholars, in the present writer's opinion correctly. But one slight qualification ought to be made. The Hebrews of the Old Testament are to be regarded as one branch of the Habiru, for the latter name probably covers a larger group of people. The references in the Amarna letters to the Habiru show that they were making persistent inroads into south Palestine, and wresting towns from loyal Egyptian deputy kings, sometimes with the goodwill and assistance of their inhabitants. The Habiru were evidently a military people, and they appear to have been employed in Babylon during the time of Hammurabi as mercenary soldiers.

The Tell-el-Amarna letters refer also to a people described as the SA.GAZ, who were playing in the north of Palestine the same part that the Habiru were performing in the south. There is good reason for believing that this name, which sometimes has the more general meaning 'plunderers', 'marauders', is equivalent to Habiru. The Habiru are usually supposed to be of Aramean stock, though Clay thinks they may be of Hittite origin. It is interesting to note that Ezekiel 16[3]—'Thus saith the Lord God unto Jerusalem: Thy birth and thy nativity is of the land of the Canaanite; the Amorite was thy father, and thy mother was an Hittite'—would lead us to believe that there was at any rate a strain of Hittite blood in the Hebrew nation.

In view of a general similarity between the situation when the Habiru were thrusting their way into Palestine and the Old Testament picture of the 'conquest of Canaan' by the Israelites under Joshua, it has been asserted that the two things are really one, and that the Habiru are actually the forces under Joshua. But the evidence in detail fails absolutely to justify this romantic theory. In the first place there is a complete want of harmony between the names of places and persons in the two accounts, and in the second place there is no suggestion in the Old Testament account that the

Canaanites against whom Joshua's forces are contending are under Egyptian suzerainty, which is clearly the situation set forth in the Amarna letters.

The Egyptian 'bondage'.

A striking feature of the early Old Testament narratives is the way in which a connexion between the Hebrews and Egypt is insisted upon. Leaving aside the stories of Moses and the Exodus, we find that the patriarchal stories represent Abraham, Jacob, and Joseph, as sojourning in that country. The historical worth of these stories in that respect is very variously estimated. There is no doubt that wandering tribes were accustomed to enter Egyptian territory to find pasturage for their flocks and herds. And in numerous details the Old Testament stories agree with Egyptian conditions. The name of Moses himself, for example, is a good Egyptian word. But however much or little historical value we may find in these earlier stories there is one thing of which we may be absolutely sure. At least some part of the Hebrew nation passed through a period of oppression in Egypt itself. Just as we can be sure that Jesus was crucified, because if that had not been so none of His followers could possibly have invented a story which attributed to Jesus a form of death so disgraceful in their eyes, so we may be sure that a proud nation could never have invented, or accepted from other sources, a false tradition that long ago its ancestors had been slaves in Egypt. The 'house of bondage', so often referred to in the Old Testament, stands for a very real experience.

We may deduce something more from this tradition. If, as we shall see reason to believe, the Hebrew nation was composed of several distinct strains, that particular element which came out of this Egyptian slavery must have become the most important of them, or the memory of this oppression would not have become so prominent a feature in the national traditions. Another point about which we may be absolutely sure is that the deliverance of the people from this Egyptian oppression must have been accompanied by some very striking events that caused it to be recounted through the generations as the outstanding example of Yahweh's intervention on behalf of his people. The entrance of a considerable body of Hebrews into Egypt is most easily accounted for in the period when the Hyksos ruled that country, roughly 1800–1600 B.C. The Hyksos were in all probability of kindred race to the Hebrews themselves, and the favourable reception of the Hebrews by the Egyptian authorities which we find recorded in the Jacob-Joseph traditions would be more easy to understand if the rulers of Egypt recognized in the Hebrews their own kinsmen. It is rather striking that one of the Hyksos rulers bears the name Ya'qobhar, the first element in which appears to be identical with the Hebrew name Jacob. The Hyksos made themselves masters of Egypt about 1780 B.C., but a little more than two centuries later they had been driven from their last strongholds. With their departure the conditions would be less favourable to the Hebrews. Whether we should deduce from the tradition of Abraham's sojourn in Egypt that there had been a still earlier body of Hebrews resident in that country is uncertain. In any case such a sojourn must have been of comparatively short duration.

The Exodus.

The date of the Exodus is very difficult to fix with certainty. Different historians have assigned it to the period of the Hyksos domination in Egypt, to the 'Amarna age', to the age of Ramses II and Merenptah, and to the time of the Twentieth Egyptian dynasty. It is impossible to be dogmatic on the subject, but the second or third of these suggestions is much more probably true than the first or fourth, and a date in the reign of Merenptah, *c.* 1225–1215, is the most plausible.

So far as extent of information goes, the story of the Exodus and the events that led up to it is one of the most detailed in the Old Testament. But the accounts—which spring from different literary sources—are not easy to reconcile when they are examined in detail, and much of the detail—as for example the story of the Egyptian plagues—is quite clearly rather legend than history. Unfortunately we have no assistance from the annals of other countries by which to check the Biblical account. The presence of so many legendary elements in the story has sometimes led scholars to doubt whether any real history is to be found in it, and one or two have denied that Moses ever existed. We have already given a cogent reason for believing that the Egyptian sojourn and the Exodus are historical events, and have no hesitation in believing that Moses did play the part of leader at this great crisis in the nation's fate. It would be difficult to-day to find any responsible Old Testament scholar who would dispute this conclusion.

Whatever difficulty there may be in locating the wonderful event which we know as 'the crossing of the Red Sea', there is no doubt that it is part of the historical nucleus round which the legendary matter has gathered. But it is almost certain that the 'Red Sea' of the Bible is not the sea known by that name on our present maps. In the original Hebrew the name of the sea in which the Egyptians were drowned is *Yam Suph*, which may mean 'Sea of Reeds', or 'Sea of Weeds', but certainly does not mean 'Red Sea'. And the Old Testament itself tells us quite definitely where the *Yam Suph* is to be found. In 1 Kings 9^{26} we read that Solomon established a navy in Ezion-geber 'which is beside Eloth, on the shore of the Red Sea, in the land of Edom', where 'Red Sea' is a translation of *Yam Suph*. Now Eloth, or, to give it the better form of the name, Elath, lies at the north-eastern corner of the top of the Gulf of Akaba, the inland sea on the east of the peninsula of Sinai. And that we should look here for the wonderful event which signalized the final escape of the Hebrews from Egyptian tyranny is confirmed by other evidence.

The ordinarily accepted view of the Exodus, which places the 'crossing' at the top of the Red Sea, supposes that subsequently the fugitives made their way along the western side of the Sinaitic peninsula to Mt. Sinai, at its southern extremity. But there is no good ground for believing this. The tradition which locates Sinai in this position cannot be traced back farther than the third century A.D. In other words, the maps which give us Sinai at the point of the peninsula are giving us not a fact but a theory. And on all grounds of probability such a route as that from the top of the Red Sea to the point of the peninsula would be the last that any company of travellers would choose, for it begins with three days' marching through waterless country.

Now the general impression that the narratives of the wanderings in the desert give us is that Sinai cannot have been far from the scene of the catastrophe that befell the Egyptians. And there is other evidence to be found in the Old Testament for connecting Sinai with the territory bordering on the Gulf of Akaba. The Song of Deborah, Judges 5, one of the oldest documents in the Old Testament, speaks (vv. 4, 5) of Yahweh, the national deity, coming from his dwelling-place to the aid of his people:

Yahweh, when thou wentest forth out of Seir,
When thou marchedst out of the field of Edom,
The earth trembled, the heavens also dropped,
Yea, the clouds dropped water.
The mountains flowed down (mg. *quaked*) at the presence of Yahweh,
Even yon Sinai at the presence of Yahweh, the God of Israel.

It is quite true that the words 'even yon Sinai' are suspected to be a later explanation inserted in the text, but even if this be granted we have here an early note which thinks of Sinai as being in the neighbourhood of Seir and Edom. And we have seen already that the top of the Gulf of Akaba is 'in the land of Edom'.

Another important reason for locating Sinai in this neighbourhood is the fact that the descriptions of Sinai in the Old Testament lend colour to the view that it was a volcanic mountain. In Exodus 19 we read that 'there were thunders and lightnings, and a thick cloud upon the mount, and the voice of a trumpet exceeding loud', v. 16: 'and mount Sinai was altogether on smoke, because Yahweh descended upon it in fire: and the smoke thereof ascended as the smoke of a furnace, and the whole mount quaked greatly', v. 18. So also Deuteronomy 4[11-12]: 'And ye came near and stood under the mountain; and the mountain burned with fire unto the heart of heaven, with darkness, cloud, and thick darkness. And Yahweh spake unto you out of the midst of the fire.' Again, Psalm 68[8]—'Yon Sinai *trembled* at the presence of God'—seems to support the inference that the mount of lawgiving was a volcano. The poem with which the book of Habakkuk ends also confirms the theory. According to the true reading of v. 7, 'The tents of Cushan and the dwellings of the land of Midian trembled' at the appearance of Yahweh.

It has been suggested that the passage of the people on dry land through the sea may have been made possible by the convulsion of earthquake, and the pillars of cloud and fire may be reminiscences of the clouds of dust which are known to hang in the air long after volcanic eruption. On the evidence as a whole we are surely justified in concluding that Sinai was a volcanic mountain. Now the geological evidence is definite that the mountains at the foot of the peninsula are not volcanic, while on the other hand the eastern coast of the Gulf of Akaba right round to Midianite and Edomite territory is volcanic. Geology, then, favours the view that Sinai should be located not far from the head of this gulf.

There is another line of evidence which supports the theory that Mt. Sinai should be looked for in this region. According to Exodus 2, when Moses fled from Egypt, because he had killed an Egyptian, he sought refuge in Midian, where he married the daughter of 'the priest of Midian', whose name is given as Reuel. In Exodus 3[1] we are told that while Moses was keeping the flock of his father-in-law, the priest of Midian—whose name here is Jethro—he came to Horeb, the mount of God. This verse comes, as the variation in the name of the priest suggests, from a different document—known to Old Testament scholars as *E*—in which the holy mountain is called not Sinai but Horeb, and the probable conclusion is that just as the two documents have different names for the priest of Midian so the different names Horeb and Sinai are given by them to the same mountain. And, if so, Exodus 3[1] furnishes yet another proof that Horeb=Sinai is to be found in the land of Midian.

If the stories of Moses as a refugee in Midian before the time of the Exodus are based, as we may reasonably believe, upon a foundation of fact, to what country so likely as Midian would he seek to lead the escaping Hebrews, a country where he was already known, and which had before afforded him a harbour of refuge? From Judges 1[16] we may further surmise that the particular Midianite clan with which the Hebrews were thus brought into close contact was that of the Kenites. A very interesting confirmation of our general theory is found incidentally in Judges 11[16], where we read 'when they came up from Egypt, and Israel walked through the wilderness unto the Red Sea'. This can only mean that the wilderness journey preceded the passage of the waters, and therefore the Red Sea cannot be the one which goes by that name on our maps.

The sojourn at Kadesh.

Although the Old Testament gives us much detail about the period which the Hebrew fugitives from Egypt spent in the 'wilderness' the stories are saga rather than history. Some of the local colouring is very faithful, but it is just this element which remains unchanged for generations, and in estimating the historical value of such stories correct detail cannot be decisive. Actually this period in the history of the Hebrews is one of the most difficult to understand, and we can be sure only of one or two outstanding features. Perhaps the best attested fact of all is that the people were settled for a long time at Kadesh. For example, in Numbers 20^1 we read 'and the people abode in Kadesh; and Miriam died there, and was buried there'; and in 20^{16} 'behold, we are in Kadesh, a city'. It is to Kadesh that the spies return after they have been to explore the land of Canaan, Numbers 13^{26}.

It is fortunate that the site of Kadesh has in late years been identified almost beyond doubt as the present ʻain Kdes, roughly half-way between Jerusalem and the head of the Gulf of Akaba, but some fifty miles west of the direct line. The similarity of the names is obvious, though not too much weight should be laid upon this, for Kadesh and Kdes are both forms of the adjective which means 'holy', and the Biblical name just means 'holy city', as the modern one means 'holy stream'. The discovery of the ancient site is one of the romances of modern travel. Up to recent years only two Christians had visited it, because the Bedaween in whose territory it lies prevent as far as possible the approach of strangers. The first of these was a clergyman named Rowlands, who visited it in 1842, and made the identification. For many years later all attempts to find it again went astray, and Rowlands was suspected of having invented his story. However, an American, Trumbull, succeeded in reaching the site in 1881. He describes how his party came from the desolate wastes of sand suddenly round the angle of a limestone ridge to find stretched out before them 'an oasis of verdure and beauty, unlooked for and hardly conceivable in such a region. A carpet of grass covered the ground. Fig trees, laden with fruit nearly ripe enough for eating, were along the shelter of the southern hillside. Shrubs and flowers showed themselves in variety and profusion. Running water gurgled under the waving grass.'

The abundant stream which waters this oasis springs from under a hill of rock, and a succession of pools and troughs of marble afford watering-places for man and beast. There is evidence that the site has been used far back into history, and the plain fertilized by the stream would sustain a large number of inhabitants. Not far distant are two other springs, one, 'ain Kderat, of considerable size, the other, 'ain Kus, small, which some scholars identify respectively with the Meribah and Marah of the Exodus stories. Whether we accept these identifications or not we can understand how stories of miraculous supplies of water would easily originate in this wonderful oasis. Even a sophisticated traveller like Trumbull felt that its presence in the dreary setting was like magic.

To whom this beautiful oasis belonged at the time of the Exodus we cannot say. We might suggest that it was in the dominions of the Amalekites, whose home is just north of Kadesh, and who fought against Israel according to the story of Exodus 17^{8-16}, the battle-field being in the neighbourhood of Kadesh. Gressmann even proposed the theory that the inhabitants of Kadesh to whom the fugitives came may have been Hebrews, like themselves, who had never been in Egypt. But these are only guesses. Nor can we say with exactness how long the sojourn at and around Kadesh may have lasted. The reckoning of the Old Testament seems to allow about thirty-seven years, and this may be a near approximation. The number of stories that centre round Kadesh lends weight to the argument for a lengthy stay there. On the other hand, if we accept the tradition that Moses was the leader of the people from the departure out of Egypt up to the entrance into Canaan, the stay at Kadesh cannot have been much more than the thirty-seven years allowed for it. And we may without hesitation accept the historical truth of the assertion that during this stay at Kadesh Moses fashioned the people into a real unity, and provided it with an organization.

The 'conquest' of Palestine.

The accounts given in the Old Testament of Israel's entrance into Canaan are impossible to reconcile, and it is difficult to deter-

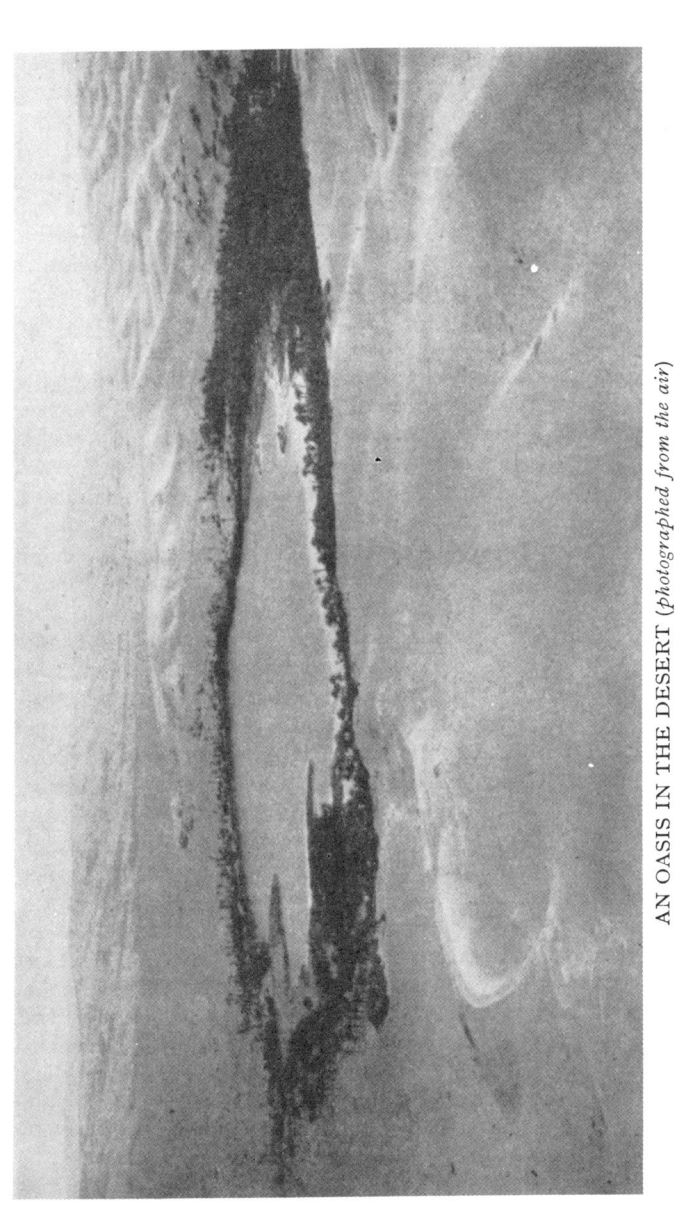

AN OASIS IN THE DESERT (*photographed from the air*)

Sometimes, as in this case, the water from the spring forms a lake, which is usually salt, owing to constant evaporation. Beyond the ring of palm-trees the rolling sands of the desert stretch away in every direction as far as the eye can see.

mine exactly what happened. Even if we were sure of the date of the Exodus we could not give an exact date for the entrance, because the 'forty years' which the Old Testament allows for the time spent in the desert-wanderings is only a round number, equivalent roughly to a generation. The story of the 'conquest' given in Joshua is the 'official' account, and, like many such, not to be relied upon. The final chapter of Deuteronomy relates the death of Moses, and represents the twelve tribes of Israel as encamped on the plains of Moab. The fertile land east of the Jordan has already been captured, and has been assigned by Moses to Reuben, Gad, and half of the tribe of Manasseh, on condition that these tribes assist the remaining tribes to conquer the territory on the other side of the river (Numbers 32). Joshua sends two spies to view the land, and in particular the strong city of Jericho (Joshua 2^1). After receiving their report Joshua musters his forces and crosses the Jordan, whose waters are miraculously parted when the feet of the priests who carry the ark touch the stream. Jericho is besieged, and falls to the invaders in miraculous fashion (Joshua 6).

Ai is the next object of attack, and is captured at the second attempt. A very amusing story is told in Joshua 9 of how the Gibeonites by false pretences make a covenant with Joshua that assures their lives. The various kings of southern Palestine unite their forces to drive out the invaders, but are vanquished, and the whole of this district save the Philistine plain is subdued (Joshua 10). In Joshua 11 a confederation of kings from northern Palestine is similarly defeated, and so the greater part of Palestine passes into the possession of Israel. Most of the original inhabitants are slaughtered. The Gibeonites, who had tricked Joshua into a covenant, are made serfs.

This account, even if it stood unchallenged in the Old Testament, would awaken suspicion. But fortunately we have other evidence by which to test it. According to Judges 1$^{16-17}$ the southern part of Palestine was conquered, not by the united forces of Israel, but by Judah and Simeon acting together, with the co-operation of Kenite allies. And in Joshua 15$^{13-19}$ we are told that it was Caleb and the Kenizzites who took Hebron and Debir. This same story is reflected in Judges 1$^{10-15}$. It seems clear, then, that

Israel's Origins

the representation of a complete conquest carried out by united forces at one time under the leadership of Joshua must be abandoned as unhistorical. In Judges 1–2⁵ we have an older account which is much more worthy of credence: it has been prefixed to the book of Judges, and professes to represent events which happened 'after the death of Joshua' (1¹). The straightforward continuation of the book of Joshua is found in Judges 2⁶. The general lesson we learn from this older account is that the conquest of the various territories was effected by individual tribes. Another correction of the official account which may be derived from this ancient document is that these attempts by the several tribes in different localities were by no means uniformly successful.

Even within this earlier account discrepancies may be detected. Judges 1⁸ tells us that 'the children of Judah fought against Jerusalem, and took it . . . and set the city on fire'. On the other hand, in v. 21 we read that the Jebusites of Jerusalem were not driven out of Jerusalem, which remained a Jebusite stronghold until it was captured by David. Judges 19¹⁰⁻¹² confirms the fact that Jerusalem remained in Canaanite possession. Another contradiction is found between Judges 1¹⁸ and 1¹⁹: the former of these verses asserts that Judah took three of the chief cities in the Philistine plain, whereas the latter admits that the successes of Judah were confined to the hill country These inconsistencies are due to insertions by a later author, who was anxious to give a more glowing account than that found in the ancient document.

The fortunes of the Joseph tribes in their attempts to make good a footing are dealt with in Judges 1²²ᶠ. The capture of Bethel is recorded as their outstanding exploit. But Manasseh met with no success against the strongly fortified cities in the Plain of Esdraelon (vv. 27 f.), and Ephraim made no impression upon Gezer. That the latter remained in the hands of the Canaanites is confirmed by 1 Kings 9¹⁶, according to which the king of Egypt captured it from them and presented it as a dowry for his daughter to Solomon. Zebulon, Naphtali, Asher, and Dan also appear to have fared badly, for in the verses which deal with the fate of these tribes the constant refrain is 'they did not drive them (the Canaanites) out'. Dan, whose original attempt at settlement was made in the south-west, seems to have been able to maintain but a precarious foothold there, and was eventually forced to migrate to the extreme north. (Cf. Joshua 19^{47}; Judges 18.)

That, despite the promises made to Israel by God, the Canaanites remained for centuries in possession of so much of the 'Promised Land' was a sore problem for later generations. All sorts of explanations are offered. Sometimes it is said that God allowed the Canaanites to remain so that they might afford Israel practice in warfare (Judges 3^2); again, it is said that God retained a number of Canaanites in order that he might use them as a rod of correction for his people (Joshua 23^{13}). In one passage (Exodus 23^{29}) it is explained that the Canaanites were suffered to live because if they had been exterminated the Israelites would not have been numerous enough to fill the whole land, and consequently wild beasts would have multiplied in the vacant territories. But the real reason for the survival of the Canaanites is given in Judges 1^{27}, 'the Canaanites would dwell in that land'. In other words, the Israelites were not strong enough to subdue them.

Another fragmentary narrative of some importance is found in Joshua 17$^{14-18}$. Ephraim and Manasseh complain that the territory allotted to them is insufficient, since they have been unable to make any impression on the plains, where the chariots of the Canaanites are all-powerful. Joshua bids them turn their attention to the 'forest', or 'hill country'. It is difficult to see how this can mean the highland ranges south of the Plain of Esdraelon, for these are presumably the territory that—in contrast to the plains —has been already occupied. Budde has suggested that the hill country meant is the district of Gilead on the east of the Jordan, which might be called 'forest', for it was well wooded. If this theory be true the subjugation of the land occupied by these tribes was—contrary to the order of events given in the official account —subsequent to their capture of the highlands of Ephraim.

The general situation finally arrived at seems to have been this. Judah, Simeon, and certain Kenite and Kenizzite allies made good their position in the southern hill country, but were held in check by the Philistines in the west, and by the Jebusite stronghold of Jerusalem in the north. The central highlands are occupied by the Joseph tribes, Ephraim and Manasseh, but a belt of country both north and south of them remains in Canaanite possession, so

Israel's Origins

that they are shut off from the other tribes. The situation of Dan, Naphtali, Zebulon, and Asher in the north is obscure, but certainly they had to be content with a situation which left the Canaanites at least as powerful as themselves in the area as a whole. We must not forget that it is possible that among the inhabitants of Canaan whom the Hebrews found on their return from Egypt there would be some clans who were themselves of the same origin as the Hebrews, and with whom it would be fairly easy for the invaders to come to terms.

The Philistines.

In the days immediately before the founding of the kingdom of Israel the Philistines even more than the Canaanites threatened the survival of the Hebrews as a distinct people. That the Philistines were perhaps of greater importance in the history of Palestine than the records of the Old Testament might lead us to suppose may be gathered from the fact that to them the country owes the name by which it is still universally known: for 'Palestine' means nothing more than 'country of the Philistines'. Evidence outside the Old Testament confirms the impression we gain from its pages that the Philistines came into prominence towards the beginning of the twelfth century B.C. The Egyptian records recount an attempt made by the 'Peoples of the Sea' at the beginning of that century to effect a settlement in the Delta. Prominent among these invaders were the Peleset or Pulesati, who are certainly to be identified with the Philistines of the Old Testament. They seem to play a part in the Mediterranean very like that of the sea-roving Danes in early English history. Their attack on Egypt proved unsuccessful, for they were heavily defeated by the reigning Pharaoh, Ramses III, in 1194 B.C. Over twelve thousand of the invaders fell in the conflict. But though foiled in this direction, they were able a little later to effect a settlement on the south-west maritime plain of Canaan, when apparently the power of Egypt had so much declined that she was unable to evict them.

The origin of the Philistines is a controverted subject. Usually it is said that they came from Crete. Amos 9[7] asserts that Yahweh brought up the Philistines from Caphtor as he had brought up the Israelites from Egypt. Caphtor is commonly supposed to denote

Crete. Breasted asserts that the Philistines were 'no doubt one of the early tribes of Crete'. But while Crete may well be one of the bases from which the sea-rovers set out to invade Egypt and Canaan, it is probable that the original home of the Philistines is to be sought in the neighbourhood of Asia Minor, and that they were of Carian or Lycian descent. The Greek Old Testament seems to favour this idea, for it renders the Caphtor of Amos 9[7] by Cappadocia. The pictures of the Philistines that have survived show them as wearing armour and the distinctive feather crest that was characteristic of Lycians and Carians. Certainly the armour of Goliath described in 1 Samuel 17 is of Greek type.

The adjective 'uncircumcised', so often applied in the Old Testament with contempt to the Philistines, marks them off from their Semitic neighbours. Their language, too, was not Semitic; Nehemiah (13[24]) complains that the children of the Philistine women who had married Jews 'spake half in the language of Ashdod, and could not speak the Jews' language'. They seem to have contributed little to the civilization of Canaan. Their military organization was undoubtedly superior to that of the folk among whom they settled. Like many conquering races, they absorbed much from the country into which they had thrust their way, though the statement that they were 'in many respects a Semitic people' is rather an exaggeration. Their god, Dagon, seems to have been taken over with the country they occupied, for he was a corn-deity well known in Syria and Palestine. The idea that he was a 'fish-god' is based on a mistaken etymology. Flinders Petrie thinks that his excavations have proved that the Philistines grew corn in their fertile district and exported it on a considerable scale. They were a source of mercenary soldiers, for the Pelethites of David's body-guard, 2 Samuel 8[18], are Philistines under another name.

CHAPTER III

THE PERIOD OF THE JUDGES

What were the 'judges'?

THE book of Judges is almost our sole source for knowledge of the Hebrews from the time of Joshua to that of Samuel. But to give history in the ordinary sense was far from being the purpose of the compiler of the book, and he did his work centuries after the events with which he deals. He had a theory that when Israel was faithful to Yahweh she prospered, but when she deserted Yahweh for other gods Yahweh allowed other nations to oppress her. Then the people cried to Yahweh in their misery, and he raised up a deliverer for them. After the death of a deliverer the same cycle of events repeats itself. These deliverers are the 'judges'. For example, after the deliverance under Deborah and Barak Israel did 'that which was evil'—by which is meant specifically the worship of other gods—in the sight of Yahweh, and Yahweh delivered them into the hand of Midian seven years (Judges 6[1]). The people cry unto Yahweh (v. 7), and he calls Gideon to their rescue (v. 14).

The stories of these hero-deliverers which are used by the author of Judges to illustrate his theory are very old traditions. But because he thought, mistakenly, of Israel as a united people during the period with which he deals, his use of the stories to enforce the moral he desired to impress on the people of his own time has resulted in a distortion of history. We know that, far from being a unity, the various tribes were isolated from one another by hostile tracts of territory. Also in some cases they were under the domination of a Canaanite majority in the districts where they actually lived. The idea of a 'judge' exercising authority over the people of Israel as a nation does not correspond with the facts of the situation. The word rendered 'judge' ought rather to be translated 'deliverer', 'saviour', or 'champion'; for the real work of those heroes to whom the name is given was to free the people in their immediate neighbourhood from foreign oppression, and their task was accomplished on the field of battle, not on the seat of judgement. No doubt after their triumphs were achieved they did, like other chiefs, exercise judicial functions; but these were only a sequel to their real work. The important point to remember is that their influence was only local; they freed, and became chiefs of, the two or three Israelite groups in a limited area. The only case of action on anything approaching a national scale was under Deborah and Barak, and even then only about half of the tribes were affected. So we must rid ourselves of the idea that the 'judges' were the rulers of Israel who followed one another in chronological succession. It is not impossible, indeed, that some may have been contemporaries.

Keeping this fact in view, we may consider the stories in Judges, not with any hope of reconstructing any ordered history of Israel during the period, but rather with a desire to learn what we can deduce from them as to the political and social conditions under which the Israelites were living. We shall find that only in a few cases can we gain much information of any real importance. Some of the 'judges' are merely shadows, and it is evident that the author of the book knew nothing about them save their names. It is indeed likely that some of them are sheer inventions just to make up the round number of twelve.

Othniel.

The first of the deliverers about whom we are told is Othniel, a Kenizzite (3^{7-11}). He is said to have delivered Israel from the oppression of Cushan-rishathaim, king of Mesopotamia, which had lasted eight years, and to have ruled the people for forty years. This, except the statement that he was a nephew of Caleb, is really all we are told in the story. Apart from the incorrect assumption that there was a united Israel at this time, the story is difficult. Mesopotamia was far away, and there is no evidence of any invasion of Canaan from that quarter during this period. Further, if there were such an invasion, it is very strange that the deliverer, Othniel, should be drawn from the Kenizzite clans in the extreme south, the district farthest from the point at which any attack from Mesopotamia would come. On the other hand, it must be admitted that the name of the hostile king, which means 'Cushan of twofold wickedness', though obviously not a genuine name but a play upon words, such as the Hebrews delighted in, is for that reason likely to have a real name behind it. Possibly there has been some confusion in the text between Mesopotamia and Edom, which might easily happen in the original Hebrew, and some obscure oppression by Edom underlies the story. At any rate, a Kenizzite deliverer would come from the district most open to Edomite attack.

Ehud.

The story of Ehud, which follows, may well be historical, though it combines two forms of the narrative, as is evident upon a careful reading. Eglon of Moab is the enemy, and Ehud's forces come from the highlands of Ephraim (3^{27}), which agrees very well geographically. The Ammonites and Amalekites of v. 13 are an expansion of the original story. This, then, is certainly the case of a local conflict between the tribes settled in the central hill country and their neighbours of Moab just on the other side of the Jordan.

Shamgar.

Shamgar, who comes next in the list, is not introduced by the usual formula, and it is noteworthy that 4^1, which begins the story of Deborah and Barak, seems to assume that no deliverer has appeared since the death of Ehud. The name Shamgar is probably Hittite. The account of Shamgar may be a pure invention based on a misunderstanding of Judges 5^6, where Shamgar is really an oppressor and not a deliverer of Israel.

Barak and Deborah.

The most illuminating of all the stories in Judges is that of Barak and Deborah, cc. 4–5. The first of the chapters tells the story in prose, the second—the 'Song of Deborah'—in verse. The two accounts differ in a number of details, and the Song, which is the older, being indeed the oldest document of considerable length in the Old Testament, is generally agreed to describe the situation far more accurately. It is likely that the Song was composed immediately after the events which it so vividly portrays, though the idea that it was sung by Deborah herself as a triumph song, based on v. 7, cannot be maintained, because the correct translation of the verse should run:

> The rulers ceased in Israel, they ceased,
> Until that *thou* Deborah didst arise,
> That *thou* didst arise, a mother in Israel.

The text of the Song, especially at the beginning, has suffered so much in transmission that it cannot be translated without hazardous conjecture; but though details may be difficult, the general picture of the conditions under which the Hebrews were living can be reconstructed in all its main features.

A time of crisis has been reached. The Hebrews are holding the hilly country, but the Canaanites still dominate the plains. The cities with their massive walls, and especially the chariots of the Canaanites, have prevented the Hebrews from making an effective conquest of the country as a whole. From their strongholds in the hills the Hebrews look down enviously upon the fertile plains, and watch the rich caravans as they pass. But the Canaanites, too, are uneasy. The Hebrews have shown themselves to be hardy soldiers, and are as thorns in the side of the dwellers in the plains. True, they seem at the time to be under a cloud, and disheartened (vv. 6–8). But their numbers are formidable and increasing. There is a situation of tension which cannot continue indefinitely. Leaders on both sides, Sisera among the Canaanites—the Jabin of the prose story is in all likelihood an imaginary character, for it will be noted that the Song completely ignores him, and that even in c. 4 Sisera is really the prominent figure—Deborah and Barak among the Hebrews, prepare for a decisive trial of strength. The Canaanites would root out the menace of the invading Hebrews: the Hebrews would entrench themselves more firmly than in their precarious holding of the comparatively barren mountain ranges. The clash of arms comes about in the Plain of Esdraelon, which has been well described as the classic battle-field of Palestine. The Hebrews, whose chance of succeeding against the Canaanites and their chariots in the plain must have been very small, are aided by a stormy deluge which causes the river Kishon, ordinarily a gently meandering stream, to become a raging torrent. The horses and chariots are reduced to helplessness, many of them

The Period of the Judges

perishing in the flood. The Hebrews interpret this natural phenomenon as being the direct intervention of their God, Yahweh, in the conflict. He has come striding from his home in the desert (vv. 4-5) to aid his people. They fight with more than human courage, and gain a decisive victory. Sisera escapes from the field of battle, only to perish treacherously by the hand of a woman—the most disgraceful of all deaths for a warrior!—the nomad Jael. The issue of the conflict decides finally the fate of the Hebrew 'conquest'. Though even now the Hebrews do not dominate the whole country, they have dug themselves in and are never again in so serious a danger of being evicted.

Two really important facts are made clear in the Song. In the first place the tribes at this time did not in any true sense form a united organization. Only half of them take part in the fighting, Zebulon, Naphtali, Ephraim, Benjamin, Machir—that is, Manasseh, which tribe was at this time probably resident only on the west side of the Jordan—and Issachar. These were the tribes whose homes were nearest to the scene of the battle. Asher, Reuben, Dan, and Gilead—that is, Gad—all held aloof, and are taunted for their cowardice or selfishness. Judah and Simeon are not even mentioned. Their home lay far to the south, and they were probably so cut off from the other tribes by hostile Canaanite territory that there was no thought of their taking part in the struggle. The other important truth that the Song reveals is that such unity as did exist among the tribes was religious rather than political. They were bound together, despite geographical separation, by their common allegiance to Yahweh. It is the 'people of Yahweh' that go down to the gates, v. 11; and the inhabitants of Meroz are cursed because 'they came not to the help of Yahweh', v. 23.

Gideon.

The story of Gideon is told with great vivacity. As we have seen in other cases, there is a double tradition of the events. In one of them Gideon's name appears as Jerubbaal. The two Midianite princes who fall victims to his prowess appear now as Oreb and Zeeb, 7^{25}, now as Zebah and Zalmunna, 8^5. The historical basis for the story is clearly the rise of a Hebrew leader whose skill is sufficient to deliver the territory of Manasseh from the repeated Midianite raids of which it had been the victim. Gideon's outstanding merit as a military chief won from the people of his district an invitation to make himself king. Like Cromwell, he declined the name, but exercised the authority associated with it. It should be observed that among those who recognized his rule were the inhabitants of Shechem, which was a predominantly Canaanite city. So here we have an example of Canaanites living at peace in a territory that is under Hebrew control, as no doubt elsewhere Hebrews dwelt under Canaanite rule. One of Gideon's wives was a Canaanite woman of Shechem, which fact had important consequences for the subsequent history of the region over which he was sheikh. For a whole generation Gideon maintained his position, and he died 'in a good old age' at Ophrah, his capital town.

Abimelech.

The story of Abimelech, Judges 9, is quite different in its general features from those that tell the exploits of the earlier deliverers. In the strict sense of the word he is not a 'judge', or saviour of the people, at all. The story has not the characteristic formulae at its beginning and end, and there is good reason for believing that at one stage in the history of Judges the Abimelech story was omitted and replaced by the colourless summary 8^{33-5}. Its chief historical value lies in the light it throws on the relationship between Canaanites and Hebrews, and on the general political situation of the country. Abimelech, son of Gideon by the aforementioned Canaanite wife from Shechem, when his father died made a subtle appeal to the Canaanite inhabitants to support him as successor to the authority wielded by his father, on the ground that it would be better for them to have as their sheikh a man who was half Canaanite himself—their bone and their flesh—rather than any of Gideon's sons who were of pure Hebrew descent. The burghers of Shechem were persuaded to advance him money from the temple treasury, the city bank of those days, by means of which he hired a band of reckless assassins and butchered all his brothers save one. He thus succeeded in establishing his position, which he seems to have held with considerable skill until he met his death by a missile cast by a woman's hand from a stronghold he was besieging.

Jephthah.

The next-mentioned judges, Tola and Jair, are quite unimportant, and one is tempted to surmise that, like the later Ibzan, Elon, and Abdon, they owe their mention, if not their existence, to an attempt to bring the number of judges up to the symbolical number of twelve—it may be, with a view to finding a judge for each tribe, though if this last intention was present it must be owned that it was very imperfectly carried out.

Jephthah, on the other hand, is a man of real importance. The section of Judges which tells his story, 10^{17}–12^{7}, is very difficult to interpret, because in it two quite different accounts of his activities have been combined, in one of which the oppressors from whom he delivers the people of Gilead are the Moabites, in the other the Ammonites. A curious feature of the story is that 11^{12-28}, which in its present form deals with the Ammonites, really is concerned with the Moabites, for Chemosh (v. 24) is the national deity not of Ammon but of Moab. It seems that there has been some attempt in this passage to edit the original in order to make the enemy Ammon throughout.

Of outstanding interest is the dramatic episode in which Jephthah sacrifices his daughter to Yahweh, in fulfilment of a vow. This shows clearly that human sacrifice, though it may have been rare, was not unknown to the Hebrews of this period. None of the attempts to construe the passage in such a way as to avoid this conclusion is in the least convincing. The laws which provide for the redemption of the first-born son have no meaning unless there was at one time the custom of actually sacrificing the first-born to the national god. Jephthah's career as deliverer of Gilead was marked by considerable success, but its duration was short.

Samson.

Like Abimelech, Samson does not properly belong to the ranks of the judges. His exploits are entirely personal efforts of valour, and in no sense was he a deliverer of his people from the dreaded Philistines. The critical evidence goes to show that his story was not included in an earlier form of Judges. But apparently the lively accounts of his deeds of valour were so popular that later editors were compelled to restore them to the book. There is little religious interest in Samson's career; it is hardly too much to describe him as a pagan. The account of his birth in Judges 13 is suspiciously like certain incidents in the story of Gideon, and the attempt of the editors to fit the sensual, boisterous hero for more respectable company by making him into a Nazirite is unsuccessful.

The Samson stories have much in common with those told of Hercules, and his Babylonian forerunner, Gilgamesh, and are decorated with *motifs* from solar mythology. But Samson was for all that probably an historical character, and though the account of him furnishes us with little history of the ordinary kind it does give us some light on the social customs of the period, and on the civilization of the Philistines.

The concluding chapters of Judges are an amalgam of various elements, some early, some late; but they afford us glimpses of the political conditions and social and moral customs of the Judges period. The account in c. 18 of Dan's migration from its original home to its later place of settlement in the north is particularly valuable, and bears all the marks of a genuine historical tradition.

CHAPTER IV

THE RISE OF THE KINGDOM

Situation at the end of the 'judges' era.

THE era of the 'judges' passed, leaving the situation of the Hebrews in Palestine on the whole very much what it had been. Only in limited areas did they effectively possess the territory. From some districts which they had originally occupied they had been expelled; in others they had become merged with the Canaanites. In some ways the situation had grown more threatening. It is true that the great victory gained over Sisera had secured them against expulsion at the hands of the Canaanites. But the Philistines had grown increasingly powerful, and now presented a menace to the independence of the Hebrews even more formidable than the hostility of the original inhabitants. This is made clear in the opening chapters of 1 Samuel, the source from which we derive our information as to the beginnings of the Hebrew kingdom. We see that the kingdom is established as an outcome of a life and death struggle between the Hebrews and the Philistines.

Nature of Samuel and Kings.

The books of Samuel and Kings really form a continuous story which covers the whole existence of the kingdom and the two kingdoms into which it was later divided. In the Greek version of the Old Testament the four books appear as four books of 'Kingdoms'. They provide a story rather than a history. The Hebrew Old Testament includes them under the head of 'Prophets', which at first sight seems to us rather strange. But there is an excellent reason for it. The intention of the editors who gave the books their present form was primarily to point a moral. They are concerned to show that the prosperity of the nation throughout its history was dependent upon the faithful discharge of its religious obligations, and that whenever the people allowed themselves to be seduced into the worship of other gods, or practised the worship of their own God in unrecognized shrines, or with improper ritual, they came to grief. The editors selected from history such material as enabled them to drive home their point, and ignored a great deal that a modern historian would have deemed to be more valuable. So it happens that some of the greatest of the kings have little or nothing said about them. It is fortunate that for the period of the kingdom the annals of other nations enable us to check and supplement the statements contained in Samuel and Kings.

The books of Samuel are really a compilation from the stories of three outstanding figures, Samuel, Saul, and David. The time covered is roughly a century, from the end of the 'judges' era, to the accession of Solomon. The contents of the books fall into five main divisions:

(1) Eli, Samuel, Saul. 1 Samuel 1–16^{13}.
(2) Saul, David. 1 Samuel 16^{14}–31.
(3) David's assumption of the kingship. 2 Samuel 1–8.
(4) A history of David's family affairs. 2 Samuel 9–20.
(5) An appendix. 2 Samuel 21–4.

To a large extent the books of Chronicles, too, cover the ground traversed by Samuel and Kings, but they are of considerably later date; moreover what information they include apart from the extracts culled by their editor from Samuel and Kings adds little that is trustworthy to our knowledge.

The struggle against the Philistines.

The situation from which the movement that developed into the monarchy arose is in many respects parallel to the crisis that produced the triumph of Deborah and Barak. The hostile power is no longer the Canaanite inhabitants—of whom we hear singularly little in the story of Saul—but the Philistines. And the menace was much more serious than the attacks of Moab, Ammon, or Midian in the earlier period. These eastern neighbours of the Hebrews had continually raided the territory of Israel, but had not attempted to conquer it in the ordinary sense of the term. The Philistines, on the other hand, appear to have contemplated an extension of their authority permanently, and to have pursued a systematic campaign for the reduction of Palestine.

The Hebrews were ill equipped to resist the pressure of Philis-

The Rise of the Kingdom

tia. The one district which they really dominated was the hill country of Ephraim. They possessed few important cities. The tribe of Simeon had been almost extinguished, and even Judah was weak and isolated. So pronounced was the superiority of the Philistines that they were able to deprive the Hebrews of their weapons (1 Samuel 13$^{19-20}$). Once again had come a time when the question of Deborah's Song, 'Was there a shield or spear seen among forty thousand in Israel?' could be asked in irony. There was little coherence among the various Hebrew settlements. The central rallying point, as far as one existed at all, was the famous sanctuary at Shiloh, to which the people who could reach it resorted. There was no military leader, and the one prominent figure was Eli, the priest of Shiloh, whose pathetic story shows him to have been the least likely man in the country to organize the national resistance. He was not able even to save the cult at Shiloh from the perversity and corruption of his own sons. Surely this was the time for the Philistines to reduce the territory of the Hebrews to a mere province of Philistia!

The story of the campaigns in 1 Samuel 4–6 begins as though the Hebrews had taken the initiative; but the narrative is evidently a fragment, and the action of Israel was much more probably a desperate attempt to ward off an overwhelming threat. The Philistines are victorious in the first battle. The Israelites then, as a last resort, take with them into the battlefield the sacred ark, in which the power and presence of Yahweh were supposed to dwell: but the Philistines, though not without some superstitious dread of this new force, triumph again, and actually carry off the ark as a trophy of war.

The narrative records the tragic fate of Eli and his sons, but then passes to an account of the fortunes of the ark, saying nothing about the disastrous effect of the defeat on the country. Happily we are able from other sources to reconstruct the main features of the subsequent history. It is noteworthy that when later the ark is returned to the Hebrews by the Philistines, who find it a most troublesome guest, it is brought, not to the famous shrine at Shiloh, which had been its abode, but to Bethshemesh, and afterwards is removed to Kirjath-jearim. Why? Evidently Shiloh must have been captured and sacked as the crowning achievement of the Philistine effort. And in the later literature this supposition is definitely confirmed. Jeremiah threatens that Yahweh will punish the evil-doers of Jerusalem by destroying the temple upon which they set such store. 'Go ye now unto my place which was in Shiloh, where I caused my name to dwell at the first, and see what I did to it for the wickedness of my people Israel. . . . Therefore will I do unto the house, which is called by my name, wherein ye trust, and unto the place which I gave to you and to your fathers, as I have done to Shiloh' (Jeremiah 7[12-14]). 'I will make this house like Shiloh, and will make this city a curse to all the nations of the earth' (26[6]). Another reference to the sack of Shiloh and the slaughter of its inhabitants may be seen in Psalm 78[60-4].

The idealized portrait of Samuel.

The narratives relating to Samuel in this early period are clearly more in the nature of idyll than of history. A strange thing is that the etymology which 1 Samuel 1[20] gives for his name really applies to the name of Saul, which does mean 'asked'. All that we can reckon on as history in the stories of Samuel's birth and call is the fact that from his early years he had a definite connexion with the sanctuary at Shiloh. Other narratives which represent Samuel as exercising, even before the rise of Saul, all the functions of a 'judge' in Israel are worthy of even less credence. The picture of all Israel from Dan to Beersheba looking up to him as the virtual ruler (1 Samuel 3[20f]) presumes a united people in possession of the whole country, which is a gross anachronism. The same criticism is valid against the story in 1 Samuel 7, according to which Samuel summons 'all Israel' to Mizpah, and offers a sacrifice to Yahweh for Israel. In response to the prayer of Samuel Yahweh miraculously discomfits the Philistines who have drawn near in battle-array, leaving the Israelites to pursue and slaughter them—another suspicious element in the account. And when we are told that as a consequence of this victory Israel recovered all the territory that had been captured by the Philistines, and that the Philistines came no more within the border of Israel—statements clean contrary to what we find in the story of Saul—we are left with no shadow

The Rise of the Kingdom

of doubt that the account must be a fiction. The reason for these romances about the prominent part taken by Samuel in freeing Israel from the grip of the Philistines is clearly to be found in a deliberate attempt, of which we shall find other cogent evidence presently, to minimize in every possible way the achievements of Saul.

Saul.

The incident related in 1 Samuel 11 probably gives us the first step in the progress of Saul to the throne. Righteous indignation against oppressors of his kindred roused him to action. The Ammonites under Nahash had invested the Hebrew town of Jabesh in Gilead, whose inhabitants, despairing of a successful resistance, asked for terms of submission. Nahash makes it a condition that their right eyes shall be put out. They plead for a delay of seven days, in which time they may send messengers to their kinsfolk appealing for succour. Nahash, apparently confident that from a people depressed and deprived of arms no response could come, agrees. When the message comes to Saul's ears he hews in pieces the oxen which he is driving, and sends the pieces throughout the district, threatening that so shall be slain the oxen of all who fail to respond to his call.

He leads those who answer the call against Nahash, defeats him, and delivers Jabesh. In their enthusiasm the people, with Samuel's approval, choose him as their king. The account of this event has been exaggerated by a statement that the followers of Saul in his exploit were 300,000 men of Israel and 30,000 men of Judah. These numbers are absurdly high, but illuminating in that they do fairly well represent the proportions of the people in the later Northern and Southern Kingdoms. This exaggeration apart, the narrative seems worthy of credence.

Much of the history of Saul's reign has been so distorted in the attempt to minimize the part he played in establishing the kingdom that it is difficult to get at the truth. This is particularly evident in the contradictory accounts of his installation as king. On this matter, it is now generally recognized, there are two quite different and irreconcilable traditions. The older one, which is very primitive in its religious ideas, tells of Saul's first introduction to Samuel. He is seeking some strayed asses, and his servant recommends him to consult a seer in a city near by, who will be able by his gift of divination to locate the asses. Saul has never heard of the seer before—which would be quite impossible had Samuel really occupied the position of national leader which the later writers attribute to him—but agrees to consult him. Samuel has previously been instructed by Yahweh that the stalwart young man who will consult him is the divinely chosen deliverer of Israel from Philistine oppression, and after satisfying Saul's demand for information as to the whereabouts of the lost asses, solemnly anoints him king. Saul duly fulfils the purpose for which God has chosen him, and, helped by his son Jonathan, achieves notable successes over the Philistine oppressors. According to this tradition, then, Saul is definitely chosen by Yahweh as the deliverer of Israel, chosen, further, to be king, and is recognized as such by Samuel without hesitation.

The later tradition is absolutely opposed to this. Its version is that the elders of Israel, seeing that Samuel's sons, who were looked upon as likely to succeed to their father's authority, are unworthy to exercise it, demand that Samuel shall make them a king, 'to judge them like all the nations'. Samuel is, perhaps not unnaturally, displeased. More important still, Yahweh, to whom, as the real king of Israel, the demand is a grievous affront, is offended, and, while bidding Samuel concede the demand of the elders, evidently does so to 'read them a lesson'. Samuel points out that a king will prove to be a tyrannical oppressor, but fails to dissuade the people from their purpose. In a solemn assembly at Mizpah, after another grave warning, Samuel chooses Saul by lot, under divine guidance, as king. In an elaborate sermon he manages to convince the people that their action has been sinful. Very soon after Saul has been proclaimed king Yahweh rejects him, and instructs Samuel to anoint David to take his place in due time.

This second account is undoubtedly for the most part fictitious. Later experience of kings tended to disillusionize the people, and the disasters which overtook the nation came to be regarded, with no little justification, as due to the folly and wickedness of its kings. It is under the influence of this bitter

The Rise of the Kingdom

anti-monarchical feeling, which saw in the monarchy a declension from the ideal state in which God alone was king, that the attempt is made in this second version of Saul's election to represent it as being from the beginning a step taken in opposition to the declared will of God as expressed by his representative, Samuel.

Saul's election as king may be dated *c.* 1025 B.C. He won notable military successes. Not only did he maintain the struggle against Philistia with advantage to Israel, but he fought against the peoples of the surrounding desert so that they did not molest the peace of the country. The territory over which he held sway comprised the central highlands of Palestine and part of Trans-Jordania. Presumably Gibeah was his capital; it might have been better had he made Shechem, a much more important city, his headquarters. Many of the chief events in his reign are recorded in the story of David, and will fall for consideration later. His career was marked by friction within his realm even more than by attacks from external foes. It is clear that very soon after his accession Samuel and he began to drift apart. His relations with Jonathan and David were unhappy. Being naturally of a passionate and superstitious disposition he became more easily the subject of a melancholia bordering upon madness. His declining years were embittered by the growing importance of his rival David. In the end he fell a victim to his ancient enemies the Philistines, who inflicted a crushing defeat upon his army at Mt. Gilboa, where his sons were slain, and he himself committed suicide to avoid a more humiliating death.

Though his reign thus ended in the tragedy of defeat it is to Saul rather than to Samuel that we must ascribe the honour of the movement which at last freed Israel from the Philistine yoke. In spite of the attempts made by later writers to thrust him into the background and make Samuel the real hero of the crisis we can discern that Saul was a greater king than they would have us believe. This is borne out by the ancient elegy from the 'Book of Jashar' (2 Samuel 1$^{19-27}$), in which the fallen hero is described as 'mighty', a warrior whose 'sword returned not empty', 'swifter than an eagle', 'stronger than a lion', and as a foe whose death would bring great joy to the Philistines. Only a strong man could have held his position on the throne in spite of the popularity of his rival, David, and in defiance of the opposition of the recognized religious leader, Samuel. That his kingdom must have been well established appears certain when we reflect that his son Ishbosheth, a weakling, was able to hold the throne for a time even when David had become actually king of the Southern tribes.

David.

While Saul must be credited with the establishment of the first Hebrew kingdom it was David who made the new institution secure. He was the greatest of all who occupied the throne of Israel, and to him later ages looked back as the model king. Often when in the dark days that followed the destruction of the kingdom prophets comforted the despairing people with pictures of the good days that were yet in store, they spoke of the happy future as a kingdom ruled by a second David. He was the most popular hero of Hebrew history, and stories of his exploits were told from generation to generation.

THE PHILISTINES. Reliefs from the Temple of Ramses III at Medinet Habu, showing typical facial characteristics.

These stories were later gathered into groups, and the richness of the material accumulated in this way for an account of his

The Rise of the Kingdom

life is one cause of the difficulty we have in gaining a clear view of his career. For the history as set down in the Old Testament has been pieced together by editors from the groups of stories, with the result that in some cases striking incidents have been duplicated, and the chronological order is often violated. The result of the editors' work appears in 1 Samuel 16–1 Kings 2, and so well, in one sense, have they performed their task that, although we can be reasonably sure that two main sources have been used, it is impossible to distinguish their limits accurately. There is also a history of David in 1 Chronicles 11–29, which is based on the contents of Samuel and Kings, and runs parallel in part to those sources. The additional matter contained in it consists chiefly of lists of officials and details as to the temple worship, so that for our purpose it contributes nothing substantial. Its greatest service is to show us a further stage in the idealizing of David, a process which had already begun in the earlier story. The bold, sensual warrior of Samuel has become in Chronicles something more like a 'plaster saint'. The Greek Bible differs considerably from the Hebrew account in Samuel and Kings, giving a different selection of material in places, and shows that additions were made to the Hebrew record as it was left by its first editors.

No incident in David's career, save perhaps the duel with Goliath, is more familiar to us than the beautiful story which tells how Samuel, under Yahweh's direction, chooses the youngest son of Jesse as the destined successor of Saul. This record, 1 Samuel 16[1-13], forms the connecting link between the biography of Samuel and that of David. It is with real regret that one is compelled to regard it as no more than a lovely idyll. But it can hardly have taken place as sober matter of fact. The story informs us that Samuel selected David and anointed him in the presence of the elders of Bethlehem. Had such a thing actually happened it is difficult to suppose that the incident would have been kept a secret from Saul, and Saul was certainly not the man to disregard such a challenge to his position. The later narratives, too, absolutely ignore this story. Had it been a record of fact we must surely have had some reference to it later.

The real story of David's emergence on the scene of history is that found in 1 Samuel 16$^{14-23}$. Saul has become subject to moods of melancholy, and music is prescribed as a cure. One of the king's young courtiers knows of David, who is skilful in playing the harp, and also a man of valour, good to look upon, and with manners that fit him for the court. David is summoned; the king takes a fancy to him at first sight, and appoints him not only court musician but also his personal attendant.

Immediately following this comes the immortal tale of the conflict with Goliath, in which David, a shepherd lad, kills the giant in single combat. This story, again, must, at any rate in its present form, be regarded as romance rather than history. For one thing, 2 Samuel 21^{19} states definitely that it was one of David's heroes, Elhanan, who slew Goliath. It is a familiar custom of ancient times to credit a leader or king with the exploits of his servants. 1 Chronicles 20^5 makes an attempt to resolve the contradiction by saying that the victim of Elhanan's valour was 'Lahmi, the brother of Goliath'. If the story had been true we should certainly have looked for some reference to it in 1 Samuel 21$^{10-15}$ or 29. But even if we brush aside all these difficulties others remain that are insuperable. According to the context immediately preceding Saul has appointed David, a man of valour, to be his court musician and armour-bearer. Now David appears as an untried shepherd lad, and neither Saul, nor his commander-in-chief, Abner, have the faintest idea as to David's parentage; indeed the impression we naturally receive from the narrative is that neither Saul nor Abner had ever seen David before.

The Greek Bible has a shorter version of the story, which is less open to criticism, but the utmost that can be conceded is that the story may be an expanded account of some famous combat in which David triumphed over a Philistine champion, though his opponent's name was not Goliath. Some such striking feat of valour would account for David's popularity, and might, if we reject the story of David's introduction to the court as a musician, have been the occasion of his coming to Saul's notice. For we read (1 Samuel 14^{52}) that 'when Saul saw any mighty man, or any valiant man, he took him unto him'.

Before long, however, Saul became jealous of David, who was

The Rise of the Kingdom

the darling of the crowd, and in whom he saw a dangerous rival, if not a possible aspirant to the throne. (In the shorter Greek version of 1 Samuel 18 the development of this jealousy is described more naturally than in the Hebrew.) Saul removes David from the centre of public attention by making him the captain of a thousand soldiers and dismissing him from his place at the court. But in his new position David is very successful, and the general esteem for him increases, so that Saul feels more uneasy than before. One cannot withhold some sympathy from the king, who found that even the members of his own family were enthusiastic admirers of the young hero. Jonathan, Saul's favourite son, was joined to David by the most intimate ties of friendship. The clothing of David in Jonathan's apparel (1 Samuel 18[4]) may be a symbolic action comparable with the exchange of blood as a symbol of brotherhood. It has been plausibly argued that this incident is part of a parallel tradition according to which David was armour-bearer rather to Jonathan than to Saul.

It is not easy to be sure from the stories whether the friendship between Jonathan and David was in any sense hostile to Saul, but it may well be that Saul so interpreted it. And there is certainly ground for believing that long before Saul's death David had set the crown before himself as something to be schemed for. Saul's daughter, too, falls in love with the brave young captain. Of this fact Saul takes advantage, setting David an almost superhuman task against the Philistines as the price of her hand, confident that if he undertakes it he will perish. But all goes wrong with Saul's projects, and David accomplishes the task. It is not impossible that the conduct of Saul in so obviously treating David as a rival may have quickened the latter's ambition to play that part.

The breach between Saul and David, like that between Saul and Samuel, grew wider with the days, and despite some attempts to close it, temporarily successful, became at last an impassable gulf. Saul's jealousy took the form of insanity—real or feigned?—and eventually he attempted David's life. David now leaves the king and goes into exile with a few followers. He obtains provisions from Ahimelech, the priest of Nob, at which shrine he had been wont to consult the priestly oracle. As the story runs in 1 Samuel 21, he seeks refuge at the court of the Philistine king of Gath, Achish, and receives from him kind treatment, because he feigns madness, and ancient peoples believed that mad folk were specially under divine protection. (This part of the narrative seems to anticipate the later story of David's acceptance as a protégé of the Philistine king (27), and to be out of place in this context.) As the story runs David had equipped himself with the sword of Goliath, which had been hanging as a trophy in the shrine at Nob, and whether he himself or another had slain Goliath it would hardly have been tactful to go thus armed to the Philistines.

We must rather suppose that he went at this time to his famous 'cave of Adullam'. This phrase, which has become a proverb in our English tongue, is unfortunately a mistranslation. Its true meaning is 'stronghold of Adullam', and it is to be regarded as describing rather a small fortified site than a cave. A number of his clansmen joined him here, and the band was strengthened by others who feared to be sold into slavery as bankrupt debtors, until David could muster four hundred followers. Saul, exasperated at the escape of his rival, wreaked a terrible vengeance on Nob. All its inhabitants were slaughtered, save Abiathar, one of Ahimelech's sons, who escaped and joined the band of outlaws, whom he served as priest.

The story of Keilah, 1 Samuel 23$^{1-13}$, illustrates the way in which David maintained his followers. Learning that the city was being attacked by the Philistines, David, after twice consulting the divine oracle, marched to its assistance and drove off the raiders with heavy loss of life. He would act as protector of cities in the district against such marauding attempts on the part of Philistines or Bedaween, and would be paid for his services. Quite possibly the citizens would pay him a regular tribute, in return for which they would have the right to call upon him for aid in any time of danger.

Learning that David was in Keilah, Saul proposed to lay siege to it. The oracle of Abiathar warned David that the inhabitants would hand him over to Saul; so David departed with his followers, whose number had now grown to six hundred, and lived the life

The Rise of the Kingdom

of a hunted outlaw, wandering from stronghold to stronghold in the border country. His method of life continued to be the same in one respect, for the story of Nabal, 1 Samuel 25, shows him threatening to root out the family of a rich farmer who refused to pay the protection levy. Nabal's wife, Abigail, intercedes with David, and the churlish Nabal dies 'smitten by Yahweh', after a drinking bout. David then marries Abigail. We read of another marriage about the same time: in fact, David was using matrimonial alliances as well as levies to strengthen his position.

But after a time David wearied of his precarious life, and offered the services of his band to the Philistine king, Achish of Gath. Under his protection David established himself at Ziklag, which probably lay on the desert border south of Judah. He supported his men by raiding the Amalekites and other Bedaween. The statement of 1 Samuel 27[10] that David represented his own countrymen of Judah as the victims of his raiding activities, in order to convince Achish of his loyalty, is not easy to believe; but in any case Achish had no suspicion of David, and when he was preparing an important campaign against Saul he was ready to take David and his company into the fray with the Philistine army. What might have happened if David had gone into battle against the army of Israel is sad to contemplate! Either to the Philistines or to Israel he must have proved a traitor. Fortunately he was spared the dilemma, because the Philistine officers, not so confiding as their king, demanded successfully that he should be dismissed from the army.

David returned to Ziklag, to find that in his absence the Amalekites had been playing his own game upon him, and raided the town. He pursued them and recovered his own property with additional booty. By distributing some part of his spoil among various local chieftains in the south country he strengthened his influence among the southern clans. Meanwhile, the Philistine campaign, which he had been so fortunate as to escape, had ended disastrously for Israel; Saul and his sons had perished in the decisive defeat on Mt. Gilboa.

By their victory the Philistines made themselves masters of the part of Saul's kingdom that lay west of the Jordan, but Ishbaal, also called Ishbosheth, a son of Saul who had escaped the fate of his brothers, established himself as king over the territory east of the Jordan, with his capital at Mahanaim. Ishbaal seems not to have been much more than a figure-head; the real force in the diminished kingdom was Abner, Saul's commander-in-chief, who continued to act as head of the army.

With the decline of the fortunes of Saul's family those of David began to rise, and he took an important step towards his final goal. After consulting the divine oracle he established himself as 'King over the house of Judah' at Hebron, a place of great traditional sanctity. His age at this time—*c.* 1010—was thirty, according to 2 Samuel 5[4]. David was now overlord of a considerable district, and added to his dignity by extending his harem. This process would bring him into alliance with the rulers of important towns, and help to base his position securely. A characteristically shrewd action is recorded in 2 Samuel 2[5-7]. David sent to the inhabitants of Jabesh, in Ishbaal's territory, a message commending them for the pious care they had shown in burying the body of Saul. The message was accompanied by a hint that they would do well to transfer their allegiance to him. For the time being, however, the hint was not taken.

Abner realized that the future lay rather with David than with the puppet-king Ishbaal, and picked a quarrel with the latter which gave him a pretext for offering to transfer his allegiance, and to bring what was left of Saul's kingdom over to David. This proposal was well received by David, but as Abner was returning from Hebron to carry out his scheme, Joab, David's chief warrior, treacherously slew him in satisfaction of a blood feud. David disclaimed any complicity in this cruel deed, but apparently had found Joab so useful that he did not attempt to punish him. Without the support of Abner Ishbaal was quite helpless, and he was presently assassinated by his own followers. The northern tribes then swore allegiance to David at Hebron, and he became king of all Israel.

Next—after he had been in Hebron seven years and a half—David marked an important stage in his career by the capture of Jerusalem. This city—as its long resistance later to the forces of Babylon and Rome shows—was an exceedingly strong natural fortress. Up to the time of its capture by David it had never been

The Rise of the Kingdom

conquered by the Hebrews, and the Jebusites who held it looked upon it as impregnable. The capture of the stronghold was a brilliant military exploit, and the transference of David's capital to Jerusalem an equally brilliant stroke of diplomacy. At Hebron David had been in a town sacred especially to his own southern kinsmen and tribes: but Jerusalem was neutral ground between north and south, and the choice of it as capital tended to abate the jealousy, now subdued, but always smouldering, between the two elements. David still further strengthened the fortifications of the site, and built himself a splendid palace, the materials and artificers for which he obtained from Hiram of Tyre. This, and a further enlargement of his harem, indicated the advance of his power, which is evident in the consideration afforded him by an important ruler such as the king of Tyre. Successes against the Philistines, who realized the serious menace to their power which was developing, and attempted to check it, had further added to his reputation.

The next step taken by David was designed to make Jerusalem the religious as well as the political centre of Israel's life. The ark, which seems to have been neglected after its return from Philistia, was brought from Baal of Judah to the new capital and housed in a specially prepared pavilion amid the rejoicings of the inhabitants. The king designed to build a temple for Yahweh as a permanent shrine for the ark, but did not carry out his intention; according to 2 Samuel 7, which, though a late document, may have behind it some historical background, the scheme was vetoed by the prophet Nathan.

The court was now elaborately organized, and the armies of David gained numerous victories over neighbouring peoples such as Moab, Ammon, and Philistia. Edom was made a tributary country, and the capital was enriched by the spoils of these wars. So successful were these campaigns that from this time onward no external power ventured to attack David. The kingdom was, however, subject to internal strife. David's son Absalom headed a formidable revolt, which at one time seemed likely to thrust him from the throne. The king was compelled to abandon Jerusalem, and escaped to the territory of Gilead. There he put his forces in order, and the first set battle between the rebels and

David's army resulted in a crushing defeat for Absalom, who was slain by Joab, though David had given orders to spare his life.

David was thus able to return to Jerusalem, but the peace of the realm did not remain long undisturbed. There had never been a real unity between the northern and the southern tribes. Both were content to have David as king, but they found it difficult to dwell together because of their mutual jealousies. The northern part of the kingdom was the greater in size and population, and resented the precedence which the people of Judah claimed on the ground of their relationship to the king. This discontent broke into open rebellion under Sheba, a Benjamite. Energetic action by Joab crushed this revolt too, and Sheba paid forfeit with his life. It should be mentioned that some historians would place the revolts of Absalom and Sheba in an earlier part of David's reign.

From this time David was no more troubled by revolt, and the only outstanding event recorded is the intrigue for the successorship to his throne, when he had become feeble with old age. The oldest of his surviving sons was Adonijah, who suspecting, not without reason, that David's wife Bathsheba would try to secure the succession for her son Solomon, determined to get the throne for himself. Like Absalom, he possessed personal charm, and was a favourite with the people. He assumed the state suitable to the heir-apparent, and, with the backing of Joab and Abiathar, gave a ceremonial banquet, to which he invited the other sons of David, with the pointed exception of Solomon. Nathan, the prophet, Benaiah, and others of David's mighty warriors were also excluded from the invitation, from which we may deduce that these formed a party in favour of Solomon. Nathan realized that prompt action must be taken, and persuaded Bathsheba to secure from the fast-failing king ratification of a promise he had made to Bathsheba that Solomon should follow him on the throne. Whether this promise had actually been given, or whether it was a fiction invented to impose on the mind of the dying king, the ratification was obtained. The feeble old man summoned up sufficient energy to make formal arrangements for the solemn proclamation of Solomon. Strangely enough, the rival faction collapsed without a struggle, and Adonijah sought sanctuary at the horns

The Rise of the Kingdom

of the altar. Thus Solomon was left with no one to challenge his right when David, after a reign of forty years, 'slept with his fathers'.

The importance of David as the founder of the united kingdom can hardly be over-estimated. His abilities were conspicuous. Whether in his exploits as a young officer under Saul, or in the guerrilla warfare of his outlaw days, or later as head of the army, he was uniformly successful. The story of his duel with Goliath may be legend, but it can have been told only of a brave man. To the skill of the soldier he added the astuteness of the diplomatist. Sometimes his actions in this field were hardly commendable, but he must be judged by the standards of his own day in this as in other respects. In the modern East—indeed, may we not say over a wider area?—let alone in ancient times, trickery of the kind he indulged in, so far from being frowned upon, is regarded with positive approval. The patient skill of his character is exhibited most clearly in the very careful way in which he made his plans to gain the throne, never rushing matters, but taking each forward step as it became safe. It is true that circumstances outside Israel were favourable to his project. He happened to live in one of those rare periods when all the great empires were so much occupied with their own affairs that they could not effectively challenge his progress. But even when this is taken into consideration we must see in his creation of the most powerful empire Palestine ever produced—an empire extending possibly as far north as Kadesh on the Orontes, and certainly covering some part of what is later known as the kingdom of Syria—a great achievement. Nor can we be surprised that when in later times the Jews reflected on their past history they saw in David the ideal king, and pictured the king-messiah, for whose coming in the future they looked, as a second David. His faults were not a few, but on the whole he was chivalrous, and though he may have been far less saintly than the David whom we have been wrongly taught to regard as the author of all the Psalms, he was a sincerely religious man, ever full of reverence for the prophet and priest, sincerely devoted to the service of Yahweh. The period of his reign may be given approximately as 1010–970 B.C.

Solomon.

David, as we have seen, was followed on the throne by Solomon, who owed his position to palace intrigue. It is sometimes said that Solomon, not being the eldest of the surviving sons of David, was not 'the rightful heir' to the throne. But this is to import a modern idea into the situation. An oriental king, as we see so often in the *Arabian Nights*, may nominate his own successor, and, so far from being compelled to choose his eldest son, may even select an outsider. All the same there was a danger that, despite the complete collapse of the movement in favour of Adonijah, the succession might be challenged again. Solomon took care to ensure that no such threat should hang over his head. The leading members of Adonijah's party had been Joab, the commander-in-chief, and Abiathar, the leading priest. The sacred office of the latter saved him from death, and Solomon contented himself with sentencing him to retirement at Anathoth, his home, and replaced him by Zadok. Joab, more formidable, did not escape so lightly. He realized what fate might be in store for him, and sought asylum at the horns of the altar in the pavilion that housed the ark. Solomon sent Benaiah to slay him, but Joab, though he knew that he was doomed, refused to satisfy Benaiah's scruples against assassination at the altar by obligingly leaving his place of sanctuary at Benaiah's command. The latter reported this obstinacy to Solomon, who gave orders that Joab should be slain at the altar itself. The story of David's dying charge to Solomon, 1 Kings 2, represents that David specially enjoined Solomon to slay Joab. It would relieve the memory of David from a slur if we could believe that this commission was invented to palliate the ruthlessness of Solomon's action, the real purpose of which, as distinct from the motives alleged, was to remove from his path a dangerous obstacle.

Adonijah also had sought refuge at the shrine, and been ordered to confinement in his own house. He too was later assassinated by Benaiah at Solomon's command. The excuse for this action is given in a story that Adonijah sent Bathsheba to Solomon with a petition that Abishag, who had ministered to David in his last sickness, should be given him as wife. This was almost equivalent to taking the concubine of a dead king as wife,

The Rise of the Kingdom 71

a proceeding that was ordinarily interpreted as preferring a claim to the succession. It is not easy to believe that Adonijah was so

'The horns of the altar.' A stone altar found at Gezer, with protuberances ('horns'?) at each corner.

foolish as to prefer this request. But whatever may have been the pretext alleged, the real motive of Solomon is evident in 1 Kings 2^{22}, where Solomon admits his fear of his elder brother's pretensions, and classes him with Abiathar and Joab. These assassinations would be regarded as 'political necessities' for establishing the throne of Solomon in security. They appear to have attained their object.

As we read the narratives of Solomon's reign we get the impression that it was almost throughout prosperous and peaceful, and, though there are indications that the picture has been touched up to remove some of its shadows, this may be taken as substantially true. Solomon set himself to consolidate what his father had established. He seems not to have shared the love of military adventure which was a quality of David's character, and indulged in no wars of conquest to extend his borders. His policy was rather to secure himself by forming alliances with some of his more powerful neighbours. And his success is proved by the freedom of his long reign from external trouble.

Soon after his succession he contracted an alliance with Egypt by adding a daughter of the reigning Pharaoh to his harem. This brought him two advantages. First he was protected against any attempt by Egypt to invade Palestine and assert her ancient suzerainty over that country. In the second place the Egyptian monarch laid siege to the important Canaanite fortress of Gezer, captured it, and presented it to Solomon as part of his daughter's dowry. Solomon rebuilt the city and maintained it as an outpost of his dominion (1 Kings 9[16-17]). The alliance with Hiram of Tyre which had been made by David was continued and extended by Solomon. This secured the safety of the north-western frontier. It also facilitated Solomon's trading projects, for as the ally of Tyre, the greatest merchant power of the time, he was able to take part in the commerce of the Mediterranean Sea.

The little notice in 2 Kings 23[13] which informs us that Solomon had built at Jerusalem altars for the deities of Sidon, Moab, and Ammon is also enlightening as to Solomon's foreign policy. The erection of such altars was primarily a matter rather of statecraft than of religion. An alliance between two countries necessarily brought their deities too into alliance, and it was regarded as only courteous to recognize this fact by giving them a ceremonial status in the allied countries. We are justified, then, in concluding that Solomon had treaties with Zidon, Moab, and Ammon. So on the east, as well as north and south, he had friendly relations with the powers. The extent of Solomon's dominion ran, if we are

The Rise of the Kingdom

to regard 1 Kings 4^{24} as authoritative, from Gaza in the southwest to Thapsacus on the Euphrates; probably this sweeping statement to some extent exaggerates the truth. We may be certain that he controlled the territory of Edom, for he made use of a port at the head of the Gulf of Akaba for his trade to Ophir.

Trade, rather than warfare, was the object of Solomon's chief activities. In this he resembled some of the Pharaohs, for whom the foreign trade of Egypt seems to have been a royal monopoly. So large was the scale of his imports that he is said to have made silver and cedars as common in Jerusalem as stones and sycamores. In partnership with Hiram of Tyre he owned a fleet which traded all over the Mediterranean Sea, bringing home 'gold, silver, ivory, apes, and peacocks' (1 Kings 10^{22}). Hiram also supplied skilled Tyrian sailors to man the fleet which traded from the Gulf of Akaba, for the Hebrews did not easily take to the seafaring life. No certainty has yet been attained as to the situation of Ophir, to which this fleet made voyages. Possibly it may be South Arabia. Horses were imported into Palestine at this time. These came from Egypt, according to 1 Kings 10^{28}, though it is probable that the name rendered 'Egypt' is intended to denote a country north of Syria. Solomon certainly revolutionized the economic life of Israel, and under his rule the country was brought for the first time fully into the current of oriental commerce and civilization, and its capital, Jerusalem, became a centre of luxurious wealth.

Solomon was a great builder. Many provincial towns were fortified, and adapted for use as arsenals, garrison centres, and storehouses. Jerusalem itself was especially transformed. Solomon was not content with the palace that David had built, and spent thirteen years in erecting a more splendid one. He also built a temple, to which he gave about half the time devoted to the royal palace, and which was, despite its fame, only a royal chapel attached to the palace. Solomon followed his father's example in drawing the materials and artisans for his building from Hiram of Tyre.

The country was organized under an elaborate scheme to obtain supplies of food and labour. It was divided into twelve districts, upon which levies were made in rotation. These districts were artificial sections, independent of the old tribal divisions. It may have been a subordinate purpose of the scheme to break down the old tribal distinctions and jealousies. From the Canaanites forced labour was exacted. The record boasts that the Israelites, on the contrary, were not made 'bond-servants'. Though this may be true in a formal sense, there can be no doubt that many of the poorer people were reduced to a condition very like slavery by the constant demands made upon them for the expenses of the grandiose building projects and the upkeep of the costly court and harem. Solomon was minded to play thoroughly the part of an oriental sultan. This economic oppression was certainly a cause of great discontent. The magnificence of the court hardly compensated the ordinary folk for the trials they suffered to maintain it. And while it is true that during the reign of Solomon the nation was freer from external threat than in any other days of the monarchy, the internal strain was preparing the rupture that became inevitable when Solomon was replaced by a king who lacked the personal force of his father.

There is evidence, too, that Solomon's reign was not quite so much undisturbed as we might think from a superficial reading. The rather obscure passage 1 Kings 9^{10-14} suggests that Solomon gave Hiram twenty cities in Galilee as compensation for the aid he had received from the king of Tyre in his building projects. It is not impossible that he was compelled to part with this territory for other reasons. The friendship with Egypt, too, cannot have lasted through the reign, for at the court of the Pharaoh one of Solomon's enemies found asylum. Jeroboam, who, significantly enough, had been in charge of the levies on the tribes that afterwards formed the Northern Kingdom, encouraged by a prophet of Yahweh, was minded to raise a rebellion among the disaffected folk of the north, and fled to Egypt when Solomon sought to slay him. Hadad of Edom, who had escaped from Joab's massacre of the notables of Edom when David subdued that country, returned after Joab's death to his own land, and though, as is shown by the fact that Solomon was able to control the trade route to Ezion-Geber, he failed to free Edom from Israel's grasp, was a source of constant trouble to the king. David had maintained a garrison in Damascus, but Rezon, an

The Rise of the Kingdom

Aramean soldier of fortune, had even in David's time recovered possession of the city, and he too 'was an adversary to Israel all the days of Solomon' (1 Kings 11^{25}). He is said to have reigned over Syria, but that kingdom was not so strong as it became later in the history, when at times it threatened the very existence of the Northern Kingdom.

But, while we have good grounds for believing that the reign of Solomon was less undisturbed than the records represent it as being, there can be no doubt that in many ways Solomon was an able king. Later ages thought of him pre-eminently as Solomon the Wise; and though at most only a fraction of the Wisdom literature credited to his account can have come from his hand, the mere fact that it is attributed to him makes it certain that he was a capable ruler. His devotion to Yahweh cannot be held in question, though he was more restrained in its expression than was David. That he erected altars to so many foreign deities in connexion with his matrimonial and political alliances—and no doubt many of his marriages were made with the idea of strengthening his influence in foreign courts—and even his participation in the rites associated with those altars, is not evidence of apostasy from his own God. These things were in his eyes mere international courtesies. Later the Jews regarded them as grievous departures from orthodoxy, and so he appears in a double part, as founder of the Temple and largely the creator of its ritual, and also as an apostate from the pure religion. When the editor of Kings writes his obituary notice the verdict is that he did the evil thing in the sight of Yahweh, that is, deserted Yahweh for other gods, and went not fully after Yahweh as did David his father (1 Kings 11^6). A more serious criticism of him is that by the very elaboration of his schemes for converting Israel into a well-organized empire he subjected the fabric to a strain that very soon after his death became a rupture.

CHAPTER V
THE DIVIDED KINGDOMS

Rehoboam

SOLOMON was succeeded by Rehoboam (c. 932?), who proved himself to be thoroughly unfitted to deal with the difficult problem he had to face. His coronation was to have taken place at Shechem, perhaps the most revered site among the northern tribes. If this was his own choice it was the one wise act of his career, for it showed some attempt to conciliate the feelings of the disaffected northerners. But the northern tribes had already recalled Jeroboam to act as their leader, and probably had resolved to break away whatever happened. They demanded less onerous conditions than had been their lot under Solomon, but Rehoboam, encouraged by the hotheads among his own companions, insultingly refused their plea, ignoring the advice of his elder statesmen. The northern tribes drew off in resentment, stoned the officer, Adoram, who was sent to discipline them, and made Jeroboam their king. Only the tribe of Judah remained loyal to the dynasty of David, and from this point we have to deal with the divided kingdoms.

Relative importance of the kingdoms

Of the two kingdoms the Northern Kingdom was by far the more important, though the fact that the Old Testament history is compiled by writers whose sympathies are entirely with Judah has meant that this truth is obscured. It will be convenient to use for the Northern Kingdom the name Ephraim, since its more common designation *Israel* is ambiguous. Ephraim was more extensive in territory, more wealthy, more numerously populated, more civilized, and in some periods more vigorous in its religion, than Judah. It counted for far more in international politics than did its southern rival: indeed, it is hardly too much to say that from the time when the kingdom was divided Judah was almost in a backwater.

The form in which the history is given by the editor of Kings makes it far from easy to follow the course of events in either

The Divided Kingdoms

kingdom. The annals of the two kingdoms are interwoven according to a stereotyped pattern, the accession of each king being dated by the number of years the contemporary king of the other kingdom had occupied his throne. The system has a close parallel in the 'Synchronous History' of Babylonia, dealing with the kingdoms of Babylon and Assyria. The chronology, in any case very obscure, is thus rendered more precarious still. We shall gain a much clearer understanding of the course of events if we study first the complete record of Ephraim, and then retrace our steps to follow the development of Judah, even if this method involves a certain amount of repetition.

Another factor of which we shall now have to take account is the influence of foreign nations upon the history. Soon after the division of the kingdom Egypt began to assert herself in the affairs of Palestine, Damascus became a serious rival of Ephraim, and, a little later, the far more powerful empire of Assyria made an effort to bring northern Palestine under her control. The chief issues at stake for these foreign powers were, first, the control of the trade routes through the Mediterranean ports, and second, the ownership of the cedar forests in Lebanon. Unfortunately for the Hebrew kingdoms, and more especially for Ephraim, they happened to be placed in the arena where these struggles were fought out.

History of Ephraim

Jeroboam I.

To turn first, then, to the history of Ephraim. Its first king, Jeroboam, was a much abler man than Rehoboam. His ascendancy over his people seems to have been unchallenged. He organized his realm in such a way as to accentuate the cleavage between the two kingdoms. His capital he fixed at Shechem, and, realizing that the only real bond between the two kingdoms was that of religion, he established rival temples to that in Jerusalem at the shrines of Bethel and Dan. There he erected bull images of Yahweh. He also instituted a rival priesthood and changed the date of the Feast of Tabernacles. In this action he was not intending to depart from the worship of Yahweh. Indeed he had been supported in his schism by one of the leading prophets, Ahijah, and there is no indication that his bull images aroused any protest among his own people. But in the eyes of the later editors of Kings this worship of Yahweh by means of images was an unpardonable heresy, and Jeroboam is often mentioned with horror as 'he who caused Israel to sin'.

Of the events in his reign we are told little or nothing, save that there was perpetual strife between him and Rehoboam. The affairs of Ephraim, outside what they regarded as its apostasy, had interest for the editors of Kings only when they directly affected the fortunes of Judah. The presumption is that Jeroboam proved himself to be a thoroughly capable and successful ruler.

Nadab.

Jeroboam was succeeded by his son Nadab, of whose short reign all that we are told is that he conducted a campaign against Philistia. He was engaged in laying siege to Gibbethon, when he met his death as a result of a conspiracy headed by Baasha of Issachar. Baasha assassinated all the royal family, and seated himself on the throne. This was the first of the series of violent changes in the ruling dynasty of Ephraim, where the monarchy seldom remained long in one family.

Baasha.

All that we know of Baasha's reign is that he removed his capital to Tirzah, and continued the struggle against Asa of Judah. He pressed Asa very hard, and the latter, to obtain relief from the pressure, was compelled to bribe Benhadad of Damascus to break his alliance with Ephraim and attack the northern territories of his ally. This is the earliest example of the practice, which hastened the destruction of both Ephraim and Judah, of seeking the intervention of foreign powers in their inveterate strife. Baasha reigned for twenty-four years.

Elah; Zimri.

Elah, who succeeded his father Baasha, had a brief reign of two years, and was assassinated by Zimri, a leading officer of his chariotry, during a drunken revel at the house of his palace steward in Tirzah. Zimri sought to make his position

The Divided Kingdoms

safe by following the approved precedent of exterminating the royal family. The army was at the time engaged in a renewed siege of Gibbethon, and when the news of Elah's murder came to the forces Omri, the commander-in-chief, seized the opportunity to proclaim himself king with the support of the army. Omri was thus well equipped for achieving his purpose, and was in any case a man of very real ability. He acted with great energy, and, marching against Zimri at Tirzah, captured the city and slew his rival usurper. Zimri's brief reign lasted just a week, according to the Hebrew text. The reading of one important Greek manuscript, which allows him seven years instead of seven days, must be merely a slip.

Omri.

Omri was the first successor of Jeroboam who was of real significance in the history of his times. Very little is told of his achievements in the Old Testament. From it we learn that before he could secure his position he had to suppress a rival contender for the throne, Tibni, and that he built a new capital, Samaria. But fortunately the annals of other powers enable us to understand what a great king he really was, and the reference to the 'statutes of Omri' in Micah 6[16] confirms this impression.

For a century and a half we find that the Assyrian annals call Ephraim *Bit Humri*, that is, Omri-land: this can be explained only on the ground that Omri was a man of real importance in the larger world of international politics. Like David, he sought to strengthen the power of his country by allying himself with Tyre, and married Ahab, his son, to Jezebel, a princess from the Tyrian court. Like David, again, he was wise in his choosing of a new capital, and in the site which he chose. The recent excavations at Samaria have confirmed the statement in the Old Testament that the site was previously unbuilt upon. Its natural advantages were, like those of Jerusalem, excellent. Proof of this may be found in the successful resistance which the city later put up against the Assyrian army under Tiglath-pileser III, 733–732, and its determined struggle, lasting three years, before it succumbed finally in 722. It was nearer to the Phoenician allies and farther from the Syrian foe than was Tirzah. Omri improved its natural strength by massive fortification. He made walls 10 feet thick, whose foundations were sunk 6 feet into the solid rock. The gate of the city was protected by a rectangular fort measuring 57 by 44 feet. Probably Tyrian masons were employed in the work. The excavations have shown that the country was organized into districts which sent supplies to the storehouses of the new capital. Omri fought successfully against Moab, and attached some of its territory to Ephraim. He was also at war with Damascus, which had developed by this time into a considerable power, and in this struggle was less successful, having to cede some thirty cities to the enemy, and to permit the establishment of trade concessions by Syrian merchants in others. With Judah his relations seem to have been comparatively peaceful. Probably Judah recognized that Omri was too strong to be contended with, and was content to play a subordinate part.

Ahab.

Omri was followed by his son Ahab, most famous of all Ephraim's kings. He, too, was an exceedingly able ruler, wise in his policy, and gallant in war. He further strengthened the fortifications of Samaria, and beautified it by the erection of an 'ivory palace', which received its name possibly from the gleaming whiteness with which its walls stood out against the blue sky, but more probably because it was furnished with ivory inlays. If Omri bears in some respects a strong likeness to David, in some ways Ahab was a second Solomon. His relationship with Judah was one of friendship, and he married his daughter Athaliah to Joram, son of Jehoshaphat, the contemporary king of Judah. The Old Testament represents Jehoshaphat and Ahab as allied kings of independent countries, but it is highly probable that during Ahab's reign Judah was not much more than a vassal state to Ephraim.

Damascus, early in Ahab's reign, made a determined effort to subdue Ephraim. Benhadad II—it is very hard to get from the Old Testament a clear idea as to the different Benhadads, and it is not unlikely that successive kings of Damascus were called Benhadad as the Egyptian kings were called Pharaoh—formed a coalition against Ahab, advanced against Samaria, and demanded

The Divided Kingdoms

the surrender of Ahab's treasure and family. This demand Ahab was prepared to concede, but when Benhadad made still more insulting demands they were rejected, and Ahab routed the Syrian forces by a surprise attack. In the following year Ahab won a pitched battle at Aphek, and compelled Benhadad to restore the cities lost by Omri and to grant trading concessions in the bazaars of Damascus to Ephraim.

Now, however, an ominous cloud appeared on the horizon. Under Tukulti-ninurta II (889–884) Assyria had begun to recover her ancient territories. His successor, Ashur-nasir-pal (884–859), had penetrated to the Mediterranean Sea, but had left Damascus and the states farther to the south untouched. He was followed by Shalmaneser III (859–824), who sought to break the power of the Aramean kingdoms. To meet this threat Benhadad of Damascus, whose name is given in the Assyrian annals as Adad-idri, formed a coalition of nations. The rival armies met in a great battle at Karkar on the Orontes, 853, and Shalmaneser in his inscription claims to have won a great victory. But his own losses were very heavy, and as he did not pursue his campaign farther we may conclude that the battle was indecisive. The interesting feature of Shalmaneser's inscription is that he names among the allied kings who confronted him Ahabbu Sir-ilai, that is, Ahab of Israel. He gives also a list of the forces contributed by the several kings, and the military strength of Ahab is shown in that his contribution was 2,000 chariots, the largest of all such contingents, and the third largest army, 10,000 men. Allowing for exaggeration on Shalmaneser's part of the forces opposed to him, it still remains true that Ephraim is one of the most considerable countries among the allies. If Judah was engaged in the battle, which is doubtful, the forces she contributed must have been counted as part of Ahab's army. The indifference of the compilers of Kings to secular history is strikingly proved by the absence of any allusion to this most important battle.

The heroic effort made to repel the Assyrian invader had gravely weakened the Syrian forces, and Ahab deemed the opportunity of renewing the traditional struggle with Damascus too good to be missed. Accordingly he set on foot a campaign to recapture for Ephraim the territory that Syria had occupied in

Trans-Jordania, and particularly the city of Ramoth-Gilead. Jehoshaphat of Judah accompanied him in the struggle, either as ally, or, more probably, vassal. The combined forces of Ephraim and Judah defeated the Syrians, but Ahab was wounded early in the fight, and died as the victory was won. The army retired to Samaria.

There can be little doubt that the character of Ahab has received scanty justice at the hands of the Old Testament writers, though even among these there are diversities of judgement. He was a shrewd and successful ruler, and a gallant warrior. His conduct in remaining on the battle-field though sore wounded, lest his army should be disheartened, was a noble last gesture. And though he was guilty in the matter of Naboth's vineyard his crime was less heinous than some that stain the shield of David. He receives severe condemnation as an apostate from Yahweh, but would have reckoned himself a loyal worshipper. As evidence for this we may advance the names of his children, all of which are compounded with the name of Yahweh, and his maintenance of a band of Yahweh prophets at his court.

A monument of great historic interest was found in 1868 on the site of the Diban mentioned in the Old Testament. It was in the form of a black basalt stela, and though it was subsequently broken the greater part of the inscription on it has been made available, for squeezes had been taken before it was shattered. It records the achievements of Mesha, king of Moab. Moab had been made tributary by David, but had probably recovered its independence soon after the disruption of the kingdom. The stone shows us that Omri had subjugated part of Moab's territory, and describes the campaigns in which Mesha regained its freedom. The chronology of the stone is difficult to reconcile with that of Kings, and would seem on the whole to be more trustworthy. Kings records the revolt of Moab from Ephraim's suzerainty, but places the movement after the death of Ahab. The stone places it during the reign of Omri's son, and if 'son' is to be taken literally, and not as equal to 'grandson', the reference must be to Ahab. The divergences are possibly to be explained on the theory that there was more than one campaign, and on the ground that the oriental annalists are given to enlarging on their suc-

THE ASSYRIANS. A sculptured slab found at Nineveh, representing a camp scene. The wall of the camp is seen at the top. In the centre a high officer is returning to his tent after a day's fighting. One of his servants offers him a drink, and another is making his bed. In a neighbouring tent (on the right) a sheep is being killed, no doubt for the officer's evening meal. Other animals lie outside.

cesses while ignoring their defeats. But apart from questions of detail the stone and Kings are substantially in agreement. There can be no doubt that Moab did take advantage of Ephraim's entanglement with Syria to shake off the yoke at this time. That the issue was decided in favour of Moab is clearly seen in 2 Kings 3[27], where it is said that Ephraim's forces, which had achieved initial victories in a campaign to repress the Moabite rising, 'returned to their own land'. The writer in Kings attributes this to the intervention of Moab's god, Chemosh, from whom there came 'great wrath against Israel', when Mesha as a last desperate resource sacrificed his son who should have reigned after him to win the aid of Chemosh. The stone proves, what on other grounds we should have suspected, that in language and customs there was very little difference between the Moabites and the Hebrews.

Ahaziah; Jehoram.

Ahab's successor was his son Ahaziah, whose reign lasted only two years. From Jehoshaphat's refusal (1 Kings 22[49]) to accept Ahaziah's offer to join in a revival of the commercial expeditions from the Gulf of Akaba it may be deduced that Judah was now to some extent freed from the vassalage to Ephraim. Ahaziah, who had no son, was followed on the throne by Jehoram, another son of Ahab. According to 2 Kings 3 it was during his reign that Mesha freed himself in spite of the fact that Jehoshaphat of Judah had joined him in the effort to crush the Moabite rising. The story is so much like a duplicate of the earlier record of Jehoshaphat's alliance with Ahab against Syria as to raise suspicions.

The stories of Elisha are related, for the most part, as though they covered the period of Jehoram. But they are so obviously largely legend that it is hard to say what nucleus of historical truth lies in them, and it is generally held that much that is told as though it happened in the Omri dynasty's time really belongs to the time of Jehu. The strife between Syria and Ephraim in the earlier part of this period seems to have taken the form of forays rather than organized military campaigns. But the last year of Jehoram's reign was marked by a serious attempt to recover Ramoth-Gilead from Syria, where Benhadad had been

The Divided Kingdoms

supplanted by the usurper Hazael. In this expedition Jehoram was joined by Ahaziah of Judah. In the fighting Jehoram was wounded, and retired to Jezreel, where there was a royal palace, to be healed of his wounds.

For some time past there had been an undercurrent of revolution. The moving spirit was the prophet Elisha, who was dissatisfied with the tolerance of Baal worship which had been part of the royal policy. The man to whom the prophet looked to execute his plans was Jehu, a leading officer in the army. The story is told with great dramatic force in 2 Kings 9. The king's absence from the army afforded just the opportunity that promised success for the conspirators. Elisha dispatched a prophet with a vial of the sacred oil used in the coronation ceremonies to Ramoth, to anoint Jehu as king. Though no hint to that effect is given in the narrative there can be little doubt that Jehu had been well prepared for such a happening. The prophet calls Jehu into an inner room and performs the ceremony that in itself made a man king. Jehu's fellow-officers demand to know what has been done. Jehu replies, 'You know quite well!' It is probable that some at any rate of them were not unprepared for the event. They press him for a direct answer, and he tells them that he has been anointed king. The officers with one accord accept the situation, and improvise a throne for Jehu by placing their garments on the top of a flight of stairs.

Jehu.

The usurper, Jehu, is now in control of the army, but cannot be sure of his position while Jehoram lives. If Samaria and its garrison remain loyal to their old master there must be a struggle ere Jehu gains his end. Precautions are taken to prevent news of the revolution reaching Jehoram at Jezreel, and Jehu makes himself the messenger of doom. A watchman on the wall of Jezreel sees the dust of a fast-moving company nearing the city. Jehoram dispatches a horseman to inquire whether it is news of a victory the company brings. The horseman is detained by Jehu. A second horseman is treated in the same way. By this time the company has drawn near enough for the watchman to deduce that it is under the command of Jehu, who was noted for the fury of his driving. In perplexity, and perhaps not without foreboding, Jehoram, and Ahaziah of Judah, who was on a visit to his convalescent ally, go forth in their chariots to meet Jehu. Jehoram challenges Jehu with the question he had sent by his messengers before; Jehu answers him by one of the most grievous insults an oriental can offer, abuse of his mother, Jezebel, and, drawing a bow, shoots him through the heart as he turns to regain the safety of the city walls. A hurried warning from Jehoram to Ahaziah was unavailing, for although the king of Judah fled in his chariot from the scene of his ally's assassination he was shot by Jehu's archers ere he could make good his escape, and, mortally wounded, died at Megiddo, whither his attendants had carried him.

Jezebel, the queen-mother, knows that her last hour has come. With a superb gesture of defiance she decks herself in her finest apparel, and paints her eyes with kohl as for a great state occasion. She shows herself from a window of the palace to Jehu below, and hurls at him the withering taunt 'thou Zimri, thou murderer of thy master'—was not Zimri one who slew his master and usurped the throne, but, and here was the subtlest sting of the taunt, reigned but a few days? Jehu appealed to the eunuchs of the harem to show their adherence to his cause by throwing Jezebel into the courtyard. Then in his frenzy he trod her body to pulp under the feet of his chariot horses. He sat down to a meal, and in cooler frame of mind regretted the horrible sacrilege, for so it would have seemed to any decent citizen, of this last act of fury, and he gave orders that such fragments of the body as might remain—for the scavenger dogs of the city had devoured much—should be buried.

Now Jezreel was in Jehu's hands. There is much in the story to suggest that there had been a party in his favour before he arrived outside its walls; else the city might have closed its gates and compelled him to a siege. At least none of the garrison did anything in defence of the king and the queen-mother. Samaria has still to be dealt with. A message is dispatched to the authorities of that city demanding that they make their choice between adhesion to the new king and fighting for the dynasty of Ahab. They bow before the impetuous storm of the new tyrant. He bids

The Divided Kingdoms

them as guarantee of their loyalty to send him the heads of the family of Ahab, and they send seventy decapitated heads in baskets to Jezreel. These are piled in two grisly heaps at the gate of the city, so that all who come in or go out may see the evidence of Jehu's power. A further massacre of all the leading retainers of the late royal house in Samaria leaves the position of the usurper unchallenged. Proceeding to Samaria Jehu falls in with a company of Ahaziah's relatives, on their way, all unwitting of his fate, to visit their king at Jezreel. These, some forty-two in number, are slaughtered by Jehu's command, and so he reduces the possibility that Judah will make any effective attempt to avenge her murdered king.

As he is entering the city he meets Jehonadab, a leader of the Rechabites. These were the puritans of the country, believing in the old simple ways of their desert-wandering fathers. They hated the Canaanitish civilization which had, as they saw it, corrupted their people. They would not build houses, or plant vineyards, for these involved a settled life. They were fanatical devotees of Yahweh, and the Baal worship was anathema to them. Jehu bids Jehonadab step up into his chariot, promising that he will do great things for the honour of Yahweh. And so Jehu makes his ceremonial entrance displaying as one of his chief supporters the leader of the Rechabite party, a stroke of diplomacy. He then, representing himself as a Baal worshipper, gathers the chief partisans of the alien religion to a solemn service in the temple of Baal, and has them all assassinated. It is not easy to understand why the victims allowed themselves to be taken in this trap. That Jehu should profess adherence both to Yahweh and to Baal is understandable—for him religion was nothing but a tool to serve his ambition, and, as Henry of Navarre said, 'Paris is well worth a mass!' But the Baal worshippers must have been singularly blind not to see that to maintain his position Jehu was bound to hold the loyalty of the Yahweh devotees, who hated the family of Ahab.

So ended the dynasty of Omri, and Jehu founded a new one. The bloody work of the usurper is approved in Kings, as the vengeance of Yahweh upon Ahab and his descendants. The revolution is one of the many examples in history of fanatical religion making use of a politician, while the politician uses the religious partisans. It is comforting to know that men of finer religious instincts abhorred this vile business, and we are content to side with Hosea, who finds in the evil fate which overtook Jehu's dynasty Yahweh's verdict upon an abominable crime (Hosea 1⁴).

The reign of Jehu was marked with disasters. Hazael of Damascus took the offensive against the eastern territories of Ephraim, and recovered for Syria the country east of the Jordan. Jehu's impulsive vigour was not equal to sustained effort, and the wholesale murders with which he had opened his career had seriously reduced the population, depriving the state at the same time of many able citizens. In a small state this was bound to be a very grave handicap when she was called to face the attack of a powerful neighbour. Had the struggle been confined to a duel between Ephraim and Syria the former might well have been completely subdued. But Assyria was once more upon the warpath in her campaign for the possession of northern Palestine. The Assyrian king attacked Syria, and won a pitched battle at Mt. Saniru in the Hermon range, in which he slew, according to his own record, 16,000 of the enemy and captured 1,921 chariots. Even allowing for the customary exaggeration of a victor the blow inflicted on Hazael must have been severe. He was compelled to seek refuge within the walls of Damascus, while Shalmaneser ravaged his country and sacked its towns. In the same account Shalmaneser records that at this time Tyre, Sidon, and Jehu 'son' of Omri', that is 'of Omri-land', paid tribute to him. The Black Obelisk inscribed by Shalmaneser, which is now in the British Museum, gives a list of the silver and gold articles included in Jehu's offering: these may have been intended as a bribe to secure Assyria's support against his Syrian rival.

For nearly a generation the armies of Assyria were engaged on other frontiers, and Syria, though sorely shaken, renewed her strength. Before the end of Jehu's reign Ephraim was deprived by Syria of the country east of the Jordan, and the ruthlessness of the Syrian attack would be the more marked because, in becoming tributary to Shalmaneser, Jehu had broken finally the alliance which had induced Ephraim and Damascus, however

THE BLACK OBELISK OF SHALMANESER

they might fight against each other in times when the danger from Assyria was remote, to stand together against the Assyrian threat.

Jehoahaz.

Under Jehoahaz, the son and successor of Jehu, the fortunes of Ephraim reached their nadir. Hazael and his son Benhadad reduced the country to a state of abject submission, and the forces of Jehoahaz were restricted, as were those of Germany by the victors in the Great War, so that his military establishment was but ten thousand infantry, fifty cavalry, and ten chariots. The account in 2 Kings 12$^{17-18}$ of a campaign in which Hazael captured Gath, and was bought off from a threatened attack on Jerusalem by a heavy bribe from the temple and palace treasures, shows that Ephraim was so completely under Hazael's control that she was compelled to allow unmolested passage to the Syrian armies.

This was the bright expiring flame of Syria's glory, for when Adad-nirari III became king of Assyria, *c.* 805, he resumed the drive against Palestine, which during the reign of Shalmaneser's successor, Shamshi-adad V, had not been prosecuted. Adad-nirari recounts how he subdued beneath his feet the land of the Hittites, the land of Amurru, Tyre, Sidon, the Omri-country, Edom, and Philistia. These countries submitted without a struggle. Damascus was less easy to deal with. Her king, whose name is given as 'Mari', which may be a blunder of the scribe, or possibly the name of an otherwise unknown successor of Benhadad, was besieged in Damascus. The city was compelled to yield, and in the list of booty taken by the captors are 2,300 talents of silver, 20 talents of gold, 3,000 talents of copper, 5,000 talents of iron, and articles of luxury such as a bed and throne inlaid with, or constructed of, ivory. This list in itself is evidence of the surprising recovery of Syria since the time of Shalmaneser.

Jehoash; Jeroboam II.

The crushing of Syria loosened the stranglehold which she had maintained on Ephraim, and under Jehoash, who followed Jehoahaz, Ephraim began to lift up her head. Three victories were won against Benhadad, and several cities were retaken from

The Divided Kingdoms

Syria. Under Jeroboam II, who succeeded Jehoash, the fortunes of Ephraim rose to a point which made the land almost as extensive and prosperous as in the days of Omri. Of this Indian summer there is little notice in Kings. Jeroboam reigned for forty-one years, but all that we hear about his political career is that 'he restored the border of Israel from the entering in of Hamath unto the sea of the Arabah', and that he 'recovered Damascus and Hamath for Israel' (2 Kings 14$^{25, 28}$). It is almost certain that this is an exaggeration, but it does rest on a considerable basis of fact. We get more enlightenment from the book of Amos, who prophesied in Ephraim when Jeroboam was king. The true rendering of Amos 6^{13} is 'Ye who rejoice over Lo-debar, and say "Have we not captured Karnaim by our own might?"' Lo-debar is a city on the east side of Jordan, and Karnaim is almost certainly an abbreviation of Ashteroth-Karnaim, a city in the same region. Thus we have contemporary evidence that under Jeroboam the boundaries of Ephraim were enlarged. The picture painted by Amos shows that commerce was flourishing under Jeroboam, and that the landowners and nobles grew rich. But under the appearance of material wealth the social system was rotten. The wealthy men built themselves splendid palaces, but the poor folk were crushed, and could obtain no redress for their wrongs in the law-courts because the judges were corrupt and took bribes from the rich oppressors.

Zechariah; Shallum; Menahem.

When Jeroboam died the rotten structure of his kingdom collapsed, and Ephraim went swiftly to her doom. King followed king in rapid succession, and all but one of them met his death by violence. Zechariah, Jeroboam's son, had been but six months on the throne when he was assassinated and succeeded by Shallum. A few weeks later Shallum suffered a like fate at the hands of Menahem. For ten years Menahem sat uneasily on his throne: Assyria was once more upon the warpath in Palestine, and there was no power able to stem the irresistible sweep of her armies. Menahem, as we learn both from Kings and the Assyrian records, paid a heavy tribute to Tiglath-pileser III, the Pul—a name by which he was known in Babylon—of 2 Kings 15^{19}.

Tiglath-pileser III was one of the ablest kings who ever ruled Assyria, and set himself to make Palestine a province of his empire. No doubt he was aiming ultimately at using Palestine as a base of operations for a campaign against Egypt. At least that was the view of Egypt herself, and she resumed her traditional policy of attaching the little kingdoms of Palestine to herself by promises of support against Assyria. In Ephraim there were two different parties, one pro-Assyrian, the other pro-Egyptian, and the changes on the throne meant, as a rule, that a pro-Assyrian king was replaced by one with a pro-Egyptian policy, or vice versa. In a striking figure the prophet Hosea, who lived through these troubled times in Ephraim, describes the statesmen of his country as silly doves, fluttering now to Egypt, now to Assyria.

Pekahiah; Pekah.

Pekahiah, the son of Menahem, after a reign of two years was assassinated by his commander-in-chief, Pekah, who adopted the pro-Egyptian policy. In opposition to Assyria he revived the old alliance with Syria, ruled at that time by Rezon. But the days when a combination of two such states could offer any effective resistance to Assyria were past, and Tiglath-pileser soon swept aside the opposition. Syria and Phoenicia were ravaged, Damascus itself fell in 732, Rezon was slain, and the population of the city deported. Thus the last poor bulwark of Ephraim's security was destroyed, and her fate sealed. Tiglath-pileser deported a great number of the inhabitants from northern Palestine and the regions east of the Jordan. Pekah was in his turn assassinated by Hoshea. Tiglath-pileser asserts that it was he who, 'because the people of Omri-land had overthrown their king, seated Hoshea over them'. This is probably true, and suggests that Hoshea had been the leader of the pro-Assyrian party against the pro-Egyptian policy of his predecessor.

Hoshea.

Hoshea confirmed his loyalty to Tiglath-pileser by the payment of tribute, but when, in 727, Shalmaneser V succeeded to the throne of Assyria, Hoshea thought an opportunity had come to free himself, and began to intrigue with Egypt, withholding his

The Divided Kingdoms

annual tribute to Assyria. Shalmaneser proved himself to be as energetic as Tiglath-pileser, and led his forces against the treacherous Hoshea, who was taken and imprisoned. Samaria was then invested, but made a heroic resistance. The siege began in 724, and not until 722 did the city fall. Shalmaneser had died just before the end of the siege, and Sargon was the king who actually received its submission. At last the unrelenting pressure of Assyria had extinguished the kingdom of Ephraim, and a large number of settlers from various parts of the Assyrian domains were planted in the country, to replace a large part of the native population who were deported, after the Assyrian custom, to the land of the conqueror.

History as recorded in such annals as we have is largely a matter of kings and their military activities. We must, however, not be blind to the fact that much happened during the history of Ephraim that was of at least as great significance as the political intrigues and battles. It was a period of much literary activity, and it is generally agreed that during these troubled years there was compiled in Ephraim the history of Israel known to scholars as E, from which source are taken large parts of the Pentateuch, and probably of Joshua, Judges, Samuel, and Kings. Nor was the religious life stagnant. Great figures like Elijah, Elisha, Amos, Hosea were prominent forces in the life of the people. There is a marked tendency to-day to credit the Northern Kingdom with some part of the more distinctively religious literature in the Old Testament, notably some of the Psalms.

History of Judah

We have watched the rise and fall of Ephraim. Let us now retrace our steps and see how Judah fared meanwhile. Something of the story we have been bound to notice, for in a considerable measure the fortunes of the two kingdoms were intertwined. Sometimes Judah appeared as the foe, sometimes as the ally, and again as the vassal of her more important neighbour. Yet it would be a mistake to regard Judah as nothing more than a satellite of Ephraim. At one or two periods in the rivalry between the two kingdoms Judah was rather more than able to hold her own, though, it must be admitted, this was due more to alliance with other powers than to her own unaided strength. The geographical situation made it inevitable that in some ways the development of Judah should run upon different lines. In the picturesque phrase of Welch, Judah, whether for the time being an ally of Ephraim or an enemy, was 'sitting apart on her eagle's nest of Judean highland'.

We have seen already that the historians of the Old Testament, who were for the most part sympathizers with the Southern Kingdom, have distorted the perspective so that the relative inferiority of Judah is obscured. And even where the numerical superiority of Ephraim is conceded figures are exaggerated so as to give to Judah a material importance that she never possessed. A particularly glaring case of such exaggeration is to be found in 2 Chronicles 13, where Abijah of Judah is said to have mustered 400,000 men of war for his campaign against Jeroboam I, whose army is put down at 800,000 men, and to have slain 500,000 of the enemy, a victory which resulted in the capture of important cities by Judah. The obviously fictitious character of the numbers in itself makes the whole story improbable.

Rehoboam.

The position of Rehoboam after the division of the kingdom was difficult to maintain, and he was ill-equipped for the task. According to 1 Kings 14[30] there was war between Rehoboam and Jeroboam continually, a statement that we can readily accept. This strife provided an opportunity for Shishak of Egypt to intervene in the affairs of Palestine with more promise of success than would have been possible while the kingdoms were united under capable rulers such as David and Solomon. This chance he was not slow to seize, and in Rehoboam's fifth year, *c.* 934, he invaded the country. In view of Jeroboam's previous intimacy with the Egyptian court it would be natural to assume that in acting thus Shishak was taking the part of Ephraim against Judah; but the famous inscription on the south wall of the temple at Karnak, in which Shishak records his victory, mentions among the cities that submitted to him some that were in the territory of Ephraim, which makes the assumption improbable. The record of 1 Kings 14 admits that he took Jerusalem, and removed from the temple

The Divided Kingdoms

and the palace their golden treasures. Curiously enough the name of Jerusalem does not appear in Shishak's inscription, but this may be accounted for by the fact that the inscription is incomplete.

Shishak's inscription on the Temple of Amun at Karnak.

Apparently Shishak made no attempt to reduce the Palestinian kingdoms to a permanently tributary position, and contented himself with this display of his power, realizing that the internecine strife between the two kingdoms would prevent either of them from becoming a serious cause of annoyance to him. The Chronicler (2 Chronicles 12[8]) is probably exaggerating again when he represents Judah as becoming subject to Egypt as a result of this campaign.

Abijah; Asa.

Of the brief reign of Abijah, wrongly called Abijam in Kings, little is known, for the great victory recorded by the Chronicler, to which reference has already been made, belongs to the realm of edifying fiction rather than to that of history. Abijah was succeeded by his son Asa, whose reign was long and fairly prosperous. Jeroboam of Ephraim died soon after the accession of Asa, and was followed on the throne by his son Nadab, who after a brief reign was slain and supplanted by Baasha. Between Baasha and Asa there was perpetual strife (1 Kings 15^{32}). The fortunes of war inclined at first to favour Baasha. He attacked the northern border of Judah, and fortified Ramah, which was only five miles north of Jerusalem, as a threat to Asa's capital. So serious was the situation that Asa appealed to Benhadad of Damascus to break league with Ephraim, and create a diversion in his favour. As this appeal was made the more persuasive because it was accompanied by a bribe consisting of the treasures that were in the temple and palace Benhadad graciously responded to it. He attacked and captured territory on the north of Baasha's dominion, so that the latter was compelled to turn his attention to defence in that quarter. The pressure on Asa being thus relieved, he in his turn took the offensive, captured Ramah, dismantled its walls, and used the stones to fortify Geba and Mizpah as covering outposts on his frontier. Baasha retired to the shelter of his capital city, Tirzah.

The Chronicler records an earlier attack on Asa by 'Zerah the Ethiopian', whose great host was repulsed by the intervention of Yahweh in support of Judah's army. Many scholars identify this Zerah with Osorkon I of Egypt, the successor of Shishak, whose reign lasted approximately from 925 to 889. That there is no reference to this campaign in the Egyptian annals might be explained by the tendency to omit any mention of defeats. It is true, also, that a conflict between Egypt and Judah, even though the latter were successful, would so have weakened the power of Asa as to have afforded Baasha his opportunity for attack. But as there is some difficulty about equating the names Zerah and Osorkon, and the name Zerah is found in the old South Arabian inscriptions, some scholars suppose that the story relates to an

The Divided Kingdoms

Arabian raid rather than to an Egyptian invasion. The Old Testament describes Zerah as from Cush, which is the term generally used for Ethiopia. But on the other hand, Cush appears in the genealogies more than once as the ancestor of Sheba and other Arabian peoples, so the problem must be left open. When Omri ascended the throne of Ephraim relations between the two kingdoms appear to have improved. They engaged in common sea-trade, and controlled the port of Ezion-geber.

Jehoshaphat.

Jehoshaphat, successor to Asa, made peace with the king of Ephraim (1 Kings 22[44]) and acted, as we have seen, with Ahab, either as his ally, or as his vassal. This enabled him to tighten his hold on Edom, which was ruled by a deputy of the Judaean king. A trading expedition, for which elaborate preparations were made, was wrecked before it could leave the port of Ezion-geber.

Jehoram.

The reign of Jehoshaphat's son Jehoram was marked by two disasters. Edom regained its independence, and the Philistines made inroads on his territory, capturing the important city of Libnah. In view of the fact that Jehoram of Judah was contemporary with Jehoram of Ephraim it has been conjectured that the two Jehorams were actually one and the same king ruling over both kingdoms, and the records are so obscure that this suggestion can hardly be ruled out. It should, however, be borne in mind that there are other cases of the same name being duplicated among the rulers of the two kingdoms.

Ahaziah; Athaliah.

In the short reign of Jehoram's son, Ahaziah, who is called Jehoahaz in 2 Chronicles 21[17], the outstanding thing is the story of his death at the hands of Jehu near Jezreel. This tragedy led to events of great importance in Judah. The queen-mother, Athaliah, a daughter of Ahab and Jezebel, was faced with the loss of her position, and the queen-mother in an oriental court exercised an influence second only to that of the king himself. She seems to have inherited her mother's imperial spirit, and her devotion to the worship of the Tyrian Baal. Her intention to retain her power was made easier of accomplishment through the murder of the forty-two princes of the Judaean royal house by Jehu. Accordingly she had all the royal personages from whom a successor to her son might conceivably have been chosen murdered, to remove any obstacle that might have stood in her path. One only escaped, Joash, who was saved by the high priest Jehoiada and his wife Jehosheba, a sister of the dead king. Joash was concealed by them in the temple. For six years Athaliah held the sceptre, fostering the Baal cult. A temple of the Tyrian Baal had been erected in Jerusalem, possibly at her instigation when she became the wife of Jehoram. This temple had its own chief priest, Mattan. Athaliah seems to have made no attempt to suppress the worship of Yahweh. She was content that her own cult should have recognition side by side with that of the national deity.

Joash.

When Joash was seven years old Jehoiada produced the young prince in the temple, and proclaimed him king. Athaliah was slain, the Baal temple demolished, and Mattan killed. This revolution was partly political and partly religious, an attempt of the Yahweh worshippers to extinguish the rival cult. Of the political events in the reign of Joash the editors of Kings tell us little. The principal thing that we learn is that Hazael of Damascus undertook a campaign against the Philistine plain, in the course of which he captured the city of Gath. He then turned his forces against Jerusalem, and Joash was compelled to buy him off by the sacrifice of the royal treasures and the gold from the temple. Joash was slain by two of his officials in a palace conspiracy. The intrigue was probably directed against him personally, rather than against his dynasty, as he was succeeded by his son Amaziah. Was it a protest against his craven submission to Hazael?

Amaziah.

Amaziah slew his father's assassins. His conduct of affairs seems to have been prudent. He reasserted the authority of Judah over Edom, but was so much exalted by his victories that he unwisely attempted to measure himself against Jehoash of Ephraim. In a contemptuous message the latter refused to take up the gage, but Amaziah was foolishly insistent, and, being ignominiously defeated

The Divided Kingdoms

in a battle at Bethshemesh, was taken prisoner by Jehoash. The latter completed the humiliation of Judah by dismantling a great part of Jerusalem's fortifications and carrying off what treasures still remained in the palace and temple. He further secured his position by taking hostages. The offensive powers of Amaziah having thus been nullified, he was allowed to return to Jerusalem. He survived his conqueror by some fifteen years, and met his death as the result of a conspiracy in Jerusalem, for though he made his escape to Lachish he was captured there and slain.

Azariah.

The people of Judah installed as Amaziah's successor his son Azariah, or as he is called in 2 Chronicles 26, and Isaiah 6, Uzziah. Of this double name there is no convincing explanation. Azariah was sixteen years old when he became king. His reign is said to have lasted fifty-two years, and was certainly prosperous. The power of Judah at any time may be tested by one question, 'Was she able to control Edom sufficiently to use the port of Elath at the head of the Gulf of Akaba?' We read that Azariah 'built Elath and restored it to Judah'. Apart from this important statement, and a moderately favourable verdict on his religious orthodoxy, the compilers of Kings have nothing to say about him save that during the latter part of his reign he was afflicted with leprosy, so that his son Jotham acted as prince regent. But the evidence of Isaiah goes to show that under Azariah Judah enjoyed a season of prosperity comparable with that which Ephraim was experiencing under the contemporary Jeroboam II.

There may be a real historical nucleus in the much more detailed account of Azariah's reign given in 2 Chronicles 26. There Azariah is credited with strengthening the fortifications of Jerusalem, irrigation schemes, reorganization of the army, the capture of Philistine cities on his western frontier, and successful campaigns against the desert-dwellers on the east. An interesting problem arises from the reference in the Assyrian annals to a king Az-ri-ya-hu of Ya'udi, who was the head of a confederation which opposed Tiglath-pileser in 738. Some scholars assert the identity of this king with Azariah of Judah; but in spite of the intriguing similarity of the names the identification is highly improbable, for the king named in the annals is associated with the country round Hamath.

Jotham; Ahaz.

Jotham, the prince regent, became king on the death of his father. During his reign the alliance between Pekah of Ephraim and Rezon of Damascus against Assyria was formed, and these two kings tried to persuade Judah to join the confederation. Judah obstinately refused, and the allies determined to compel her adhesion by force. They marched against Jerusalem, where, before the crisis had come, the throne of Jotham had passed to his son Ahaz. Pekah and Rezon proposed to capture the city and replace Ahaz by a nominee of their own, a certain Syrian named Ben-Tabeel. In Isaiah 7 we have a vivid contemporary account of the situation. The prophet in a striking simile tells us that the heart of Ahaz and the heart of his people were trembling as the leaves of the forest in a wind. It has been thought that this may have been the occasion on which Ahaz offered his son as a sacrifice, just as Mesha of Moab did when in a similar plight. If so, it is a little surprising that there is no mention of the deed in Isaiah. In vain the prophet sought to persuade Ahaz to remain calm, assuring him that the threat would come to nothing. Ahaz appealed to Tiglath-pileser for assistance. His refusal to join the anti-Assyrian league entitled him to Assyria's support, and no doubt this would in any case have been given, as Isaiah was wise enough to see. But Ahaz thought it necessary to back up his appeal with a costly present from the treasures of Jerusalem.

The campaign of Tiglath-pileser in which Damascus fell is represented in 2 Kings 16[9] as the response to this appeal. In any case it removed all danger so far as the threat of the allies went. But the action of Ahaz had brought Judah definitely into the position of a tributary power. Ahaz was summoned to Damascus to meet his overlord, and caused an altar to be built in the temple after the likeness of an (Assyrian?) altar he saw at that city. Various other modifications in the temple furniture and ritual 'because of the king of Assyria' were made rather to show that the Assyrian suzerainty was thoroughly recognized than as any intentional departure from the worship of Yahweh.

The Divided Kingdoms

Hezekiah.

Ahaz was followed on the throne by his son Hezekiah, who for a time remained a faithful vassal of Assyria. But, undeterred by the fate of Samaria, he renounced his allegiance, and attacked the Philistines. An inscription, unfortunately incomplete, of Sargon's relates that Philistia, Judah, and Moab withheld their tribute, and sent gifts to 'Pharaoh, the king of Egypt, a prince who could not save them', in order to gain his support against Assyria. This may very well refer to the action of Hezekiah mentioned in 2 Kings 18[7]. It has been suggested that the campaign of Hezekiah against Gaza was an attack upon a loyal vassal of Assyria; some confirmation of this theory is found in the subsequent action of Sennacherib, who handed over to the king of Gaza a part of Hezekiah's territory by way of compensation. Nor is the theory inconsistent with Sargon's statement that the Philistines had refused to pay tribute, for on other occasions we find that some Philistine cities remained loyal when others were in rebellion. Most interesting is Sargon's contemptuous reference to the weakness of Egypt, which agrees well with the verdict of the Rabshakeh in 2 Kings 18[21], 'this bruised reed ... Egypt'. The figure is that of a hollow cane, used as a staff for walking, which, so far from supporting the hand that leans upon it, collapses so that the jagged edges of the fracture penetrate the hand. There is no evidence that Sargon's forces advanced against Jerusalem on this occasion, though they were sent to reduce the Philistines to submission, a task which, as Egypt lent no assistance, they found comparatively easy.

Hezekiah remained quiet until Sargon had died and been succeeded by Sennacherib, *c.* 705. The prince called Berodach-baladan in 2 Kings 20[12] and—more nearly corresponding to his actual name, Marduk-apal-iddina—Merodach-baladan in Isaiah 39[1] had given much trouble to Sargon. He had seized the throne of Babylon on Sargon's accession and held it for more than a decade, the most that Sargon could exact from him being tribute. In 709 he had formed a powerful alliance to challenge Sargon's position, but Sargon by prompt action prevented the army of Elam from joining Merodach-baladan, and drove him into the fenland country at the head of the Persian Gulf. Merodach-baladan, however, was irrepressible, and Sennacherib's first task was to remove him from the throne of Babylon, which he had again seized. Sennacherib quaintly describes him as 'that prop of evil devils', 'that worker of iniquity'. Though Sennacherib captured Babylon and drove Merodach-baladan out, he had by no means seen the last of him. It is highly probable that the embassy of Merodach-baladan to Hezekiah recorded in 2 Kings 20$^{12-19}$, though it is placed in the Old Testament narrative after the retreat of Sennacherib from Jerusalem, took place in connexion with his early attempt to secure the throne of Babylon at Sennacherib's accession. Evidently Hezekiah was disposed to listen to him, for the display of his treasures and armaments was intended to prove his power as a possible ally rather than as a vainglorious exhibition.

About 700 B.C. Sennacherib was free to turn his attention to the refractory states in Palestine. Tyre he failed to subdue, but Edom, Moab, and, among the Philistine cities, Ashdod, submitted. Askelon, Ekron, and Judah were defiant. Sennacherib, after defeating near Eltekeh the forces of Ekron, who were assisted by large contingents from Egypt, and capturing it, took Ekron and Askelon by assault, proceeding next to reduce one by one the outlying cities of Judah. He boasts that he took from Judah 'forty-six fortified cities and innumerable small towns', and more than 200,000 prisoners: this must surely be the exaggeration of a conqueror, even if we concede that Hezekiah had considerably extended the boundaries of his kingdom.

Hezekiah was particularly obnoxious because he was holding prisoner in Jerusalem Padi, the pro-Assyrian king of Ekron, who had been dethroned by the opposition party and handed to Hezekiah for safe keeping. However, Sennacherib made no actual assault on the city. He distributed much of Judah's territory among petty kings on its borders who had been loyal to Assyria, and blockaded Jerusalem itself. In his own picturesque phrase he shut up Hezekiah 'like a bird in a cage'. Hezekiah thought discretion the better part of valour, handed over Padi, and attempted to placate Sennacherib with an offer of submission accompanied by a gift of 300 talents of silver and 30 talents of gold (2 Kings 18^{14}). Sennacherib's own list of his booty adds 500 more talents of silver, ivory furniture, elephant skins, and women from

The Divided Kingdoms 103

Hezekiah's harem, male and female musicians, and daughters of the king.

The prophet Isaiah is probably describing the terrible condition of Judah's ravaged kingdom at this time in Isaiah 1$^{7-9}$: 'Your country is desolate; your cities are burned with fire; your land, strangers devour it in your presence, and it is desolate, as the overthrow of Sodom (so read for *strangers*). And the daughter of Zion is left as a booth in a vineyard, as lodge in a garden of cucumbers, as a besieged city. Except the Lord of hosts had left unto us a very small remnant, we should have been as Sodom, we should have been like unto Gomorrah.' But though Isaiah had strenuously opposed Hezekiah's policy in joining the anti-Assyrian league, he held fast in the darkest hour to his faith that Yahweh would not suffer his holy city to be taken by the enemy, and his faith was justified by the issue.

It is difficult to make out from the account in Kings just what were the successive steps in Sennacherib's offensive against Jerusalem. The story told in 2 Kings 18$^{17-37}$ seems to relate to a demonstration made by a force detached from the main Assyrian army before the city was invested: this demonstration was intended to incite the inhabitants of the city to revolt against their king, and so spare Sennacherib more serious trouble in reducing the city. Eventually Sennacherib was compelled to return home without subduing Jerusalem. If 2 Kings 19$^{10-13}$ is not a partial duplicate of this narrative it must record an attempt by Sennacherib to frighten Hezekiah into keeping his recently renewed pledge of loyalty.

According to 2 Kings 19$^{35-6}$ the cause of Sennacherib's departure from Palestine was the outbreak of a devastating plague among his forces. He was influenced also by the renewal of trouble in his own country, where Babylon had again revolted; and though he crushed the revolt he was too busy in his remaining years defending his eastern frontier against Elamite pressure to make a further expedition into Palestine. He was assassinated in 681 at Nineveh, by one of his sons, who, as we learn from the annals of Ashurbanipal, had Babylonian support. There is a confused reminiscence of this event in 2 Kings 19^{37}. Another son, Esarhaddon, put down the rebellion, and ruled Assyria from 681 to 669. Some reference to these events may be the foundation of the prophetic words ascribed to Isaiah in 2 Kings 19⁷.

Freed from further Assyrian pressure, Hezekiah no doubt recovered some of the territory of which Sennacherib had stripped him. Although his anti-Assyrian policy brought disaster upon his country he was a capable ruler. His religious reforms, which win him the praise of the editors of Kings, would have as a secondary result the consolidation of the kingdom by centring the interests of the nation round the temple in Jerusalem. His name will always be associated with the making of the Siloam tunnel, which assured the city against having its water-supply cut off by besiegers, and was, for its day, a remarkable feat of engineering.

Manasseh.

Hezekiah was succeeded by his son Manasseh, a boy of twelve. There is no mention in Kings of the relationships between Judah and Assyria during his reign. The story of 2 Chronicles 33¹⁰ff. to the effect that the Assyrians invaded Judah and carried Manasseh captive to Babylon is regarded by many scholars as a fiction. But the absence of any reference to it in Kings and the Assyrian annals is not positive proof of its incredibility. Necho of Egypt was removed by Ashur-banipal and afterwards restored to his throne. The references in Ezra 4², ¹⁰ to the settlement of more colonists in Samaria by Esarhaddon and Ashur-banipal are probably based on fact.

The description of the cults introduced into the temple by Manasseh goes to show that he was a loyal vassal of Assyria. In an inscription recording building operations at Nineveh Esarhaddon gives a list of twenty-two kings from Cyprus and the Mediterranean coastlands whom he summoned to pay him homage and provide materials for the building: among them appears Manasseh of Judah. A subsequent successful campaign by Esarhaddon against Egypt no doubt strengthened the respect shown by Manasseh towards his overlord in Assyria.

Amon; Josiah.

In contrast with the long reign of Manasseh was the very brief rule of his son Amon, who was slain by a group of palace conspirators. This violent action had no popular support, and the conspirators were themselves slain by the people of Judah, who placed Amon's son Josiah on the throne. As Josiah was but eight years old at the time, the conduct of the foreign policy was in the hands of his statesmen, who seem to have kept the country free from rash adventure. The chief event in his reign was the repairing of the temple and the purification of the cult, with the centralization of sacrifice in Jerusalem. This reform involved the removal of the cult objects of other religions which had been introduced into the temple, including those that had symbolized the overlordship of Assyria. Evidently such a step could be taken only if the power of Assyria had notably declined, and this was actually the case.

Esarhaddon appointed as his successor Ashur-banipal, who was one of Assyria's greatest kings; his military campaigns were extensive and successful, and under him the culture of his country reached a high level. But the many campaigns against Egypt, Elam, and other countries, added to embittered conflict with Babylon, over which city Ashur-banipal had placed his brother Shamash-shum-ukin as deputy ruler, must have exhausted the resources of the state. Egypt under Psammetichus threw off the yoke of Assyrian suzerainty, and Ashur-banipal could make no effort to meet the challenge. Even before the death of Ashur-banipal the signs of Assyria's inevitable collapse were evident, and the king himself in pathetic words describes his sense of failure: 'I cannot away with the strife in my country . . . with cries of woe I bring my days to an end.' It was shortly after Ashur-banipal's death that Josiah carried out his reforms, and we can see that Assyria was no longer in a position to interfere with his actions.

But though the shadow of Assyria had been lifted from Judah's path a new enemy had appeared on the horizon—the Scythians. These were soldiers of fortune, who lived by hiring themselves to such rulers as would pay for their services, and by harrying peaceful country-sides. The weakening of the Assyrian empire, which had acted as a barrier between the Scythians—whose homes were in the wide plains of Central Asia—and the countries bordering on the Mediterranean, allowed these raiders to pass south-west.

The History of Israel

About the time of Ashur-banipal's death, on their swift-moving horses they penetrated as far as Philistia, and, Herodotus tells us, were prevented from attacking Egypt only by the gift of a ransom. These raiders can hardly have left Judah unmolested, and the terror they inspired is vividly depicted by Zephaniah and Jeremiah. This highest wave of the Scythian incursion, however, receded, and Judah was troubled by them no more.

THE SCYTHIANS. A relief showing two Scythian horsemen (notice their 'trousers') one of whom is hobbling a horse.

Meanwhile the state of Assyria went from bad to worse. Ashur-banipal's successor Ashur-etil-ilani (626–621?) had to oust a usurper before he secured the throne, and internal strife so weakened the country that Nabopolassar was able to establish himself as independent king in Babylon, 625, and most of the outlying subject-kingdoms freed themselves. Nabopolassar set himself to destroy utterly the power of Assyria during the short reigns of Sin-shum-lishir and Sin-shar-ishkun, who followed Ashur-etil-ilani. During the struggle Psammetichus of Egypt supported Assyria, realizing that to maintain his ancient enemy was the only way of preventing the creation of an enemy more powerful still in the form of a great Babylonian empire. The Medes, on the other hand, allied themselves with Babylon. Nabopolassar's efforts met with varying success, but whenever he was repulsed he returned more vigorously to the attack. The Medes under Cyaxares sacked Ashur, the old capital of Assyria. The final blow to Sin-sharishkun was the desertion of his Scythian supporters to the enemy, who sacked Nineveh in 612. In the book of Nahum we have an ecstatic expression of delight at the prospect of ruin overtaking the hated city.

Even then the Assyrian empire was not finally extinguished. Remnants of the army that had escaped at the fall of Nineveh set up Ashur-uballit as king at Harran, and though the Babylonians and Medes drove him out in 610 he was still seeking to recapture the city two years later. The rest is silence. Necho of Egypt led his armies again and again against the Babylonians, whether in the hope of resuscitating an Assyrian power, or simply to crush his rival of Babylon, we do not know. And Egypt's hopes were finally extinguished when Necho suffered a decisive defeat at Carchemish in 605. From that time Babylon was the dominant power. It was in connexion with one of Necho's marches towards Babylon that Josiah met his death. The circumstantial account of this in 2 Chronicles 35^{20-5} may be dismissed as unhistorical. The sentence in 2 Kings 23^{29}, 'and king Josiah went against him (Necho); and he slew him at Megiddo, when he had seen him', is tantalizingly obscure. So perished one of the best kings of David's line, of whom the prophet Jeremiah, no lenient critic, said: 'He judged the cause of the poor and needy; then it was well' (22^{16}).

Jehoahaz; Jehoiakim.

The history of the Southern Kingdom now moved rapidly towards its tragic close. Jehoahaz, a son of Josiah, was chosen by the people to succeed him, but held the throne for three months only. Seemingly his policy was pro-Babylonian, for Necho, who was campaigning in the north-east of Palestine, summoned him to Riblah on the Orontes, and sent him as a prisoner to Egypt. Necho replaced him by another of Josiah's sons, Eliakim, changing the name of the new king to Jehoiakim. By this action he signified that the new king was entirely his creature. Naturally

Jehoiakim was compelled to send heavy contributions to his Egyptian overlord, and since the diminished treasures of the capital would not suffice to provide these, the people were taxed oppressively for this purpose.

The picture of Jehoiakim given by Jeremiah (22^{13-19}) is sketched in vivid colours. Despite the distress caused to his subjects by the heavy demands of Egypt the king lavished money on ambitious building schemes for his own selfish display, and cared little or nothing for justice. Opposed by prophets who continued to teach the ethical precepts of their great forerunners, and who foretold the doom of the city as a punishment for the wickedness of its rulers, he defied them. One, Uriah, escaped from his threats to Egypt, but Jehoiakim persuaded Necho to send him back, and put him to death. Jeremiah barely escaped the same fate. Before long the foresight of Jeremiah that the power of Egypt was doomed was proved to be true, and Necho was decisively beaten at Carchemish by Nebuchadrezzar II of Babylon, better known to us by the incorrect spelling of his name in the Old Testament, Nebuchadnezzar. Babylon now became the unchallenged arbiter of Palestinian politics.

Jehoiakim, who possessed no loyalties save to himself, transferred his allegiance to Babylon. But the city had its pro-Egyptian party still, and, possibly owing to intrigues with Necho, Jehoiakim changed his policy, and rebelled against Nebuchadrezzar, c. 598. For a time Nebuchadrezzar did not intervene in person, but sent mobile forces from his own army to act with the neighbouring Arameans and Moabites, whom he incited to harass his disobedient vassal. Against these Jehoiakim seems to have held his own with fair success. For the closing part of his reign, which lasted eleven years, we have no reliable information. The account in Kings, naturally interpreted, would show that of all Judah's kings since Josiah he alone came to a peaceful end, in spite of Jeremiah's predictions that his death would be violent and his end shameful.

Jehoiachin.

To Jehoiakim there succeeded his son Jehoiachin, an inexperienced youth. But before he could exercise his authority the

THE SITE OF NINEVEH TO-DAY

Babylonian army led by Nebuchadrezzar in person had appeared at the city gates, and within three months Jerusalem capitulated, 597. The king and his harem, the chief personages of the court, and a considerable number of the wealthier and more skilled inhabitants were deported to Babylon. In the view both of Jeremiah and Ezekiel the Jews who were thus exiled were the best of the people morally as well as materially. The palace and temple were despoiled of their treasures.

Zedekiah.

In place of Jehoiachin Nebuchadrezzar installed a son of Josiah, Mattaniah, changing his name to Zedekiah, as Necho had earlier changed the name of his nominee to Jehoiakim, and with a similar design: from the new king he exacted, as we learn from Ezekiel 17^{13}, an oath of obedience. For a time Zedekiah was faithful to his bond, and even, if we may assume that the letter of Jeremiah to the exiles referred to in Jeremiah 29 was sent with Zedekiah's approval, exhorted the exiled Jews in Babylonia to rest content under the Babylonian régime. This was now the only wise policy for Judah, and it was consistently advocated by Jeremiah. But Zedekiah was not a strong man, and when there was a general movement among the small subject states Edom, Moab, Ammon, Tyre, and Sidon against Babylon he allowed himself to be seduced from his pledge of loyalty. Under pressure, no doubt, of the pro-Egyptian party in Jerusalem he began to intrigue with Egypt, which was once again threatening to dispute the overlordship of Palestine with Babylon. Nebuchadrezzar forthwith sent an army to besiege Jerusalem. The Egyptian Pharaoh, Hophra, made some attempt to draw off the attack, and the siege was temporarily raised. But Hophra was defeated, and Jerusalem had to face the issue alone. The investment of the city was resumed, and after a resistance lasting a year and a half the end came.

Jeremiah throughout the siege consistently advocated a policy of surrender, and was naturally looked on as a traitor. Dissension was inevitable, seeing that there was a pro-Babylonian party as well as a pro-Egyptian party among the inhabitants. Famine also reduced the city's power of resistance. The walls were breached, and as a desperate resort Zedekiah with the army sought to break

The Divided Kingdoms

through the investing forces, and reach the country beyond Jordan. The attempt failed, and the fugitives were captured. Zedekiah was brought before Nebuchadrezzar at Riblah. His sons were slain in his presence, and he himself was blinded. He ended his days as a prisoner in Babylon.

The fate of the city was not determined until another month had passed. Then a Babylonian general, Nebuzaradan, came, and systematically destroyed the chief buildings. The palace, temple, and great houses were burned, the city walls broken down. Such treasure as was even now in the temple was carried off as loot. The inhabitants who belonged to the better classes were added to the prisoners taken during the siege and carried off to Babylonia. A selected group of priests, courtiers, and officers were executed at Riblah. Among the captives was Jeremiah, but he was released. It may well be that the Babylonian authorities knew that Jeremiah had stoutly opposed the anti-Babylonian policy of his king, and thought that he would be a useful influence in securing obedience from the inhabitants who were left in the city.

Nebuchadrezzar appointed as governor over what was now a small province in his empire a Jew named Gedaliah, whose family had supported Jeremiah. The governor's head-quarters was at Mizpah, a few miles north-west of Jerusalem. Gedaliah strove honestly to promote the interests of the survivors by a policy of loyalty to Nebuchadrezzar, in which he must certainly have had the full concurrence of Jeremiah. Had this course been pursued the land might have become peaceful and prosperous. But a certain prince of the royal family, by name Ishmael, who was backed by the Ammonite king Baalis, assassinated Gedaliah. This mad deed, which in no case could have enabled Ishmael to succeed Gedaliah with Babylon's consent, soon met its reward, for Johanan, who had in vain warned Gedaliah of Ishmael's evil intent, led a force against Ishmael, recovered the captives he had taken, and drove him across the border into Ammon.

The supporters of Gedaliah feared that all these happenings might be interpreted by Nebuchadrezzar to their disadvantage, and decided to seek refuge in Egypt. Jeremiah strongly opposed this plan, but to no purpose, and was himself compelled to accompany the fugitives. This was the end for Judah as a kingdom.

While the greater part, probably, of the people still dwelt in their homeland, the best of them were exiles in Babylonia and Egypt. Like Ephraim, when once Judah became involved in the politics of the great world-powers her doom was fixed. More prudent statesmanship might have deferred, but could not in the end have avoided, the day of reckoning.

CHAPTER VI

THE EXILE AND THE PERSIAN PERIOD

THE beginning of the Exile makes a line of sharp division in the history of Israel, but unfortunately our information about the subsequent years is very sparse. Our sources of history in the Old Testament for this period are fragmentary, and we get very little help from the annals of other nations.

Number of exiles in Babylonia.

Let us first see what we can learn about the exiles in Babylonia. We are accustomed to think of the Jews in Babylonia as a nation in exile. This is far from being the true state of the case. Some recent writers, indeed, have put forward the view that the 'exile' was so insignificant in numbers that it may be ignored. This is an extreme position, and involves, among other consequences, the treatment of Ezekiel as fiction. But it is undoubtedly true that only a fraction of the population of Judah was removed. The statement of the numbers taken captive in 597 found in 2 Kings 24$^{14-16}$ seems to contain duplications, but even if we take all its numbers together the total will not be very great. The round numbers do not point to accurate reckoning, and the statement that no one was left save 'the poorest sort of the people of the land' is not easy to reconcile with the fact that a number of military and state officials were surviving to form part of the captives taken eleven years later. There can be little hesitation in accepting the figure given in Jeremiah 52^{28}—3,023—as being nearer the truth.

The record in 2 Kings 25 of the deportation when the city was destroyed in 586 would naturally be understood to mean that most of the inhabitants who still remained were removed to Babylonia. Here, again, the statement in Jeremiah 52^{29}, which gives the total as 832, is probably near the truth. A third deportation of 745 persons is mentioned in Jeremiah 52^{30} as occurring five years later still. We must allow for the numbers given in Jeremiah including only men, and in that case, reckoning women and children, we might estimate the total number of Babylonian exiles as round about 15,000, perhaps about 10 per cent. of the population.

Condition of the exiles.

What we know as to the life of these Babylonian exiles is derived mainly from Ezekiel, and to a small extent from the writings of 'Second Isaiah'. The letter of Jeremiah (29) is also illuminating. Nebuchadrezzar was certainly not harsh in his treatment of conquered peoples, and the exiles were probably better off in a material sense than they had been in Judah. They were certainly brought into touch with a higher type of civilization. It appears from Ezekiel that they were settled in groups at various places, some of them in cities (cf. Jeremiah 29[7]). They were allowed to follow various occupations, and, no doubt, with characteristic Jewish industry, some of them became wealthy. At any rate Jeremiah exhorted them to build houses and plant gardens, regarding themselves as for seventy years citizens of their new country.

Several references in Ezekiel to the elders of the people who come to consult him lead us to suppose that in some measure the exiles enjoyed local self-government. The references in Second Isaiah, who wrote nearer the end of the Exile, are, however, of a rather different kind, and suggest that some, at any rate, of the exiles were in his day ill-used (Isaiah 42[22], 51[23]). The details given in connexion with the return go to show that some Jews had risen to positions of considerable importance in the land of their captivity.

Condition of Jews in Judaea.

What of the Jews who remained on their native soil? After the assassination of Gedaliah, Nebuchadrezzar must have appointed a new governor. Whether he was a Babylonian or a native we cannot say, but it is worthy of note that the later governors of the restoration period, Zerubbabel and Nehemiah, were of Jewish nationality. It is also likely that the Sanballat who was governor of Samaria in Nehemiah's time was of Jewish race, for though his official name is Babylonian we learn from one of the Elephantine papyri that his sons had good Jewish names. The situation of the Jews in Palestine was in some ways unhappy. Their resources were limited, and they would certainly be heavily taxed. Their reduced territory was encroached upon by the neighbouring Am-

The Exile and the Persian Period

monites, Moabites, Edomites, and Philistines. The exact borders of the several territories of these peoples would not be a matter of great concern to the Babylonian authorities so long as each was submissive to Babylonian rule. But while Babylon seems not to have exerted herself to protect the Jews from their neighbours, she appears not to have oppressed them on her own account.

Decay of Babylon's power.

The next great change in the fortunes of the Jews was a minor consequence of vaster changes in the relationships of the world-powers, which replaced Babylon by Persia as the dominant empire. Nebuchadrezzar died in 562, and his son, Amel-Marduk, the Evil-Merodach of Jeremiah, reigned for two years only. He was killed in a revolution, and succeeded by Neriglissar, whose reign lasted about four years. Neriglissar's son, Labashi-Marduk, was assassinated before he could establish his position, and succeeded by a usurper named Nabunaid. The history of Babylonia during this troubled period is reminiscent of the days of Ephraim's decline, and displayed symptoms which showed that the greater power was declining to a similar end. Nabunaid, more familiarly known as Nabonidus, was not without ability, and though he was an old man, nearly sixty, when he assumed the crown, conducted his affairs with sufficient skill to keep his throne for seventeen years. He was not a popular king, partly because of his especial devotion to the moon-god, Sin, who was not the national deity. Much of his time he spent in the pleasant city of Teima, in north Arabia, and his long absences from the capital must have involved some loss of control.

Cyrus and the Return.

Meanwhile the strength of Elam was growing, under the leadership of a virile king, Cyrus. Croesus of Lydia watched the consolidation of Elam with anxious eyes, and challenged Cyrus in battle. After an indecisive engagement he disbanded his forces, thinking that the snows of winter would prevent further campaigning. But Cyrus had original ideas as to the close season for fighting, and fell upon Croesus when he was helpless. He thus added Lydia to the kingdom of Elam.

Babylon was obviously the next objective, and Cyrus began to attack it in 547, obtaining control of the upper waters of the Tigris. He continued with persistence the process of seizing outlying portions of the empire, and the people of Babylon realized that they could make no permanently successful resistance to his unrelenting pressure. Nabonidus seems to have made little real effort to counter the activities of Cyrus, and was absent from his capital until just before the end came. In 539 Cyrus struck his final blow. He won a battle at Opis, and Babylonia turned to him as a deliverer rather than as a conqueror. Sippar willingly received the victor within its walls. Babylon itself submitted without resistance to the Persian army under Gobryas, and handed over Nabonidus to his enemies. Cyrus entered Babylon in triumph, and appointed Gobryas as its governor. He acted with far-seeing statesmanship, representing himself to the people as called to deliver Babylon by its own god, Marduk. Nabonidus was given a subordinate position in Carmania. There were in the city numerous divine images, captured from many nations and retained as trophies of war. These Cyrus restored to their owners, and in this way ingratiated himself with countries that had been unwilling subjects of the Babylonian empire.

What effect had this great change on the fortunes of the Jews? It would be natural to think that the rise of Cyrus as a formidable opponent of Babylon would wake in the minds of those exiles who still looked for an opportunity to return to their native land new hope. This hope is expressed by Second Isaiah, who, writing on the eve of Babylon's fall, speaks of Cyrus as the chosen agent of God in restoring His people, and pictures in glowing terms the return of the exiles across a miraculous road which God will build for them through the desert (Isaiah 40^{1-11}). But there were many among the exiles in whose heart there burned no desire to leave the country in which they had settled.

The Chronicler—the author to whose hand we owe the books of Chronicles, Ezra, and Nehemiah, which really form one continuous history—writes as though the hope expressed in Isaiah 40 was actually fulfilled in large measure. His narrative is found in Ezra 1. Another version of this account is to be read in 1 Esdras, which, though of later date than Ezra, many scholars think to be a version of a text of the book of Ezra in some ways

A model of the Ishtar Gate and procession-way at Babylon, in the Vorderasiatische Museum, Berlin. The Gate was built by Nebuchadrezzar, and enough survives to enable a fairly accurate reconstruction to be attempted.

purer than that of the Hebrew Bible. According to Ezra 1^{2-4}, Cyrus, immediately after his conquest of Babylon, issued a proclamation to the effect that Yahweh, who had given him the kingdoms of the earth, had bidden him build the temple in Jerusalem. The proclamation further exhorted the exiles to return for this purpose, and their Babylonian neighbours to furnish them with gold and silver, and means of transport. The Chronicler recounts the execution of these commands, and states that Cyrus returned the treasures of the temple which Nebuchadrezzar had looted to Sheshbazzar 'the prince of Judah', who was in charge of the returning exiles. The families who were included are named, and the total number is reckoned at nearly fifty thousand. Arrived at Jerusalem, the exiles join with their kinsmen of Palestine to restore the ritual, under the leadership of Joshua, the priest, and Zerubbabel. The foundation for a restored temple is laid, but opposition from surrounding peoples prevents the project from being carried to completion till the reign of Artaxerxes.

Another form of the decree supposed to have been issued by Cyrus is given in Ezra 6^{3-5}, which at once raises suspicion by its dating 'In the first year of Cyrus the king', for certainly Cyrus himself would have dated from the beginning of his reign, and not from the capture of Babylon. In fact the wording of these decrees is such that it is impossible to think of them as genuine. When we remember that the Chronicler cares little for the accuracy of history in comparison with the enforcement of his particular theories, and when we find, as we shall presently see to be the case, that his account of the building of the temple is quite inconsistent with the little contemporaneous history that has come down to us—in Haggai and Zechariah—we may reject without hesitation the details of his story. The nucleus of truth round which it has grown is the return of a comparatively small body of exiles from Babylonia, with the approval of Cyrus, directly after he became ruler of Babylon. The Chronicler may well be correct in his supposition that for the purpose an official decree would be issued.

Haggai and Zechariah.

We are on much surer ground when we turn to the writings of Haggai and Zechariah. In the latter case only cc. 1-8 come into the

The Exile and the Persian Period

reckoning, the remaining chapters of the book bearing his name coming from other hands. Haggai tells us that he received from Yahweh 'in the second year of Darius', that is 520, word to rouse Zerubbabel the governor of Jerusalem and Joshua the high priest to undertake the rebuilding of the temple. He knows nothing of such a rebuilding in 537. If, moreover, Zerubbabel and Joshua had been concerned in such an earlier project as the Chronicler reports, it is hard to see why Haggai does not mention it. Further, according to Haggai, the rebuilding is primarily the work of the people who had always lived in Jerusalem, rather than of the returned exiles. Such reference as we have to the worship which was carried on in Jerusalem before the rebuilding tends to show that the temple ruins were still its centre, and that the destruction by Nebuchadrezzar had left it in such a state that it could be used, despite the dilapidation. Haggai's book deals only with the year 520, and, though the writings of Zechariah cover a year or two longer, neither prophet brings the story down as far as the completion of the building.

The references in Haggai and Zechariah to Zerubbabel raise a fascinating problem. Though the name Zerubbabel suggests that he must at one time have resided in Babylon he was certainly a Jew, and presumably descended from the Davidic line. That such a man should have been appointed 'governor of Judah' (Haggai 1^1) accords well with the statesmanlike policy which Cyrus pursued in dealing with subjected nations. The passage Haggai 2^{4-9} seems to hint that the prophet, studying the political situation generally, was expecting the power of the Persian empire to collapse. In the general 'shaking' of all nations, which he believes to be imminent, he sees the opportunity of Judah once again to resume her independence, and to recover her former glory. And we may reasonably believe that in Zerubbabel he saw the ruler of the restored kingdom.

In Zechariah the same idea appears in a more definite shape. He looks forward to a time when Yahweh's 'cities shall yet overflow with prosperity, and Yahweh shall yet comfort Zion, and shall yet choose Jerusalem' (1^{17}). According to the vision described in 4 the two chief supports of the restored community are to be Zerubbabel and—presumably—Joshua. But the name of the latter is not actually mentioned; whereas that of Zerubbabel appears four times, and obviously the leading part of the drama to be enacted is written for him. In the incident of Zechariah 6^{9-15} we may find a more open indication of the hopes which filled the prophet's mind. Certain of the returned exiles are required to furnish gold and silver, from which are to be fashioned crowns. Probably the original text had simply *a crown*. The text has clearly been corrupted, for it now names Joshua as the person for whom the crown is destined (v. 11), whereas the reference to the 'Man whose name is the Branch' in the following verse must certainly, in view of 3^8 and 4^{7-9}, mean Zerubbabel. The curtain, then, after these tantalizingly brief glimpses of the action, is dropped, and does not rise again. The sequel is left in complete obscurity. The most obvious continuation of the story is that Zerubbabel was urged by the prophets to proclaim himself prince of Judah, and that he followed out their policy. This action would inevitably strain the tolerance of Persia to breaking-point, and presumably the attempt to reassert independence was crushed. Zerubbabel would meet with the customary reward of a traitor. Since no information on the subject is available from the annals of Persia, the reconstruction of these events can be regarded as no more than probable.

Nehemiah and Ezra.

As the text of the Old Testament now stands the next glimpse we get of the fortunes of the Jews is in connexion with the coming of Ezra to Jerusalem, an event for which the date given by the Chronicler is 457 B.C. But before we can profitably deal with the work of Ezra it is necessary to examine this problem more closely, because it seems almost certain that the Chronicler, writing long after the event, has made the serious blunder of transposing the order of Ezra and Nehemiah. According to Ezra 7^8 it was in the seventh year of Artaxerxes king of Persia that Ezra, with a company of exiles, returned to Jerusalem under the king's authority. Nehemiah 2^1 gives the twentieth year of Artaxerxes the king as the date of Nehemiah's return. There were three kings of Persia named Artaxerxes, Artaxerxes I, Longimanus, 464–424, Artaxerxes II, Mnemon, 404–359, and Artaxerxes III, Ochus, 359–338.

The Exile and the Persian Period

That the Artaxerxes of the Chronicler is intended in both cases to be Artaxerxes I there is no reasonable doubt, and, if so, Nehemiah followed Ezra at an interval of thirteen years. Moreover, in one or two places it is represented that Ezra and Nehemiah were contemporaneously at work in Jerusalem. Thus Nehemiah 8^9 states that Nehemiah was present when Ezra republished the Law to the inhabitants of the city.

But it is difficult to believe that the part played by Nehemiah could have been so insignificant in comparison with that of Ezra in so solemn a ceremony. Nor in the memoirs of Nehemiah himself is there any indication that he had anything to do with such an event. And the suspicion that the mention of Nehemiah in Nehemiah 8^9 is no part of the original record is made almost a certainty when we find that the Greek version of the record—1 Esdras 9^{49}—has no mention of Nehemiah. The Attharates of that passage is doubtless equivalent to the Attharias of 1 Esdras 5^{40}, who is distinguished from Nehemiah. Nehemiah 10^1 gives Nehemiah the Tirshatha as the first of those who signed the Covenant: but here again the Greek has a variant text, omitting 'the Tirshatha', so that, though the name of Nehemiah appears in both Hebrew and Greek, there is an element of uncertainty in the text sufficient to make it of dubious authority. Nehemiah 12^{26} also mentions Nehemiah and Ezra as contemporaries, but there are good reasons for regarding this verse as an addition to the text. In short, none of the passages in which Ezra and Nehemiah are named as resident together in Jerusalem is of sufficient weight to invalidate the highly probable theory that Ezra was considerably later than Nehemiah.

Again, according to Nehemiah 3^1, the name of the high priest at the time when Nehemiah was active in rebuilding the walls of Jerusalem was Eliashib. There can be little doubt that the Jehohanan of Ezra 10^6 is the high priest Jonathan of Nehemiah 12^{11}, called Johanan in vv. 22 f., who is a son of Joiada the son of Eliashib. It is true that he is called son of Eliashib in Ezra 10^6 and Nehemiah 12^{23}; but *son* in these cases is used in the looser sense of descendant, for he is clearly the grandson of Eliashib. The inference from these passages is that Ezra was at work under the high priest who was a grandson of the high priest of Nehemiah's time. Confirmation of the view that Ezra must therefore have worked during the reign of Artaxerxes II rather than Artaxerxes I, is found in the Elephantine papyri. In two of the most famous of these documents, of date 408, concerning the petition of the colonists in Elephantine to the governor of Judaea for help in rebuilding the Jewish temple of the colony, Jehohanan is named as high priest.

Further, when Nehemiah began his work, he found that 'the city was wide and large: but the people were few therein, and the houses were not builded' (7^4). Ezra, on the other hand, gathers a 'very great congregation of men and women' (10^1), and speaks of the people as being numerous (10^{13}). The population of the city would presumably be increasing rather than decreasing, so that these statements would favour the view that Nehemiah preceded Ezra. The natural interpretation of Ezra 9^9 would be that the wall of the city is already rebuilt, and the rebuilding of the walls is clearly the outstanding achievement of Nehemiah. While it must be allowed that the problem is not easy of solution it seems best, then, to accept the view that Nehemiah precedes Ezra, and we shall deal with their activities on this assumption.

Nehemiah, like many of his race, had so distinguished himself as to obtain a prominent position in a foreign court, and was cup-bearer to Artaxerxes I. But he was intensely patriotic, and much concerned about the fate of the struggling population in Jerusalem. While he was in attendance on the king at Shushan he learned from some Jews recently come from Jerusalem that his fellow-countrymen there were in a sorry plight. The wall is broken down, and the gates burned with fire. This can hardly refer to the damage inflicted on the city after the final siege, or it would have been no news to Nehemiah. It would seem that some attempt must have been made to repair the damage, but that the results had been undone by enemies, presumably from Samaria. Nehemiah is made so sorrowful by the report that his face reveals his distress to the king, who asks what is the matter, and at Nehemiah's request gives him leave of absence and letters of authority which constitute him in fact, if not in name, governor of Jerusalem.

Nehemiah's arrival at Jerusalem, in 444, incenses Sanballat, who

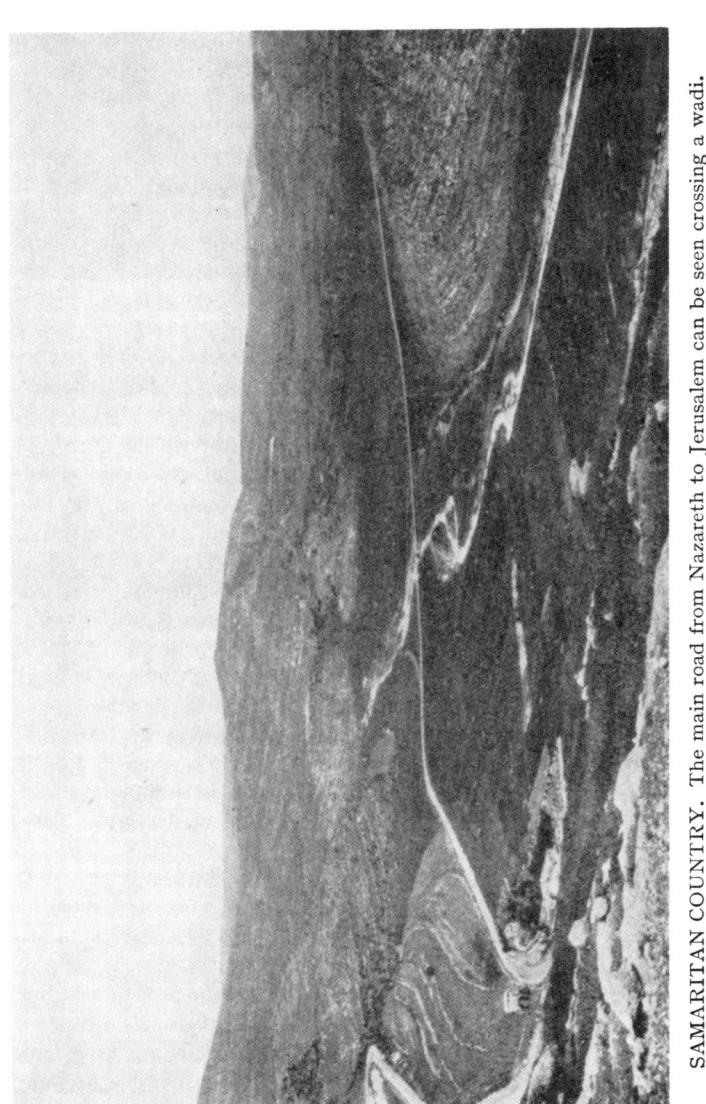

SAMARITAN COUNTRY. The main road from Nazareth to Jerusalem can be seen crossing a wadi. The photograph is taken looking west.

was governor of Samaria and no doubt looked upon Nehemiah's position in Jerusalem as a diminishing of his own authority. Nehemiah examines the condition of the walls, by night, as though he feared some opposition from the inhabitants, many of whom may well have been on good terms with Sanballat, and not anxious to see Jerusalem re-established as a walled city. The Chronicler's account of the ready acquiescence of the inhabitants in the project relates rather what he supposed should have been their attitude than the actual fact. Indeed, the difficulties Nehemiah encountered within the city seem to have been more serious than the opposition of Sanballat and those outside, who confined themselves to abuse and the fomenting of trouble for Nehemiah in the city. Presumably they were afraid to act more directly against a court favourite armed with the royal authority. Nehemiah was, however, a man of strong personality, and, despite all hindrances, succeeded in accomplishing his main project of renewing the walls and gates. His stay in the city lasted twelve years, and when he returned to Persia he left the city in the charge of his brother Hanani and Hananiah, governor of the castle (7^2).

After an indefinite time ('certain days' 13^6) Nehemiah returned once more to Jerusalem, this time not to repair material walls but to erect religious barriers which should keep the people of Jerusalem apart from the neighbouring peoples, for in the atmosphere of Babylon the orthodox Jews had come to believe that their only chance of saving the people from losing their identity was by insistence upon the observance of certain religious customs which should mark them out clearly from their neighbours. Nehemiah 13 shows us of what nature these practices were. First, all who were not Jews of pure blood must be excluded from the temple and its cult. So Tobiah, a friend of Sanballat, who had been allowed to establish himself in the temple precincts, was summarily evicted, and the buildings and vessels were reconsecrated. The fact that Tobiah's residence had been sanctioned by Eliashib, the high priest, is evidence that a party in Jerusalem, including some of the leading officials, was quite out of sympathy with Nehemiah's ideals.

Strict regulations as to the keeping of the Sabbath were enforced, for Sabbath-keeping in a very narrow sense had now come to be regarded as an essential mark of the orthodox Jew. Mixed

The Exile and the Persian Period

marriages were strongly condemned, and, though Nehemiah did not go to the length of annulling such as already existed, he issued orders that no more should be contracted. Another matter on which he busied himself at this time was the organization of the tithe system.

Ezra, whose arrival in Jerusalem, as we have seen, is probably to be dated in the seventh year of Artaxerxes II, 397 B.C., is described as a priest, a scribe of the law (Ezra 7^{21}). The language of the decree, Ezra 7^{12-26}, which authorizes Ezra's mission, and its intimate acquaintance with the details of Jewish worship, at a glance reveal that it is a fiction of the Chronicler's. Had Artaxerxes issued a decree, which may well have been the case, it must certainly have been couched in quite different terms.

The Chronicler seems to have possessed some genuine memoirs of Ezra, but he has expanded them with so much of his own material that a cloud obscures the activities of that leader. Indeed, some scholars have not hesitated to say that Ezra is altogether a figment of the Chronicler's imagination. That, however, is an extreme and improbable hypothesis.

The two great achievements of Ezra were the promulgation of a more exacting code of law and the enforcement of stricter regulations as to marriage with women of other than pure Jewish birth. On this latter point Ezra was harsher than Nehemiah had been, for he insisted that such existing marriages as were contrary to the regulation should be dissolved, the husbands compelled to send their wives away, and to offer sacrifices for their guilt. The Chronicler's story of the promulgation of the new law is to be found in Nehemiah $7^{73b}-8^{12}$, which is an extract from the memoirs of Ezra. The new law is described as 'the book of the law of Moses'. This has been variously interpreted as the Pentateuch, the Priestly Code, or that particular part of the latter known as the Law of Holiness. Of these guesses the last is the most plausible. All, however, of which we can be certain is that it comprised new and stricter developments of the older laws. These developments had become the orthodox practice among the Babylonian exiles, and Ezra's great aim was to ensure that the community in Jerusalem attained the same standard of orthodoxy.

In comparison with Nehemiah, Ezra stands out as a man of

harsh disposition and narrow views. But it must be conceded that he was largely the creator of that hard shell of particularism which made it possible for Judaism to survive during the struggles of succeeding centuries. Without it Judaism would probably have been completely Hellenized. Yet when we have allowed all this our sympathies go out to the men of wider outlook and broader tolerance to whom Ezra's policy must have been repellent. It is likely that to such men we owe the book of Jonah, with its noble attitude to the Gentiles, whom it represents in much more kindly character than the selfish Jonah—a man after Ezra's own heart; possibly the book of Ruth, which represents David as a descendant of such a mixed marriage as Ezra would have condemned, may come from the same circle. The continuation of Ezra's story is not preserved for us, and over the history of the Jews the curtain falls, not to rise again until the times of the Maccabees.

CHAPTER VII

THE BACKGROUND OF THE RELIGION

The Religions of Israel.

IF we interpret the words strictly there is no 'religion of Israel'. It is often assumed that the Hebrews as a whole professed a religion which can be traced throughout their history, becoming more spiritual as the generations passed. But this is not true to fact. Still less is it true to think of 'the religion of the Old Testament' as being the same thing as this hypothetical 'religion of Israel'. In a loose way we say that the religion of England is Christianity, but only a minority of the English people can be counted in any very serious sense as Christians. Many who would call themselves by the name 'Christian' are almost indifferent to the religion. So among the Hebrews different men held very different views, and adopted varying practices, in the sphere of religion.

The Hebrews were, no doubt, all worshippers of Yahweh, their national God. But the great majority in most ages thought of Yahweh in much the same way as each of the surrounding peoples thought of its deity. 'For all the peoples walk every one in the name of his god, and we will walk in the name of Yahweh our God', as it is put in Micah 4[5]. And as with most Hebrews the conception of Yahweh differed little from the conception held, say, of Chemosh by the Moabites, so their forms of worship and religious customs were hard to distinguish from those of their neighbours. But side by side with this popular religion was a religion of loftier type which is represented chiefly by the prophets, and has a much more exalted view of God, and a much more spiritual kind of worship. For convenience this may be called the 'prophetic religion'. We need always to remember that this higher religion was the religion of a spiritual aristocracy, not the religion of the whole people. The problem of tracing the development of religion in Israel is complicated by the fact that through a large part of the history we find these two religions existing side by side. Another difficulty arises from the fact that the books of the Old Testament as we have them have been edited by men who were in sympathy with this prophetic religion, or who belonged to the post-exilic Judaism which grew out of it. The editors sometimes read back their present into the past, and the documents must be critically considered before we can determine to what extent their picture of religion in the earlier times is true to life.

Totemism.

The popular religion contained many elements that belong to prehistoric times, and much that is common to Semitic religion generally. There are, for example, certain features of Hebrew life which seem to be most easily explained as remnants of totemism. In early societies groups of men regarded themselves as allied in a very special sense to something, generally an animal or a plant, which was their totem. For such a group the totem was sacred, and they came to look upon themselves as descended from it. If it were an animal that animal might never be hunted or killed by the members of the clan. The one exception to this rule was that on very special occasions a totem animal might be slain and eaten by the clan. This ceremonial eating was supposed to reinforce the members of the kinship with divine power, for the totem came to be looked upon as a supernatural being; indeed it came to be thought of almost as a god.

Many names in the Old Testament are animal names, and this is particularly noticeable in the case of tribal and clan names. For example, Caleb, which is really the name of a clan rather than of an individual, means 'dog', and Simeon is 'hyena'. It is difficult to avoid the inference that in earlier times such clans had as their totem the animal after which they were called. Totemism may well be the original cause for which the prohibition of the use of certain animals as food came into existence. More important still is the probability that sacrifices may have been developed out of the custom of solemnly eating a totem animal on special occasions. But whatever traces of totemism we may find in the Old Testament are inherited from a much earlier time, and we are not to think of Hebrew religion as being consciously affected by it.

The Background of the Religion

Sacred trees, stones, and streams.

In early thought certain natural phenomena were regarded as having a spiritual cause. A tree, with its branches swaying in the wind; a stream, with its rushing movement, and its power of creating fertility—these were looked upon as animated by a spirit, who easily develops into a demon or a god. For reasons less easy to understand, special stones were also regarded as the habitations of spirits or deities. We find in the Old Testament numerous indications that this type of thought survived in popular Hebrew religion.

Very striking is the prominence of sacred trees in the stories. We read that Yahweh appeared unto Abraham 'by the oaks of Mamre', Genesis 18[1.] and at the 'oak of Moreh', Genesis 12[6.] In the former passage the Greek reads 'oak', and is most likely correct. In each case the oak is named originally with some further meaning than simply to tell where the event happened. God reveals himself at such places because the trees named have a special sanctity, and were in earlier times regarded as the dwelling-places of deity. The oak of Moreh is worth special notice, because its name means 'oak of the instructor', and was probably derived from the belief that through the movements of its leaves the deity gave oracles to such as sought them. So at the shrine of Zeus at Dodona the sacred oak gave oracles by sound. When Abraham built an altar by the oak of Moreh he recognized the oak as a dwelling-place of God. The 'burning bush' connects the deity closely with a tree. It would be easy to multiply examples of sacred trees in the Old Testament, and not difficult to show that behind the references to them lies the idea that they are, or have been, dwelling-places of God.

Altars and shrines are very often found to be closely associated with trees. The reiterated complaint of Jeremiah that the people have played the harlot 'under every green tree' shows that their places of worship were usually under trees. To 'play the harlot' is constantly used as a metaphor for the desertion of Yahweh in favour of other gods, but it is probable that those who are rebuked by the prophet addressed their worship to Yahweh, though its form was the form used by other peoples for worship of the

Baalim. To worship Yahweh with foreign cultus was regarded by the prophets as hardly to be distinguished from the worship of other gods.

In this connexion the cult of the Asherah is very important. The Asherah, wrongly translated by 'groves' in the A.V., was a tree, or, more frequently, a wooden pole, regarded as a substitute for a living tree, which was almost invariably found beside an altar. Thus Gideon, Judges 6[25], is bidden cut down the Asherah which stands beside his father's altar in Ophrah. This was to be used as firewood for the sacrifice made by Gideon the same night, so it was presumably a dry pole rather than a living tree. The Asherah is probably in origin the symbol of a female deity, once worshipped at the shrine, though it seems to have become nothing more than a sacred object. It is highly probable that there was a goddess named Asherah, one form of the mother-goddess. And if it should be thought incredible that an Asherah, even if it be no more than the *symbol* of a feminine deity, should find a place beside the altar of Yahweh, it must be remembered that in the fifth century B.C. the Jewish colony at Elephantine worshipped in their temple side by side with Yahweh three or four other deities, one of whom at least was female, and yet regarded themselves as good Jews.

Sacred stones play a part almost as prominent as that played by sacred trees, though it is not quite clear how they came to be regarded in early times as abodes of deity. Just as the typical altar of early times was looked upon as incomplete without its Asherah, so it needed beside it one or more tall standing stones. The excavations at Gezer, Taanach, Megiddo, and other holy places have brought such stones to light. Some of these had hollows scooped out for the purpose of offering liquid sacrifices such as wine, blood, or oil to the deity supposed to inhabit them. Such stones were found among the Hebrews, and, although in later times they became abhorrent to the orthodox religion and were prohibited, in earlier times they were approved of.

Such a stone is known as a *massebah*. The most striking illustration of the massebah is in the beautiful story of Jacob at Bethel, Genesis 28. Jacob, suddenly overtaken by nightfall, selects a stone which he uses for a pillow. His vision of the ladder

TREE WORSHIP. An Assyrian relief showing King Ashurnasirpal with a priest wearing wings, engaged in a magical ritual in front of a sacred tree.

leads him to conclude that the stone upon which his head has rested is a dwelling-place of his God. That is why he is terror-stricken, and exclaims 'How awesome is this place [and by "place" he clearly means the stone]. This is none other than a dwelling-place of deity!' He has used a divine stone for a profane purpose, and committed what we should call sacrilege. That it is the stone, and not the locality, which is Bethel (= a house of God), is clear from v. 22, 'this stone, which I have set up as a massebah, shall be God's house'. The pouring of oil upon the top of the stone, v. 18, is an offering to the indwelling deity, partly as atonement for the act of sacrilege. It is highly probable that beside the altar at Bethel, a famous shrine of the Northern Kingdom, called by its priest, Amaziah, the royal and national sanctuary (Amos 7^{13}), there stood such a stone, which was regularly anointed by the priest, and that the story of Genesis 28 is told in explanation of the origin of this practice. At any rate the story is evidence that at the time of its inclusion in the sacred literature the massebah cannot have been regarded as an offence against Yahweh's commandments.

That water, and more especially running, or, as the Semitic idiom has it, 'living', water, should be looked upon as divine, is easily understood. Where the stream flowed vegetation flourished, and animal life abounded, though all the land outside the area irrigated by the stream might be sterile. The stream appeared to be in a very real sense a creator of life. In the words of Robertson Smith, the waters are thought to be 'instinct with divine life and energy'. It is against this background that we should see the very ancient 'Song of the Well' preserved in Numbers 21^{17-18} where the well is addressed as a person. Sacred streams were often resorted to for the purpose of seeking oracles. An offering might be cast into the stream, and according as it sank or floated the indwelling deity was thought to accept or reject the offerer. Or by drinking of the sacred water a man might receive prophetic inspiration.

Traces of this idea that streams are divine and may give oracles are not infrequent in the Old Testament, but in most cases they are rather faint. According to Genesis 14^7 an alternative name for Kadesh (see p. 37) is En-mishpat, that is, the

The Background of the Religion

Spring of Decision. It can hardly be doubted that this spring obtained its name because it was supposed to give oracles in response to inquirers. Presumably, too, the 'holy water' of Numbers 5[17], which was used by the priest in the ordeal determining the guilt or innocence of a woman charged with adultery, means water taken from a sacred stream and accordingly endued with supernatural power.

Holiness.

The ideas connected with taboo play a great part in Hebrew religion, and are closely allied to the Old Testament conceptions of holiness. Among primitive peoples certain things and persons are taboo, that is, may not be touched without danger, because they are closely connected with the gods, or, in some cases, with evil spirits. Any one who defies the rules of taboo places himself in grave danger. In the Hebrew religion such things and persons are described as 'holy', or 'unclean', and in either case the rules about them are probably derived from taboo restrictions.

The precise line between what is holy and what is unclean is difficult to draw. Generally speaking, what is holy is so because it is connected with the deity, and what is unclean is repugnant to him. Such repugnance may very well go back to times when the things causing it were regarded as specially connected with rival spirits. Certain animals, notably the swine, are unclean for the Hebrews. This was true also for the Syrians. Such restrictions will naturally go back to the time when the animals were totems, and therefore sacred animals, which might not, save in the case of a solemn community meal or sacrifice, be eaten. Places and things connected with the deity are especially under taboo restrictions, and therefore called holy. The word 'holiness' does not in early usage carry with it the ethical ideas which we associate with it. A god is holy simply because he is some one altogether apart from normal human experience. To call him 'holy' does not mean that he has any special ethical characteristics. And the holiness of a god extends to all his possessions. The conception is almost that of a semi-material essence which flows through the deity and those things with which he is in contact. Any unqualified person who touches any of these things is in danger of receiving something analogous to an electric shock, which may be fatal. A person who is himself 'holy' may be regarded, so to speak, as immune, or, if we may change the figure, inoculated against the consequences of infection.

The conception of 'holiness' may best be made clear by illustrations. The dwelling-place of a deity is, very naturally, holy. It is carefully bounded by limits, so that no one may inadvertently touch the holy soil. So in the record of the revelation at Sinai, which mountain was regarded in older times as the residence of Yahweh, at which he could be consulted by Moses, Yahweh gives the instruction 'Thou shalt set bounds unto the people round about, saying, Take heed to yourselves, that ye go not up into the mount, or touch the border of it: whosoever toucheth the mount shall be surely put to death' (Exodus 19^{12}). In this case the transgressor is to be 'stoned, or shot through', because he will have infected himself with the quality of holiness, and therefore have become a danger to his fellows. It is not a punishment for disobedience, for even an animal which strays beyond the bounds is treated in the same way. A particularly instructive case is the story of Uzza, 1 Chronicles 13$^{7-11}$. Uzza is driving the oxen that pull the cart upon which the ark is being transported. The oxen stumble, and the ark is in danger of falling from the cart. Uzza almost instinctively puts forth his hand, to hold the ark in safety. But the holiness with which the ark, so intimately connected with Yahweh, at one time thought of as his dwelling-place, is charged, instantly kills him, as though he had clutched an electric cable. Yahweh 'smote him, because he put forth his hand to the ark ... and David was displeased, because Yahweh had broken forth upon Uzza'.

The quality of holiness is infectious, so to speak. What comes into contact with something holy is liable itself to become holy. So Haggai (2$^{11-13}$) puts certain inquiries to the priests. If a man is carrying in his garment holy flesh, that is, flesh which has been offered to Yahweh, and, having become his property, is charged with 'holiness', and the garment touches any other food, bread, pottage, wine, or oil, or whatever it may be, will the food become infected with holiness? The priests say 'No'. Again, Haggai asks whether if any one who is taboo because of touching a corpse

The Background of the Religion

should touch these foods they too will become taboo, and the priests answer 'Yes'. In earlier times the answer to both questions would probably have been 'Yes'. It was obviously necessary to have the limits of infection closely defined, and the priests were the people who understood and defined the rules.

The sentence 'Stand by thyself, come not near to me, for I am holier than thou' (Isaiah 65^5) is a warning by one who is in a state of 'holiness' to one who might by touching him acquire 'holiness', given as a leper might ring his warning bell. Clothes worn in a sacred building become 'holy'. At Mecca, in pre-Mahometan times, the Arabs performed the circuit of the Caaba naked, or in clothes specially borrowed for the purpose, because if a man trod on the sacred enclosure in his own clothes these became holy, and he could neither use them again nor sell them. They must be left at the entrance to the sanctuary. So one takes off one's shoes when treading on holy ground, or they may not be used again.

In 2 Kings 10^{22} there is a reference to certain vestments kept at the temple of the Tyrian Baal in Samaria. These were to be worn by the worshippers in place of their own garments, to prevent the latter from acquiring holiness. The vestments worn by priests go back to this early custom, and in it we may find the origin of our own 'Sunday clothes'. In some circumstances 'holiness' might be removed from a garment by washing it. Shoes would, however, be taken off before touching the sacred soil, because, unlike linen or cloth garments, they would be difficult to wash. We remember how Moses is warned (Exodus 3^5), 'put off thy shoes from off thy feet, for the place whereon thou standest is holy ground'.

The ban.

Within the same circle of ideas falls the usage of the *herem* or ban. This is well illustrated by the story of Achan, Joshua 6–7. When the leader of an army was about to attack the enemy or lay siege to a city he would appeal for the help of his deity on the understanding, expressed or implicit, that the whole or some definite part of the booty should be the share of the deity. As the property of the deity such promised spoil, which might include captives, became taboo. So when the Hebrews under Joshua captured Jericho (Joshua 6[21]) 'they utterly destroyed all that was in the city, both man and woman, both young and old, and ox, and sheep, and ass, with the edge of the sword', sparing only Rahab and her family. 'They burnt the city, with fire, and all that was therein' (Joshua 6[24]), but the metal part of the booty was transferred to Yahweh, not by destroying it, but by putting it into the treasury of his shrine. The English Bible uses for action of this kind the word 'devote'; removing the promised spoil from human control or contact by destroying it, or by including it among those things which are taboo, is 'devoting' it to Yahweh.

A subsequent attack on Ai fails. Yahweh reveals the cause of this failure to Joshua. Some Hebrew has 'taken of the devoted thing' and put it among his own stuff. Yahweh, having been thus defrauded of some part of the promised booty, declines to continue his assistance to the Hebrews. Joshua proceeds to cast lots, by which method he discovers first the tribe, then the particular member of it, Achan, who has offended. Achan confesses that he has concealed from the spoil of Jericho raiment, gold, and silver, which are buried beneath his tent. These are dug up, and finally Achan, all his family, his animals, his possessions, are stoned and burned, together with the loot he had concealed. The loot having been originally 'devoted' to Yahweh was 'holy', and contact with it, direct or indirect, caused Achan and all that belonged to him to become 'holy' too. As they have thus become part of Yahweh's property, so to speak, the property must be transferred by destruction to its owner.

Magic.

Closely allied to primitive religion is magic. In Egypt, Babylonia, and Palestine magical practices were widespread, and the Hebrews themselves were much addicted to them. The general attitude of the Old Testament towards magic is one of condemnation. In the oldest code of Hebrew law, the Book of the Covenant, we find the injunction 'Thou shalt not suffer a sorceress to live', Exodus 22[18]—which reminds one inevitably of Clough's version of the sixth commandment: 'Thou shalt not kill, but needst not strive officiously to keep alive.' It is noteworthy that

BABYLON THE HOME OF MAGIC. Two Babylonian devils: Humbaba, whose face consisted of a single line, and Pazuzu, a god of sickness.

in the Book of the Covenant the practiser of the forbidden art is assumed to be a woman; witches have generally been more numerous than wizards.

The variety of these magical and allied arts may be gathered from the list given in Deuteronomy 18$^{10-14}$ of those who must be extirpated from Israel—diviners, augurs, enchanters, sorcerers, charmers, consulters with familiar spirits, wizards, necromancers. From Jeremiah 27^9 we learn that such persons were numerous in the last troubled days of the Kingdom, and Micah 5$^{12-13}$ shows that the prophets looked upon magic and idolatry as closely connected. The taunt-song of Isaiah 47 makes it clear that Babylon was regarded as pre-eminently the home of magic. The prophet speaks of the multitude of her sorceries, and the great abundance of her enchantments, wherein she has laboured from her youth. The excavations in Babylonia have brought to light a vast literature of magical formulae which amply justifies the prophet's indictment.

A very instructive passage is found in Ezekiel 13$^{17-23}$, where the prophet inveighs against the sorceresses—women, once more, it will be noted—who 'sew knots (so read, for *pillows*) upon all elbows' and 'hunt souls (i.e. human beings)'. The symbolical tying of knots as charms by means of which a victim might be brought into their power was a common practice of Babylonian sorcerers. The victim might be released by snapping the knots. One Babylonian exorcism text appeals to the fire-god to 'break the cords' whereby a sorcerer has bewitched a victim, and so release the latter from the spell. The prophet's indignation is the greater because such deeds were done for trifling fees, 'for handfuls of barley and for pieces of bread', v. 19.

One particular form of magic in vogue was the use of wonderful words as incantations. The name of the deity was regarded as a specially powerful charm, and the probable meaning of the commandment 'Thou shalt not take the name of Yahweh thy God in vain' is 'Thou shalt not employ the divine name for magical purposes'. A minor form of the practice of magic was the wearing of all manner of charms and amulets.

Rarely magic is regarded in a more favourable light. There is no hint of condemnation in the narrative which speaks of the

The Background of the Religion

cup of divination belonging to Joseph; this was a treasure to him, not so much because it was of silver, but because he was accustomed to use it for the purpose of divination (Genesis 44[5]). The prophets themselves, as we shall see, practised a form of 'sympathetic magic'. Closely allied to the use of magic, too, is decision by means of the lot, which was quite a reputable proceeding.

Life after death.

In their ideas of life after death the Hebrews shared the beliefs of some of their neighbours, beliefs which go back into a very remote past. The conception which appears most often in the Old Testament represents the shade of a dead man as departing to Sheol, a name variously rendered by 'hell', 'the grave', 'the pit'. This is a gloomy cavern beneath the earth's surface. It is 'a land of thick darkness... without any order, and where the light is as darkness' (Job 10[22]). Sometimes it is spoken of as possessing bars and gates, like a fortified city, but these are for preventing the escape of its inhabitants, not for shutting out those doomed to enter. As Job says in the verse preceding that just cited, 'I go whence I shall not return'. With rare exceptions these gates are for one-way traffic.

Life in Sheol is so empty and dreary that it hardly deserves to be called life. Usually Sheol is thought of as being outside the sphere of Yahweh's influence—'The dead praise not Yahweh, neither any that go down into silence' (Psalm 115[17]). There is no knowledge of Yahweh, or communion with him in Sheol: 'Shall thy loving kindness be declared in the grave, or thy faithfulness in Destruction? Shall thy wonders be known in the dark, and thy justice in the land of forgetfulness?' (Psalm 88[11f.]). This last-mentioned Psalm speaks, v. 5., of the dead as those whom Yahweh 'remembers no more'. In Sheol life's poor distinctions vanish. Job laments that he has not passed into Sheol as a babe, for then, instead of suffering anguish, he would have been at rest; 'There the wicked cease from troubling; and there the weary be at rest ... the prisoners hear not the voice of the taskmaster ... the servant is free from his master', because all men are reduced to a colourless monotony of mere existence (Job 3[17-19]). On the other hand, in the picture drawn by Ezekiel

(32^{17-32}) it seems that the warriors of the several nations sleep on their swords in separate areas of Sheol.

This view of life after death finds a very close parallel in Babylonia. The Babylonian equivalent of Sheol is Arallu. Arallu is a gloomy cavern in the underworld, dim and dusty. The shades who inhabit it have for their food dust and clay. In the myth of Nergal and Erishkigal Arallu appears as an inner court surrounded by fourteen concentric walls, each with its gate. Another myth tells the story of Ishtar's descent into Arallu, and gives the number of the encircling walls as seven. The gates and bolts are covered with dust. But as in the case of Sheol, though the gods may with difficulty descend into Arallu, the shades cannot pass out again. It is 'the place of no return', a description that at once recalls 'the bourne from which no traveller returns'.

With that curious facility common to mankind of holding at the same time inconsistent ideas as to the fate of the dead, Hebrews and Babylonians alike believed that though the shades in the underworld were removed from any real share in life their conditions might be dependent upon what happened to their dead bodies. If a body were unburied its shade found no rest. The greatest cruelty that could be inflicted upon an enemy was to deprive his body of decent burial. This conception appears again and again in the Old Testament. The charge brought by Amos against the king of Moab (2^1) is that 'he burned the bones of the king of Edom into lime', or, in other words, pursued his vengeance into the underworld.

CHAPTER VIII

MOSES AND YAHWEH

Ethical monotheism.

WHILE it is true that the religion of the Hebrews contained much that was inherited from primitive times, and much that was shared in common with the other inhabitants of Palestine, that which makes it of supreme interest is its difference from the religions of Phoenicia, Moab, Edom, and other neighbouring peoples. In the later centuries we find the prophets teaching that there is one God, and one only. Perhaps even more important is their belief that this God is an ethical deity, and, being good himself, demands not in the first place, if at all, sacrifice, but good conduct on the part of his worshippers. This teaching is technically called 'ethical monotheism'. What is the origin of this noble religion? Why did the Hebrews come at last to so lofty an idea of God, whereas their neighbours never advanced to it? This is the question for which we must try to find an answer.

If we could regard the stories of the patriarchs told in Genesis as historical in detail the answer would be easy to find. This sublime view of God, we should be able to say, was revealed to mankind in the beginning, and all inferior religion and worship is the result of sinful departure from the truth. But these stories in their present form are not older than the eighth century B.C., and we cannot draw this, the traditional, conclusion with any safety. At the other extreme is the view held by many scholars that this ethical monotheism is a comparatively late development, not older than the great prophets themselves. Amos, the earliest of the writing prophets, holds this doctrine in essence, and by the time of Deutero-Isaiah it is definitely stated.

The view that this lofty doctrine of God does not go back into the times before the great prophets became fashionable in that part of last century when the doctrine of evolution, then imperfectly understood, swayed the minds of all scientific scholars. It was thought that all historic religions began with crude ideas and forms which were in the course of time gradually refined and improved until they became pure and lofty. But this notion of the working of evolution in all spheres is now discredited. Development does not proceed by gradual and continuous improvement. There are sudden leaps, and sometimes equally sudden falls. And in religion, as elsewhere, this truth holds good. Certainly the prophets do not speak as if the lofty doctrine of God which they are proclaiming is a new discovery on their part. Their attitude is rather that they are recalling the people to an old truth, and bidding them return to the purer religion of their ancestors.

Moses and the Decalogue.

Great religions are always associated with great personalities. In the world of science truth advances not at a measurable yearly rate. It is when a man of genius makes a great discovery that science strides forward. It is to men such as Newton and Einstein that the leaps in human knowledge are due. And religious truth advances much in the same way. Tradition in the Old Testament associates the distinctive revelation with Moses. He is the founder alike of the nation and its religion. And here we feel that tradition is to be trusted. Indeed, if Moses is not to have this credit we shall be driven to invent some one else for the honour. Not many years ago some scholars were convinced that Moses was not an historical character, but the reaction from that view has been so pronounced that hardly any one holds it to-day.

Moses is, of course, especially associated with the revelation of the Law. It is certainly true that a large part of the legislation attributed to him is of much later date. Even this fact, however, seems to confirm the belief that he was a law-giver, for otherwise such an attribution would never have been made. The vital question for our present search is whether the Decalogue, in Exodus 20$^{3-17}$, really comes from the hand of Moses. If that be granted then we may certainly find in Moses the source of that lofty idea of God which distinguishes the later Hebrew religion.

The main objections raised against attributing to Moses the authorship of the Decalogue are three. It is urged, first, that the prevalence of image worship in later times shows that it cannot

Moses and Yahweh

have been forbidden by Moses. Then it is said that the Sabbath is a comparatively late institution in Israel, and therefore the fourth commandment cannot go back to Moses. And finally it is objected that the last commandment, forbidding covetousness, represents a stage of ethical development which cannot be thought of as obtaining at so early a date.

Before trying to meet these objections it may be said that when we assert that the Decalogue may well go back to Moses we do not mean the commandments just as they are stated in Exodus 20. Primitive commandments are brief, and almost always negative. The Decalogue in Exodus 20 contains some of the injunctions in their primitive form, but others have been expanded. Originally it would run something like this:

> Thou shalt not worship any god other than Yahweh.
> Thou shalt not make a graven image.
> Thou shalt not use the name of Yahweh wrongly.
> Thou shalt not break the Sabbath.
> Thou shalt not dishonour thy parents.
>
> Thou shalt not murder.
> Thou shalt not commit adultery.
> Thou shalt not steal.
> Thou shalt not commit perjury.
> Thou shalt not covet.

In such a short form these commandments might well have been written on two stone tablets, and the tradition to this effect is too constant to be lightly brushed aside.

Apparently similar lists of actions that were forbidden existed among the Egyptians and the Babylonians long before the time of Moses. The Egyptian *Book of the Dead*, a kind of guidebook to the after-life, which was placed in the coffin of a dead man, contains a list of denials and affirmations which the dead man will be required to make in the hall of judgement, before Osiris and the forty-two judges of the dead. Among them are:

> I have not killed.
> I have not committed adultery.
> I have not stolen.

The Religion of Israel

We cannot be far wrong in deducing from this that there was in Egypt some well-recognized code containing the prohibitions

> Thou shalt not kill.
> Thou shalt not commit adultery.
> Thou shalt not steal.

And when we remember that some copies of the *Book of the Dead* are of a date nearly fifteen hundred years B.C. we can believe that a much simpler code such as the Decalogue may well have existed among the Hebrews from the time of Moses.

This conclusion is reinforced by a study of the Babylonian exorcism tablets. The second tablet of the *Shurpu* series contains a long list of questions which are to be put to the gods by a priest in order to discover in what particular an afflicted man has transgressed, and thus incurred his affliction as the punishment of his sin. Some of these questions are concerned with ritual, others with ethics. Among the latter are these:

> Has he entered his neighbour's house?
> Has he approached his neighbour's wife?
> Has he shed his neighbour's blood?
> Has he stolen his neighbour's garment?
> Has he despised father and mother?

Here again we may reasonably infer that there existed in Babylonia a code of laws equivalent to

> Thou shalt not commit burglary.
> Thou shalt not commit adultery.
> Thou shalt not commit murder.
> Thou shalt not commit theft.
> Thou shalt not despise father and mother.

It is true that the Babylonian document is comparatively late, of the seventh century B.C., but in these matters men are very conservative, and we may be sure that the contents of the exorcism tablets are centuries older than the form in which they have survived for us.

Now let us look more closely at the three specific arguments advanced against the theory that the Decalogue may be Mosaic. We will take first the assertion that the injunction against

Moses and Yahweh

covetousness reaches an ethical level too lofty for so primitive an age. What has been already quoted from ancient documents might make us pause before accepting such an assertion. And those documents give us further ground for such hesitation. Among the affirmations which, according to the *Book of the Dead*, must be made by the soul in the judgement hall of Osiris are these:

> I have given bread to the hungry.
> I have given water to the thirsty.
> I have given clothes to the naked.

These are just like the tests which Jesus himself in his picture of the judgement regards as crucial. Surely an injunction against covetousness is not impossible in a decalogue of considerably later date than the *Book of the Dead*!

The Babylonian exorcism texts also suggest a high level of ethical obligation, though in view of the uncertainty of their age we cannot use them quite so confidently. The questions asked by the priest include such as:

> Has he set friend against friend?
> Has he failed to free a prisoner or loose a captive?
> Has he said *Yes* where he should have said *No*?
> Has he said *No* where he should have said *Yes*?

The prohibition of images may very well have been part of the teaching of Moses in spite of the fact that subsequent generations used them. Not to make capital of the point urged by some scholars that the commandment does not prohibit images, but only a particular sort of image, which might seem merely an expedient to evade a difficulty, what subsequent generations do is not necessarily that which the founder of their religion intended them to do. We are certainly not disposed in any case to believe that the religion of the Hebrews maintained the lofty standard set by Moses. So far as his more spiritual type of religion survived it was never until very late times the religion of more than the choicer souls. Infractions of a rule do not prove that the rule is non-existent.

The problem of the Sabbath is very much controverted. In a Babylonian inscription we find a day called *shabattu*, on which a festival is held for propitiating the gods, and no work is to be done. On a calendar for sacrifices and festivals the 7th, 14th, 21st, and 28th days of a certain month are marked as days when the king must not eat roast meat, offer sacrifice, ride in his chariot, change his robes, or pronounce judgement; the wise man must not prophesy; the physician must not practise the healing art. It is not surprising that in the first flush of enthusiasm which greeted the valuable discoveries made in Mesopotamia during the last century men jumped to the conclusion that here was an exact parallel to the Hebrew Sabbath.

Closer examination of the records will show that the parallel is by no means so clear as these quotations might seem to make it. But without going into any of these details we have good reason for doubting the theory that the Hebrews borrowed the Sabbath institution from the Babylonians, especially in the form that would date such borrowing from the time when exile in Babylonia had made the Jews familiar with Babylonian customs. After the exile the outward symbols which the Jewish leaders insisted on as visible evidence that their people were definitely marked off from surrounding peoples were circumcision and the Sabbath. It is not easy to understand how this could be satisfactory had the Sabbath been an institution but recently borrowed from Babylon.

Whence, then, did the Sabbath come to the Hebrews? Or did it originate among them? The most plausible theory yet advanced is that the Sabbath was originally a festival of the full-moon day, afterwards transformed into the Sabbath of Judaism. But this is by no means proved. What may be regarded as reasonably certain is that the Sabbath is as old among the Hebrews as the worship of their national God, Yahweh. Emphasis is laid so strongly on the idea that the Sabbath is Yahweh's day that it is difficult to think of Sabbath apart from Yahweh. It will be noted, for instance, that in the Decalogue the commandment which enjoins the keeping of the Sabbath follows immediately upon that which forbids the misuse of the divine name. Yahweh's name and Yahweh's day, in other words, are thought of closely together. So the answer to the question when and how did the Sabbath come to the Hebrews is likely to be dependent upon the

Moses and Yahweh

answer to a prior question, when did Yahweh become the national deity of the Hebrews.

Yahweh, the God of Israel.

According to Genesis 4²⁶, it was in the time of the patriarch Enosh that men began 'to call upon the name of Yahweh'. 'To call upon the name of' a deity is the technical expression in Hebrew for practising the cult of that deity. This particular passage comes from the document known as *J*, the oldest of the chief sources into which the first six books of the Old Testament have been analysed by scholars. So the tradition of this document traces the worship of Yahweh right back to the times of the patriarchs. But in Exodus 6²⁻³ we have a statement which stands in flat contradiction with this. God, speaking to Moses, says, 'I am Yahweh: and I appeared unto Abraham, unto Isaac, and unto Jacob, as El Shaddai, but by my name Yahweh I was not known to them'. This passage belongs to *P*, the latest of the main sources. The teaching of this tradition is, then, that before the time of Moses the name Yahweh was unknown to the Hebrews, and the patriarchs Abraham, Isaac, and Jacob worshipped a God whom they called El Shaddai. This name, which the English Bible renders by 'God Almighty', probably means 'God, my rock'.

Another of the main sources, *E*, tells us that Moses, when ordered by God to go to the Israelites in Egypt to be their deliverer, said, 'When they ask me what is the name of the God who has commissioned you, what am I to say?' The answer is, 'say to the Israelites I AM hath sent me to you' (Exodus 3¹⁴). The Hebrew word translated by *I AM* is part of the verb meaning 'to become', or 'to be', and the point here is that the writer assumes *Yahweh* to be a third personal form from that verb meaning 'he who is', or 'he who causes to be'. In other words, the aim of the narrative is to show that God reveals to Moses as something previously unknown that his name is Yahweh, and secondarily to provide an etymology explaining its significance.

The real truth of the case lies with *P* and *E*, namely, that the name of Yahweh is first used among the Hebrews under the authority of Moses. It is worth notice that with one dubious exception no name into which *Yah*, the shortened form of Yahweh, so often found in the Hebrew proper names, enters as an element occurs in the Old Testament before the time of Moses, though such names are exceedingly common later. At a subsequent time the name came to be regarded as too sacred for use, and at the time when the Jewish scholars of about the sixth century A.D. added vowels to the text of the Old Testament, which had only the consonants of the words, it was usual to substitute for it in speech the title Adonai, meaning *Lord*. So they fitted to the consonants YHWH the vowels of the word which they pronounced instead of the old name, and the combination is transliterated in our *Jehovah* (J = Y, V = W), which is really not a word at all. The result is that we cannot be absolutely sure of the way in which YHWH was actually sounded. The most widely held view is that it was called Yahweh, though it is not impossible that it was pronounced *Yahu*.

Recent discoveries have shown that the name *Yahweh* in its shorter forms *Yahu* or *Yah* was known in early times beyond the borders of Israel. Certain names found in contract tablets dated in the First Dynasty of Babylon appear to contain a divine name Ya-ve or Yahu as one of their elements. The excavations of Sellin at Taanach brought to light another tablet, inscribed with cuneiform characters, mentioning the name Ahi-yahu, which is the exact equivalent of the Hebrew name Ahijah, and accordingly contains the divine name Yah. This tablet may be of any date between 2000 and 1500 B.C., but is almost certainly older than the time of Moses. Again, in an inscription of Sargon II, we read of a king of Hamath, whose name is Ya-u-bi'-di, in which it is definitely proved that the first element is a deity's name. This is a little older than 700 B.C. So it seems to be clear that the name Yahweh, in one or other of its forms, is known among other peoples than the Hebrews, and earlier, in some cases, than the time of Moses. This is most naturally explained on the assumption that the name is in origin not a proper noun but a descriptive term. Just as in English we use the common noun *lord* as a description of God, then spell it with a capital L, and so develop it into a proper name, so many Semitic peoples may have used the descriptive name *Yahu* of their deities. The word is so old

Moses and Yahweh

that we can no longer offer any certain explanation of its meaning. But each people that used it to describe a deity might, and the Hebrews certainly did, come to treat it as a proper noun.

If we may believe, then, that the name Yahweh is older than

A coin of south Palestine, of about 400 B.C., showing Yahu as a solar Zeus. The name Yahu appears in Aramaic lettering near the figure's bearded head.

the time of Moses, how did he come to adopt it as the proper name of the Hebrews' God? This question cannot be answered with certainty, but it is highly probable that Yahweh was the name of the Midianite deity worshipped by Jethro, the father-in-law of Moses; Exodus 18 clearly represents Jethro as one to whom Moses looked for instruction in important affairs. This theory is supported in some measure if we accept the view that the Rechabites, who were the most fanatical devotees of Yahweh, were descendants of nomads whose home was in Midianite territory.

The Religion of Israel

The vitally important thing in this connexion is, however, not the name of the God of Moses, but the character of that God. Great religions go back to great personalities, and the leap forward which produces a new religion is due to some religious experience which comes to a devout soul. We may surely find the spring of Mosaic religion in that revelation which came to Moses in the mystic experience vouchsafed to him in the vision of the burning bush. And, believing that the Decalogue comes from Moses, we see that the God whom he worships is one who brooks no rival, and whose demands are primarily for the right conduct rather than for sacrifice. This is as much as to say that in practice Moses is a monotheist, though he may never have formulated any logically ordered doctrine of monotheism. Perhaps it would be more correct to use the term *monolator* rather than monotheist; for Moses may have recognized the reality of other gods but regarded them as outside the interests of the Hebrews.

Monotheism outside Israel?

Despite much argument to the contrary no satisfying proof that monotheism existed outside Israel before the time of Moses has yet been given. The only plausible rival to Moses is the famous Akhenaten, who, under the name Amenhotep IV, became ruler of Egypt *c*. 1375 B.C. He certainly effected a great reform in religion when he substituted for the worship of Amen the worship of Aten, the sun-god who was symbolized by a solar disk. He sought to root out from the religion of the Egyptians all the other gods whom they had been wont to worship, and to purify the cult from its grosser elements. He composed a magnificent hymn to Aten, the giver and nourisher of all life. Its language is so much like that of Psalm 104 that we can hardly doubt the indebtedness of that psalm to Akhenaten's hymn.

Very eminent scholars have asserted that Akhenaten is the earliest teacher of monotheism, and if this be conceded it must be admitted that Moses might have been indebted to Akhenaten for his conception of God. But it is very doubtful whether Akhenaten was really a monotheist. His reform was quite as much a political as a religious adventure. He allowed himself to be worshipped, and in other ways acted in such a fashion as to imperil his claim to be reckoned a monotheist. While we may agree that Akhenaten was a great reformer and a man of unusual spiritual insight, it is hard to see how he can be regarded as a forerunner of Moses in the teaching of a religion approaching a pure monotheism.

CHAPTER IX
THE INFLUENCE OF CANAANITE RELIGION ON THE RELIGION OF THE HEBREWS

Local shrines.

IT must always be remembered that, however lofty may have been the religion of Moses, the religion of the ordinary people, right up to the time of the Exile, was something very different. This will be more readily appreciated if we try to picture to ourselves the conditions under which, at any rate until the days of David and Solomon, the Hebrews lived. The various clans were under no central government, and were separated from one another by belts of territory that had never been wrested from the Canaanites. In some places they were living at peace with Canaanite inhabitants among whom they had settled down. Groups of Hebrews were for the most part not very large in numbers, and the towns in which they dwelt were, though the Old Testament dignifies them with the name of cities, not any larger than an English village. Only where a king dwelt, or a local sheikh of unusual importance, was there a city in the ancient East.

A Hebrew village-town would be built, as a rule, upon a hill, its houses huddled together and surrounded by a lightly constructed wall sufficient to keep out wild beasts and to enable the inhabitants to protect themselves against forays. The really large cities of the original inhabitants, such as Jericho, were elaborately fortified and able to endure a siege: but of such fortresses the Hebrews had hardly any. The villages would be isolated from one another by strips of wild country that could not be cultivated, by mountains and ravines. Each village of any account would have its own shrine, generally situated on a rising piece of ground outside the wall and known as its 'high place'. The service of such a shrine would be in the hands of a particular family.

A good example may be found in the story of Gideon, Judges 6. Joash, the father of Gideon, is the owner of 'the oak which is in Ophrah', the village where they dwell. This oak is a sacred tree,

Influence of Canaanite Religion on Hebrews 153

by which is situated the village sanctuary. There is an altar, and beside it an Asherah. The 'angel of Yahweh' bids Gideon throw down the altar, and chop up the Asherah to provide kindling for a sacrifice. Gideon carries out this command by night, so that he may not be observed by the inhabitants. Surely the shrine must have been some little way out of the village, or the operations of Gideon and his ten men would have been heard. But the striking feature about the shrine is that though Gideon's clan is a Hebrew clan, the altar is dedicated not to Yahweh but to Baal!

We see, then, that it is not regarded as something abnormal for the shrine of a Hebrew village to be used for the worship of the local Canaanite deity. This is easy to understand. Most of the villages possessed by the Hebrews were taken from the Canaanites, and the sanctuary would be there in Canaanite times. When it was adopted by the Hebrews it would be very natural for them to retain the worship of the local deity, for it was firmly believed that the fertility of a district was the gift of the local deity who resided in it. The Hebrews would offer their sacrifices to the local deity rather than to Yahweh, who was, so to speak, not 'at home' there. Even when they substituted for the local Baal their own God, Yahweh, the tendency would be to transfer to his service the local religious customs. Cult that belongs to a particular religious site will often maintain itself even though the religion may be considerably changed. Thus to-day at a cathedral in Spain an ancient pre-Christian dance is tolerated before the high altar. Though the name of the god might be changed from Baal to Yahweh at a village shrine the worship would often remain unaltered, and in effect the inhabitants would be Baal worshippers.

These considerations enable us to understand the motives that underlay the 'law of the central sanctuary' which was enforced by Josiah as part of his reform in 621. The fact that each district had its own Baal led to the Hebrews losing the sense that Yahweh, their God, was one God; for, though two villages might each offer worship to Yahweh, the feeling would develop that the Yahweh who presided over the prosperity of one village was a different deity from the Yahweh who blessed the other with fertility. As late as Jeremiah's time the prophet can say 'according to the number of thy cities are thy gods, O Judah' (2^{28}). Even more urgent, in the view of the reformers, than the correction of this error was the necessity of abolishing the pagan customs, some of them immoral, which clung around the local sanctuaries, by insisting that the temple at Jerusalem should be the sole place for practising the cult of Yahweh.

The use of Canaanite cult at the shrines where nominally Yahweh was the object of worship would be the more easy because the customs used in worship by the Canaanites were very similar to those which Hebrew law prescribed for the worship of Yahweh. Sacrifice was common to all the religions of the neighbouring peoples. While, as we have seen (p. 128), sacrifice may have developed from a totem meal eaten as a means of strengthening the communion between the totem and its devotees, certainly in historic times it was regarded more as a method of placating the gods by offering them gifts. This is made clear in the Babylonian stories of creation, according to which the purpose of the gods in making man was the provision of beings who would bring them sacrifices, which, in the crudest conceptions, are regarded as food for the gods. After the Deluge, in the Babylonian story, the gods were so desperately hungry because sacrifice had been suspended that when the Babylonian Noah prepared a sacrifice on emerging from the ark they gathered round it 'like flies'. A trace of this crude idea survives in the language of Genesis 8^{21} where it is said that 'Yahweh smelled the sweet savour' of Noah's sacrifice.

Human sacrifice.

In the methods of sacrifice, and in the prescribed materials, the differences between the Canaanite customs and the Hebrew customs were insignificant in comparison with the likenesses. Both at an early stage practised human sacrifice. The story of Jephthah's daughter furnishes one example. Among the Hebrews such sacrifices were relatively rare. They do not, as is sometimes supposed, point to a low estimate of human life. Indeed, the reverse of that statement is true. When specially great favours were needed from the deity a man might offer his most precious possession, his son. We have seen earlier (see p. 84) how Mesha

Influence of Canaanite Religion on Hebrews

of Moab, when desperately hard pressed by Jehoram, 'took his eldest son that should have reigned in his stead, and offered him for a burnt offering' to his god, Chemosh. It is worth noting that the Hebrew narrator regards this sacrifice as having achieved its object. This must be the meaning of the obscure words 'there was great wrath against Israel'; Chemosh, thus heavily bribed, rose to the occasion. We can understand how it was that in the later troubled times of Judah, when the people supposed that Yahweh had deserted them, the practice of child sacrifice was revived.

Apart from the case of Jephthah's daughter a definite example cannot be produced from the Hebrews of the early period. But originally the firstborn of human as well as of animal kind was regarded as the property of the deity, and was conveyed to him by means of sacrifice. Only so can we explain the regulation, Exodus 13[13], 'all the firstborn of man among thy sons shalt thou redeem'. In other words, a substitute for human sacrifice is recognized by more humane standards of thought. The well-known story of Abraham's attempt to offer Isaac is told with the purpose of showing that such sacrifices are not pleasing to Yahweh. Naturally the prophets of later times were utterly opposed to the custom, but the protest in Micah 6[7] where the prophet ironically asks, 'Shall I give my firstborn for my transgression, the fruit of my body for the sin of my soul?' is evidence that such an idea was not inconceivable among the less spiritually-minded of his contemporaries.

The festivals.

The great festivals of the Hebrew year, again, were akin to those observed by their Canaanite neighbours, and, indeed, probably go back to a very early period. They were three in number: the Feast of Unleavened Bread, the Feast of Weeks, and the Feast of Ingathering at the turn of the year. These are all festivals associated with important events in the agricultural year, and would be much more closely bound up with Palestine than with the nomad life from which some part of the Hebrew stock was derived. With the Feast of Unleavened Bread, the Passover, which was originally an offering of the firstlings of the flock, and as such may well have been a custom of the nomad life, was afterwards linked. The Feast of Weeks, of Pentecost, marked the completion of the corn harvest. The Feast of Ingathering, or Tabernacles, celebrated the gathering-in of fruit, oil, and wine. These feasts were later connected with certain events in the history of the Hebrews, but that was done only to give these widespread festivals some distinctively national explanation.

Teraphim; ephod; sacred lots.

The cult objects, in addition to those that have been already discussed in connexion with the inheritance from primitive religion, would be very similar in Canaanite and Hebrew worship. The teraphim were probably small portable images such as have been dug up often in the course of excavation. They were so small that when Rachel stole the teraphim of her father, Laban, she was able to conceal them by sitting on them (Genesis 31$^{19-35}$). Difficulty has been caused by the statement in 1 Samuel 19^{13} that Michal took 'the teraphim, and laid *it* in the bed', in order to mislead the agents of Saul who were seeking for David. This has quite naturally been thought to imply that teraphim might be of life size. But the correct rendering of the passage is 'placed *them* (so the Greek) towards the bed'. Mr. Sidney Smith has pointed out that the Babylonians buried small terra-cotta or metal figures under the floor or in the wall of a room where a sick person was lying. The idea was that they would drive away evil spirits and plague demons. What Michal did was to set out the teraphim near the bed, after arranging goats' hair on the pillow, to suggest that David was lying ill in the bed. Saul's emissaries would not approach beyond the distance of the teraphim. Another interesting fact brought out by the same scholar is that among certain people closely akin to the Horites, who are named in the Old Testament as dwellers in Canaan, the possession of teraphim constituted a sort of legal title of ownership for the house to which they belonged; in this case Laban's anxiety to recover his teraphim can well be understood. The teraphim are closely associated with the practice of divination (1 Samuel 15^{23}, Zechariah 10^2). It may be that some of them had movable heads which could be made to nod in answer to questions put by a priest.

The ephod presents a most puzzling problem. In many places the ephod is certainly a garment of linen, sometimes highly ornamented, worn by a person taking part in religious ceremonies. Samuel was 'girded with a linen ephod', 1 Samuel 2[18], and David wore one when dancing before the Ark, 2 Samuel 6[14]. On the other hand, there are passages which are more naturally explained if the ephod is some kind of image. According to Judges 8[26-7] Gideon used over 1,700 shekels of gold to construct an ephod at Ophrah, 'and all Israel went a whoring after it there'. The object of this idolatrous worship can hardly be a mere garment! The ephod, like the teraphim, was used for divination. When we are told that 'Abiathar fled to David with an ephod in his hand', 1 Samuel 23[6], we are to understand that he brought with him from the shrine a means by which oracles might be obtained from the deity. If the garment known as the ephod was originally the garment of the image rather than of its worshipper, we might find a link between the two seemingly irreconcilable meanings of the ephod, in the primitive idea that the clothes may stand as a symbol for their owner.

Urim and Thummim, again, are mysterious objects. All we really know about them is that they were used to give oracles expressing the decisions of Yahweh. They were carried in a pouch or pocket, and the manner in which they were drawn out of the pouch answered the question put. T. H. Robinson has suggested that they were two stones, each having one black and one white face. If both were drawn out with the white face showing, the answer would be 'yes'; if with black faces, 'no'; if with opposite colours, 'no decision'.

The Ark.

While we may be fairly sure that similar objects to teraphim, the ephod, the sacred lots, would be familiar features of Canaanite religious practice, the Hebrews may have possessed something more distinctive in the Ark. In the older texts it is known simply as the 'Ark of Yahweh': later it is called 'the Ark of the covenant of Yahweh', or 'of God'. Tradition says that within it were the stone tables upon which the Decalogue was written, a pot of manna, and Aaron's rod. In form it was a chest, with two poles projecting at each end, by means of which two men carried it after the fashion of a sedan chair. Originally it must have been regarded as a dwelling-place of Yahweh. When the Israelites took it with them into battle against the Philistines, it really meant that Yahweh of hosts was leading his army in person. When the Philistines saw it they exclaimed 'God is come!', 1 Samuel 4[7]. The divine power within it is sufficient to throw down the image of Dagon, as earlier it had caused the walls of Jericho to collapse. Although we cannot accept the tradition as to what it contained, that tradition may possibly have been based on the presence within the chest of stones from the holy mountain, Sinai, where Yahweh was supposed to reside. An Egyptian picture shows something very similar in construction to the ark. In Babylonia the images of the gods were ceremonially transported in carriers made like boats. Later Jewish thought spiritualized the cruder conceptions by treating the Ark as an empty throne upon which the deity might descend at his pleasure.

The local Baal.

Seeing that there was so much in the Canaanite cult that was indistinguishable from their own, we cannot wonder that the Hebrews were in constant danger of treating the two as equivalent. And there was one very special reason which in many places would induce the Hebrew to devote at any rate part of his worship to the local Canaanite Baal. Baal is a word common to the Semitic languages, meaning 'lord' or 'husband'. Any local god was the Baal of his peoples' territory. To his beneficence was due the fertility of its soil, and the increase of its flocks and herds. Much of the Canaanite worship consisted of ceremonies designed to win from the local Baal the gifts of plenteous crops and multiplying flocks. It was for this purpose that sacred prostitutes were maintained at the shrines. What seems to us to be no more than sensuality was for the Canaanite a very sincere religious practice.

The Hebrews would be sorely tempted to add the worship of the local Baal to their own worship of Yahweh, on the ground

Influence of Canaanite Religion on Hebrews

that the local Baal, the age-long fertilizer of his territory, would be able to give them something that might be beyond the power of Yahweh, whom they had brought with them, and who was, like themselves, a settler in the country. Or they would adopt the Canaanite practices and use them in the worship of Yahweh. It is not easy for us to realize that religious prostitution was associated even with the temple of Jerusalem, from which the prostitutes were removed at so late a time as that of Josiah (2 Kings 23[7]). The general idea that a god is the husband of his people or land, a figure of speech which is used by Hosea about Yahweh himself, explains the frequent use of the phrase 'to go a whoring after' a foreign deity, by which the Old Testament describes the desertion of Yahweh by Israel.

The Northern Kingdom was undoubtedly more affected by Canaanite religion than was Judah, for Judah was smaller, its population less mixed with other than Hebrew elements, and more easily controlled from its centre. The fact that in Ephraim from the very beginning Yahweh

---

Bas-relief of a Semitic Baal found at Amrith in Phoenicia. The sculpture shows a mixture of Assyrian, Egyptian, and Hittite elements.

was worshipped under the figure of a bull, which form of image was used regularly for the local Baals, would make contamination of the religion more easy. But in Judah itself the national religion differed very much from the religion of the prophets. We have seen already that in the temple at Jerusalem religious prostitutes were established, and the general state of the official religion may be gathered from the accounts of the attempts to reform it. One such reform is attributed to Hezekiah, who, among other things, broke up a 'brasen serpent that Moses had made', which was evidently treated as an image of Yahweh, for incense was burned to it (2 Kings 18^4).

Reformation under Josiah.

A more thoroughgoing reformation occurred during the reign of Josiah. During repairs to the temple a lost law-book was found, the contents of which, to judge from the reforms based upon it, were very much what is found in the Code of Deuteronomy. Evidently much of the cult practised in Judah had been absolutely pagan, for among the cult objects destroyed were those devoted to the service of Baal, the Asherah, and all the host of heaven (2 Kings 23^4). Clearly the relationships with Assyria had popularized star worship in Judah. At this time, too, the various altars which Solomon had erected for the service of deities worshipped by his foreign wives were destroyed. Presumably they had remained in use since his day. The most important element in the reform of Josiah was the edict that all the local sanctuaries should be abolished, and the sacrifices offered at Jerusalem only. The dispossessed priests were compensated by some minor share in the dues of the Jerusalem temple (2 Kings 23^9). Josiah sought also to suppress the practice of divination by means of spirits, teraphim, and idols (23^{24}).

The Tyrian Baal in Ephraim and Judah.

Once in the Northern Kingdom, and once in Judah, there was a deliberate attempt to establish the worship of another deity side by side with Yahweh. The first of these attempts was in the reign of Ahab. Out of courtesy to his Phoenician wife Jezebel, and as a symbol of his alliance with Tyre, Ahab sanctioned the establishment of the cult of the Tyrian Baal. There seems no

Influence of Canaanite Religion on Hebrews

reason to doubt the personal loyalty of Ahab to Yahweh. We have seen that he maintained at his court 400 prophets of Yahweh, and that the names of all his children so far as they are preserved contain the name of Yahweh as one of their elements. Ahab was of a tolerant and easy-going nature. Jezebel, on the other hand, appears to have made a serious effort to establish the worship of her national Baal as the religion of the kingdom. It was the great achievement of Elijah that he protested successfully against this attempt, if not to supplant Yahweh, to set the Tyrian Baal beside him.

A similar position occurred in Judah a little later. One of Ahab's daughters, Athaliah, married Jehoram of Judah. At the accession of her son Ahaziah, she used her influential position as queen-mother to favour the worship of Baal in Jerusalem. A temple was erected for him there, with a duly appointed priest (2 Kings 11^{18}). Yet even when her son was slain, and she, by murdering all claimants to the throne, enjoyed unchallenged power for six years, she seems not to have made any attempt to suppress the worship of Yahweh. She was content that the Tyrian Baal should be recognized. But such recognition was seen by men of Elijah's stamp to be fatal. Yahweh was a jealous god, and would tolerate no rival to his throne or companion upon it. When Athaliah was slain the worship of the Tyrian Baal perished with her.

The failure of these attempts to transplant the worship of the Tyrian Baal to the soil of Ephraim and Judah was finally assured in both cases by political revolution. Just as in the great struggles of the European Reformation rulers often professed Protestantism, or the Roman faith, according as they thought their political aims might best be promoted, so in the political intrigues of the Hebrew kingdoms Yahwism sometimes became a means to an end. This is most obvious in the story of Jehu's extirpation of the Omri dynasty in Ephraim. He rallied considerable support by holding himself out as a fervent devotee of Yahweh. His bloody career of assassination wins the approval of the editors of Kings on the ground that he 'destroyed Baal out of Israel' (2 Kings 10^{28}). But even they are bound to concede that his devotion to Yahweh was far from being perfect. In fact Jehu 'cared for none of these things' save in so far as he could make them serve his ambitions.

Rechabites and Nazirites.

Among the elements of support enlisted by Jehu was the party of the Rechabites. Meeting one of their leaders, Jehonadab, he took him into his chariot and paraded him through Samaria. This would be evidence of a fervid devotion to Yahweh, for the Rechabites were fanatical puritans of the Yahweh religion. We read of their special tenets in Jeremiah 35. They would drink no wine, till no soil, build no houses. They regarded the nomad life with its austerity as the true life for those who would worship Yahweh, and scorned the civilization of Canaan as something that corrupted and destroyed the purity of Israel's religion. Therefore they abjured all that bound them, as vineyards, cornfields, and houses might have done, to a settled life. Undoubtedly, with all their fanatical narrowness, they had grasped the truth that it was largely through the connexion of the Hebrews with agriculture that the allure of the Baal worship had seduced Israel from Yahweh.

It has been suggested that the Nazirites formed another such fanatical group, chiefly because their vows included abstinence from any product of the vine. But we know too little about this particular class to dogmatize. The law of the Nazirite in Numbers 6^{1-21} is of late origin. According to this the vows were only temporary. The story of Samson represents him as a lifelong Nazirite, but no stress can be laid on this, for the idea accords ill with what is related of his exploits, and is only an attempt to make him more reputable. Amos names the Nazirites with approval, joining them with the prophets: Yahweh, he says, 'raised up some of your sons to be prophets, and some of your young men to be Nazirites' (2^{11}). The association in this passage would rather favour the idea evidently held by those who dressed up Samson in a Nazirite habit that the Nazirites were bound by more than temporary vows. The ordinary prophet was generally an extreme nationalist, and the Nazirites may have shared this position. Extreme nationalism and fanatical devotion to the national God often went hand in hand.

Influence of Canaanite Religion on Hebrews

That the religion of Israel was saved from syncretism, that is, the toleration of different deities side by side, whether this salvation be attributed to great religious personalities like Elijah, or, in a measure, to self-seeking adventurers like Jehu, or to the excesses of fanatics such as the Rechabites, was of the first importance. For only so could Israel's religion ever have developed into the purer form of later days. Had syncretism been firmly established, the religion of the Hebrews would have sunk into the general morass of Canaanite cults, and like them have perished utterly.

CHAPTER X
LAW

The development of the Law.

FOR a Jew the most important part of the Old Testament is 'the Law'. He divides his sacred books into three parts, 'The Law', that is, the Pentateuch; 'The Prophets', which includes not only the oracles of the prophets but what we regard as historical books, Joshua, Judges, Samuel, Kings; and 'The Writings'; of these three the first has supreme authority.

It is self-evident that an organized people must have its laws. But in the case of Israel a special reason existed for the prominence of the law. Most oriental peoples regarded their national deities as akin to themselves. Often they might speak of this kinship as physical; they were the descendants of their god. But the relation between Yahweh and His people was of a different kind. They were not akin to Him. He had existed independently of them, and had chosen them to be His people. And the relation between them was based upon a covenant. He would be their God on condition that they observed the terms of this covenant. It was necessary, therefore, that this covenant should be formulated as a definite code. Undoubtedly this conception of the relationship between Israel and Yahweh ensured that the religion of Israel was more ethical than the religions of the neighbouring peoples. If a nation's god is but the highest member of a kindred, he may be expected to look after his kinsmen 'right or wrong'. At times Israel took this lower view, and, despite its own corruptness, presumed on Yahweh's aid for success; but the stern voice of a prophet would say, 'You only have I chosen of all the peoples of the earth: therefore will I visit upon you all your iniquities' (Amos 3^2).

What, then, were the covenant obligations of Israel to Yahweh? In Exodus 24^3 Moses is represented as reciting to the people 'all the words of Yahweh, and all the judgements'. The people answer with one voice, 'All the words which Yahweh hath spoken will we do'. Moses writes all the words of Yahweh, and the Covenant is sealed by a solemn blood-rite. Evidently the intention of the

Law

narrative is that all the laws previously set down in Exodus, and represented as spoken by God on the holy mountain, are the conditions of the Covenant. But many of these laws are of later date, and if, as we have reason to believe, the substance of the Decalogue is Mosaic, we may rather see in its religious and ethical demands the conditions which Israel must satisfy as its part of the Covenant obligation.

All communities have their rules, even though they be no more than usages hallowed by custom. Such tribal laws would be in force among the several stocks from which the Hebrew nation was formed, and some of these would persist. The Decalogue would need to be amplified in many particulars, and some of these age-long customs would be useful for that purpose. An instructive incident is recorded in Exodus 18[13-27]. At an earlier date than the revelation upon the holy mountain Moses sits 'to judge the people'. The problems submitted to him are so numerous that all his time is taken up, and when his father-in-law protests, Moses replies, 'The people will keep on coming to me to inquire of God'. And so through the generations fresh problems emerged, and their solutions were sought from the recognized authorities. But, not unnaturally, all these subsequent expansions of the law are incorporated in the body of the law which comes from the founder, Moses, and attributed to him. Ultimately, however, they are thought of as coming from Yahweh himself, just as Hammurabi receives his code from the god Shamash.

The words used for 'law' are interesting. Chief of them is *torah*, which comes from a verb which may mean either 'to direct' or 'to cast'. When a question is brought to the priest he will, if no precedent is known to him, consult Yahweh. Thus we read in Jeremiah 18[18], 'torah shall not perish from the priest'. Yahweh's answer will be given by the casting of lots, which decides the point at issue. 'They should seek the torah at the priest's mouth', Malachi 2[7], because the lots which gave the oracular response would be in his keeping. The decision is at first only an oral one, but later will be embodied in written form. Such written codifications may well be very old in Israel. They existed in Babylonia at least 1,000 years before the time of Moses. While a torah, or direction, would generally be given by a priest, the word is extended to cover a wider field. It might cover a decision given by a lay judge. Prophetic instruction, too, is sometimes called torah. Isaiah may say, 'give ear unto the torah of our God', and Jeremiah more than once appeals to the torah of God. Even a Psalm, like 78, may begin 'Give ear, O my people, to my torah'. In short, torah, since it embraces divine decisions upon all points of cult and conduct, comes eventually to mean almost what we understand by 'religion'.

Another interesting term is *mishpat*, which generally means a decision given on some point that is disputed, or for which there is no precedent. Thus David, when a dispute arises as to the division of spoil, determines that those who guard the camp shall share equally with those who win the battle, 1 Samuel 30$^{24f.}$. And this decision 'he establishes as a statute (*hoq*) and as an ordinance (*mishpat*) for Israel'. This decision is embodied afterwards as part of the Mosaic teaching, and is said to have been revealed by Yahweh to Moses (Numbers 31$^{25-7}$). Had it really been a recognized rule going back to Mosaic times it must surely have been known to David and his followers. Just as in England our law is built up largely from case law, that is, decisions given by individual judges on fresh points of detail that arise, so the codifications of Hebrew law from time to time would embrace such decisions. Presumably such codifications would be undertaken by the priests. At any rate it is the priests who are charged by the prophets with falsifying the law. Thus Ezekiel 22^{26} says the 'priests have done violence to' Yahweh's law, and the same indictment is uttered in Zephaniah 3^{4}.

Decalogue of Exodus 34.

The Decalogue of Exodus 20 appears in a slightly expanded form in Deuteronomy 5, but the modifications are insignificant. On the other hand Exodus 34$^{14-26}$, which is from the old source *J*, contains a decalogue that varies considerably from these. All its ten commandments are connected with the cult. There is nothing in it parallel to the ethical commandments such as 'Thou shalt not steal'. Many scholars believe this *J* decalogue to be the oldest of all, largely because it confines itself strictly to cult. It is true, also, that the *E* document, from which the Decalogue of Exodus

Law

20 comes, is probably a generation or two later than *J*; but a later document may contain elements of any older date. The argument from cult can be used both ways. As a religion grows older its cult tends to become elaborated, and its priests sometimes become absorbed in its ceremonial side. Therefore we may still look upon the Decalogue of Exodus 20 as fundamental in the religion.

The Book of the Covenant.

The oldest collection of laws in the Old Testament, leaving aside the Decalogue, is contained in Exodus 20^{22}–23^{33}, and is called, because of the reference in 24^7, the 'Book of the Covenant'. The date of its formation is uncertain. Some scholars would take it back into the time of the Judges. Others, who urge that the codification of law is likely to have taken place only in a comparatively organized state, governed by a central authority, would say that it cannot well be older than the reign of Solomon. It is noteworthy, however, that the code contains no reference to a king, or royal authority. The date is not, however, of the first importance, because we have always to bear in mind that the laws of any codification must always be older than the time when the codification is made.

The laws in the Book of the Covenant must have been largely identical with those which governed the Canaanites; for they are suited to an agricultural rather than to a purely nomadic people. A comparison of the Book of the Covenant with the Code of Hammurabi shows likenesses, even in point of detail, so extraordinary that it is impossible to suppose that there is no connecting link between them. To take one example out of many, and that not the most striking:

Exodus 22^{9-12}.	*Code of Hammurabi.*
For every matter of trespass, whether it be for ox, for ass, for sheep, for raiment, *or* for any manner of lost thing, whereof one saith, 'This is it', the cause of both parties shall come before God; he whom God shall condemn shall pay double unto his neighbour. If a man shall deliver unto his	If a man has caused an ox or sheep which was entrusted to him to be lost, ox for ox, sheep for sheep, he shall replace to its owner. . . . If in a sheepfold an act of God has taken place, or a lion has slain, the shepherd shall take

Exodus 22⁹⁻¹². (Cont.) neighbour an ass, or an ox, or a sheep, or any beast, to keep; and it die, or be hurt, or driven away, no man seeing it: the oath of Yahweh shall be between them both, whether he hath not put his hand to his neighbour's goods; and the owner thereof shall accept it, and he [the trustee] shall not make restitution. But if it be stolen from him, he shall make restitution to the owner thereof.

Code of Hammurabi. (Cont.) an oath of purgation before God, and the owner must bear his loss. If a shepherd has caused a loss in the fold by negligence, the shepherd ... shall make good the oxen or sheep.

It is clear that the same general principles are operating in the two codes.

Again we have fairly close parallels from an old Sumerian code and from a Hittite code.

Sumerian Code. If a lion devours one of a fold the owner must bear his misfortune. If an ox is lost from a fold, ox for ox [must be replaced for the owner].

Hittite Code. If any one shall harness an ox[1], a horse, a mule, and it dies, or a wolf (?) destroys it or ... if he says 'It died by the act of God' he shall take an oath of purgation.

[1] i.e. a borrowed one.

We see, then, that the whole of the Nearer East in those days possessed laws with the same general principles, varied to suit the particular circumstances of the countries to which they related, and the laws of the Canaanites must have been very similar to the other codes which have survived. There may possibly have been direct influence on Canaan from the Code of Hammurabi, for Canaan was for a long time within the sphere of Babylonian control.

The regulations of the Book of the Covenant fall into two classes: those concerned with religious matters, and those dealing with civil law. The two classes are now in confusion, but probably they existed originally as separate codes, and have been shuffled in the process of editing. The civil law is obviously case law, assembled as a guide for local judges. The typical form of it is: 'If a man shall do so and so ... such shall be his penalty'. Some-

Law

times, however, we find a general injunction: 'Thou shalt not do so and so'.

Civil law in ancient Israel would be largely the business of laymen. There is no elaborate organization of police and prisons. The elders of a village would investigate a case and give their decision. If the accused did not submit to it he became an outlaw, and the position of an outlaw was intolerable. There is no provision for torture as a means of extracting evidence. The custom in doubtful cases of taking an oath of innocence at the local shrine still prevails in Mohammedan countries. So great is the fear of the consequences that may follow perjury under these conditions that a man will often confess rather than take the oath. The place of judgement would be the gate of the city. The ordeal, which plays a prominent part in Egyptian law, stands quite in the background of Hebrew and Babylonian legislation. It would be used only in special cases (cf. Numbers $5^{15ff.}$).

General comparison with the Code of Hammurabi makes it clear that the Book of the Covenant is dealing, as we might have presupposed, with a much less elaborate civilization. Whereas in the latter the only mention of coinage is in Exodus 21^{32}, the former takes coinage for granted as the medium of exchange. In spite of the attention given in the Book of the Covenant to agriculture there is a still more considerable element dealing with pastoral conditions. In regard to humanity there is little to choose between the two codes. The Babylonian law as to freeing a slave gives him an earlier release than does the Hebrew law, and has a more exalted conception of the position of women. On the other hand, the Book of the Covenant is alone in its prohibition of usury. Law and practice, it must be admitted, do not always coincide. On the one hand, the Old Testament stories show that the wife was often treated as much more than a chattel, while, on the other hand the insistence in Old Testament law on the iniquity of bribery, perjury, and usury, is itself indicative of their prevalence.

The Deuteronomic Code.

The next important stage in the development of Hebrew law is found in the Deuteronomic Code, contained in Deuteronomy 12-26, 28. This in some form is probably the book found in 621 at the temple in Jerusalem during the reign of Josiah. It is based on the Book of the Covenant and such other laws as had grown up in the interval. An analysis shows that it is very carefully arranged in sections dealing with different subjects. We have already noted (see p. 160) its most striking feature, the law of the central sanctuary.

The most prominent characteristic of the Deuteronomic Code is its large humanity. Justice and kindness are its key-notes. Its compilers held up the ideal of a community from which poverty should be banished—'howbeit there shall be no poor with thee', 15^4. Such an ideal they recognize will not be easy to attain, so they provide for the amelioration of poverty while it continues to exist. No one must be hard-hearted or miserly in dealing with a poorer brother, 15$^{7-11}$. The workman must not be exploited, even if he is a foreigner, 24$^{14f.}$. Those easily oppressed classes, the orphan and the widow, who had no strong man to stand up for them 'in the gate', and the resident alien, who had no legal rights, must be treated with consideration. The gleanings of the harvest fields, orchards, and vineyards are to be left for them, 24$^{19-21}$, and the tithes of every third year devoted to them and to the Levites, 14$^{28f.}$. When a feast is celebrated they must be invited to share it, 16$^{10-14}$. When pledges are taken they must not be the necessary implements of domestic life, such as the corn-grinding mill, 24^6, and if the pledge be an outer garment it must be restored before nightfall, that it may be used as a coverlet, 24$^{12f.}$. The taking of interest, at least from a fellow-countryman, is forbidden, 23^{19}.

Other examples of this humane outlook might be quoted. One with far-reaching consequences is the limitation of blood-revenge. The old law, eye for eye, tooth for tooth, life for life, cruel as it seems to us, was in its day a reform of earlier usage, because it limited the extent to which revenge might be pursued. But it was still cruel, because revenge might be exacted from any kinsman of the offender, so deep-seated was the feeling that the family, rather than the individual, was the unit. Deuteronomy limits the revenge to the actual offender; a father must not be killed for the wrongdoing of his son, or a son for that of his father. Every man must bear in his own person the consequences of his own wrong-doing, 24^{16}. This further limitation must have tended to an increase in the respect paid to the individual man, and prepared the way for such prophets as Jeremiah and Ezekiel, who taught that the relation of the individual to God was of supreme importance.

Ezekiel's Code.

With Ezekiel we reach another stage in the development of the law. In the nine chapters at the end of Ezekiel a new scheme for the organization of Israel's political and religious economy is sketched out. This, whether it be from Ezekiel's own hand or from the hands of his disciples, is an ideal which was never put into practice, but it certainly shows the lines upon which the leaders of religion in the Exile were disposed to modify the previous practice. The break-up of the state leads to the exalting of religious practice as the central thing in the national life. The main function of the prince in the ideal state is to see that proper provision is made for the priests to carry out the obligations of the cult. Regulations concerning the cult have now become of more importance than the laws which promote justice. The Levites, for whom the Deuteronomic Code had claimed a share in the cult at Jerusalem—perhaps ineffectually—are now reduced to the position of menials, who are to perform the duties formerly carried out by the temple-slaves. Only the Zadokite family may fulfil priestly functions.

The Holiness Code.

Very closely akin to what we find in these chapters of Ezekiel is the 'Code of Holiness', conveniently known by the symbol H, which embraces Leviticus 17–26, and possibly 11. The main idea running throughout it is the holiness of God, and the obligation of His people to be holy too. Although it is concerned chiefly with cult, it has many points of contact with the Deuteronomic Code, and in places has the real humaneness of its predecessor. While in language and style it has so much in common with Ezekiel that he has been credited with its authorship, it is less nationalist in outlook than that prophet. The injunction, Leviticus 19[34], that a resident alien must be treated as well as a native is quite in the spirit of the Deuteronomic Code, and the chapter in which it occurs reaches some remarkable ethical heights. The farmer is enjoined not only to give the gleanings of his field to the poor but also to leave the corners uncut for their benefit, v. 9. In the command 'Thou shalt not hate thy brother in thine heart: thou shalt surely rebuke [i.e. give warning to] thy neighbour, and not bear [i.e. incur] sin because of him. Thou shalt not take vengeance, nor bear any grudge against the children of thy people, but thou shalt love thy neighbour as thyself', vv. 17–18, the Law reaches its supreme point. Though Ezekiel was not the author of this code it must be of about the same date as that prophet, and comes from a source in general sympathy with his position. It makes, however, no distinction between priest and Levite.

The Priestly Code.

The last important collection of laws is known as the Priestly Code. This forms part of a document[1] beginning with Genesis 1, the purpose of which is to represent the whole of history as an ordered scheme by means of which God brings into existence the Jewish Church. It is concerned primarily with cult. The main object, for example, of the creation story with which Genesis begins is to provide a divine sanction for the Sabbath. So high is the estimate of the cult in this document that it carries back the complete sacrificial legislation to the time of Moses, and regards it as having been revealed to him by God. The simple tent of the wilderness days is transformed into an elaborate tabernacle similar to the temple at Jerusalem. The code is narrowly nationalist in its outlook.

The Priestly Code makes a sharp distinction between priests and Levites. The idea of a central sanctuary at which alone the cult may be practised is taken for granted. A distinction, unknown to the earlier codes, is made between clean and unclean animals. The latter may not be sacrificed. The forgiveness of sin may be obtained only by the bringing of a sin-offering. Religion has become a matter of law almost to the exclusion of grace. The idea of God is exalted and pure. Crude anthropomorphic conceptions are banished. But between God and man there is a great gulf fixed, which can be bridged only by the mediation of priest and sacrifice. On the other hand, this code changes Passover into

[1] The 'Priestly Document', referred to by the symbol *P*.

a family rite, which need not, as in the Deuteronomic Code, be celebrated at the temple. The code contains some elements that are primitive, almost magical, for a great deal of the material in it is much older than the time of its codification.

When did this codification take place? Presumably it must have been later than Ezekiel, for if he had been aware of its existence he would surely have appealed to it as an authority for distinguishing sharply between the priest and the Levite. The Priestly Code was probably codified towards the end of the fifth century B.C. It will represent the Law as it was known to Ezra in the early part of the following century. The Law of Holiness was probably embodied in this codification.

Later still, perhaps as late as 350 B.C., the existing law codes, *J*, *E*, *D*, *H*, and *P*, were united into one great compendium of Jewish law and history. This must have been earlier than the Samaritan schism, for except in the matter of some trifling details the Samaritan Pentateuch is identical with that of the Hebrew Bible, and the Samaritans would certainly never have accepted as their authority any compendium produced by the Jews after the schism. The whole was attributed to Moses, and in its final form shaped the religion of the Jews and greatly influenced both Christianity and Islam.

CHAPTER XI
THE DEVELOPMENT OF PROPHECY

The function of a prophet.

WE are accustomed to think of a prophet as being primarily one who forecasts future events. In recent years we have been learning that the great prophets of Israel were in the first place ambassadors of God, interpreting his will to his people. The distinction has been put into an epigram—'the prophet is a forth-teller rather than a fore-teller'. This conception of the prophet's function is admirably illustrated by Exodus 7^1: 'And Yahweh said unto Moses, See, I have made thee a god to Pharaoh: and Aaron thy brother shall be thy prophet.' In other words, a prophet is the interpreter of his god's commands. The same idea is put more explicitly in Exodus $4^{15f.}$: 'And thou shalt speak unto him, and put the words in his mouth: and I will be with thy mouth, and with his mouth, and will teach you what ye shall do. And he shall be thy spokesman unto the people: and it shall come to pass, that he shall be to thee a mouth, and thou shalt be to him as God.' The assumption of the great prophets that no distinction can be made between their words and God's words is here expressly stated.

If this wider conception of the prophet's true work had been more generally realized, the Christian Church would have been spared the eccentricities of those interpreters who try to extract from the book of Daniel a time-table of future events, or seek the explanation of universal history in the Great Pyramid. At the same time it must be recognized that the foretelling of future happenings sometimes formed part of the divine message with which the prophet was entrusted, though such predictions were generally not detailed, and related to events in the imminent future. Certainly this part of the prophet's message was spoken to the generation in which he lived, not given as a programme for generations yet to come.

Early prophecy.

Like many great things, prophecy springs from simple, even crude, beginnings. We may get an excellent idea of early prophecy from a study of the story of 1 Samuel 9–10. Saul and his servant

The Development of Prophecy.

are travelling in search of some lost asses. They fail to find them. Saul is for abandoning the search, but his servant suggests that they may be able to find the lost animals by consulting 'a man of God' in a neighbouring city, who, though Saul seems never to have heard of him before, is none other than Samuel. Saul objects that he has no money to pay for the consultation, but the servant produces the necessary fee. At the subsequent interview Samuel tells Saul that the asses have already been found, and before Saul departs forecasts several things which will happen to him on his return journey. All these prophecies are fulfilled.

Here we have one characteristic of prophecy, the gift of second sight, or clairvoyance. Not that the Hebrews themselves would have described it in this way: from their point of view these things are revealed to the prophet by God Himself (cf. 1 Samuel 9[15f.]). The prophet is not only as mouth, but also as eyes, to his God.

Another quite distinct characteristic of prophecy is displayed in the band of prophets who, as Samuel had foretold, met Saul on his way back. They come down from the local shrine with instruments of music, a psaltery, a timbrel, a pipe, and a harp, and are prophesying. These are men who work themselves into an ecstatic condition by means of music, and, possibly, of dancing, like the modern dervish. Another illustration of this use of music is found in 2 Kings 3[15]. The kings of Ephraim and Judah desire an oracle from the prophet Elisha. He demands the services of a minstrel, who will play until 'the hand of Yahweh' comes upon the prophet, that is, until an ecstatic condition is produced in the prophet. In that condition he can utter the word of Yahweh.

It is probable that in early times these two characteristics of prophecy were represented each by separate types of prophet, the seer, and the corybantic ecstatic. The former was called *ro'eh*, the latter, *nabi'*. Later both characteristics might be combined in one man, and the term *nabi'* superseded *ro'eh*. So the editorial note, 1 Samuel 9[9], explains that 'he that is now called a Prophet (*nabi'*) was beforetime called a Seer (*ro'eh*)'. When the two types were distinct the seer would usually be the priest of some local shrine, while the prophet would move freely from place to place. It has recently, however, been plausibly argued that the prophets were recognized functionaries of the shrines.

An interesting feature of the ecstasy which came upon the prophet is that it is contagious. When Saul falls in with the band of prophets 'the spirit of God comes mightily upon him, and he prophesies among them': 'prophesying' here means the uttering of abnormal words or sounds. Another incident in Saul's story exhibits the same phenomenon: the messengers whom he sends to take David are infected by prophetic ecstasy when they see a company of prophets, headed by Samuel, in this ecstatic condition, and when Saul himself comes he too falls a victim. One of the effects on Saul is that he strips off his clothes.

To each of these stories is appended the comment that out of it arose the popular saying, 'Is Saul also among the prophets?' The point of the saying is that the raving prophet was looked upon as not quite respectable. He was thought to be more or less mad. Jehu's fellow officers speak contemptuously of the prophet sent by Elisha as 'this mad fellow' (2 Kings 9^{11}). So, too, Shemaiah speaks of 'every man that is mad, and maketh himself a prophet' (Jeremiah 29^{26}). The story of Eldad and Medad, however, which recounts an ecstatic experience of the seventy elders (Numbers 11^{23-9}), affecting at the same time those who were in the tent and two who were left in the camp, sets a high value on this kind of prophesying, for Moses exclaims 'Would God that all Yahweh's people were prophets!'

In the ecstatic condition the prophet was able to perform feats which would be impossible to a normal man. The prophets of Baal on Carmel, who are evidently closely akin to the older Hebrew type, dance round the altar, and cut themselves with knives and lances, seemingly insensitive to pain. They remind us very much of the Indian fakir. And after the conflict on Carmel is ended Elijah runs before the chariot of Ahab right to Jezreel, because 'the hand of Yahweh' is upon him, that is, because he is in an ecstatic condition.

Ecstasy in the writing prophets.

How far away this seems from the spiritual teachings of the great prophets! Yet undoubtedly the manifestations associated with the early type of prophet do not utterly disappear even in their case. They still have experiences of ecstasy, and speak of

The Development of Prophecy

the 'hand of Yahweh' being upon them. Their message comes to them often in vision, and some of these visions are certainly of the ecstatic type, as, for example, the great vision of Isaiah 6. Some scholars assert that all the utterances of the prophets are spoken in conditions of ecstasy, and are originally very brief. The distinctively literary form in which their writings come to us makes this difficult of belief. Of all prophets Ezekiel most resembles the old type, with his trances and extraordinary examples of clairvoyance. Perhaps the chief development in this direction is that the writing prophets did not seek to excite the ecstatic condition in themselves by artificial means such as music and dancing. Amos expressly disclaims the title of prophet, though he recognizes the prophets as raised up by God. On the other hand, Isaiah in referring to his wife uses the term prophetess, meaning, not that she possessed the prophetic gift, but that she was the wife of a prophet, and so implicitly accepts the title for himself.

Use of symbolism by the prophets.

A most interesting feature of the prophets' activities is their use of symbolism. In some cases the symbolism may be merely illustrative metaphor; but usually the symbolic actions were actually performed by the prophet, and were regarded as powerful agents for bringing about the event which they symbolized. This may be seen clearly in the strange little story of 1 Kings 20$^{35-43}$. A certain prophet seeks to attract the attention of Ahab by posing as a wounded soldier, and to predict his death. For this purpose he places over his head a helmet to disguise himself. The helmet is evidently intended to conceal something that would cause him to be recognized as a prophet. This may well have been a tonsured head, and if so would explain the epithet 'bald head' applied to Elisha. The other recognized mark of the prophet was a particular kind of mantle. But the prophet in the story also insists upon being actually wounded before he takes his stand at the side of the road. Why could he not have been content to simulate some injury? The reason is that the actual wound is a kind of magic which will help to bring about the injuries whereof he asserts the king will die. The spoken word in the thought of the Hebrews has a real power and energy which fulfils itself. A curse once uttered cannot be recalled, or a blessing. Their very utterance equips them with independent power that ensures their fulfilment. So Isaac cannot recall the blessing once pronounced upon Jacob, however much he may desire to do so. If a man's uttered word has such self-fulfilling force, how much more the word of God as spoken by his prophet! The word of Yahweh does not 'return to him void', that is, without accomplishing itself. And if a mere word can bring about its own fulfilment, how much more certainly will an *acted* parable ensure the coming about of what it symbolizes!

Examples of such dynamic symbolism are numerous. When Zedekiah equips himself with horns of iron (1 Kings 22[11]), and thrusts with them like an angry bull, he is doing something that will help to achieve the thrusting of the Syrians which he predicts. When Jeremiah makes bands and bars and puts them on his neck (Jeremiah 27[2]) he believes that his action will help to ensure the captivity of the nations against whom his words are spoken, and Hananiah in breaking the yoke on Jeremiah's neck is equally confident that he is, so to speak, breaking the spell which lies in Jeremiah's action. Ezekiel is particularly given to this use of symbolic action.

Who were the false prophets?

A very difficult problem arises when we attempt to draw a distinction between the true and the false prophets. We are conscious of the fact that over against the prophets whose writings are preserved for us we find numerous prophets who are opposed to them, and who are commonly called 'false' prophets. The distinction is certainly not in the first place between those whose words 'came true' and the rest. There are clear cases in which the predictions of the true prophets failed of accomplishment. Nor can we distinguish them simply as those who were inspired by God and those who pretended to be. It is admitted that a false prophet may be inspired by Yahweh. Micaiah in 1 Kings 22 recognizes that the four hundred prophets of Yahweh who predict victory for Ahab are not hypocrites. They really believe that Yahweh has given them their message. Micaiah agrees with them

The Development of Prophecy

on this point, admitting that they have been inspired by Yahweh, but asserts that Yahweh has deliberately deceived them (v. 22).

The real distinction seems to be one of character. The ordinary prophet expected payment for his services. Some, like the four hundred maintained at Ahab's court, had an established position. Others were free lances, prepared to undertake a problem for any customer. Amaziah, the priest of Bethel, assumes that Amos as a prophet earns his living by his gift, and bids him return to his own land, and not take money out of Ephraim (Amos 7^{12}). The obvious temptation of such men was to speak not true things, but pleasant things, to those who supported them. The people 'say to the seers, See not; and to the prophets, Prophesy not unto us right things, speak unto us smooth things, prophesy deceits' (Isaiah 30^{10}). So Jeremiah (23^{16}) accuses these prophets of speaking 'a vision of their own heart, and not out of the mouth of Yahweh'. In the same chapter Jeremiah charges them with gross immorality.

The prophets as statesmen.

The prophets were much concerned with the politics of their day. Indeed, some scholars have described them as 'political agents'. But the attempts of the true prophets to shape the policy of the state were only consequences of their sense of duty to God as God's representatives. The line they took was usually unpopular. Isaiah attempts to dissuade his king from making alliances with other nations, because God will be his sufficient aid. Jeremiah spoke continually against resistance to Babylon, and even during the siege of Jerusalem encouraged the desertion of the defenders to the enemy. No wonder he was detested as the equivalent of a 'little-Englander' or a pro-Boer! The false prophets, on the other hand, were usually fanatic nationalists. They always proclaimed victory for the nation's arms. It was they who encouraged in the minds of the people the idea that a 'Day of Yahweh' was coming, when Yahweh would intervene on behalf of his people, subject their enemies to them, and make them luxuriously prosperous. It is the true prophet who takes the words out of their lips and proclaims that a Day of Yahweh is indeed coming, but that it will be a day of doom and disaster, when the people will be punished for their sins. 'Shall not the Day of

Yahweh be darkness, and not light? even very dark, and no brightness in it?' asks Amos (5^{20}), first of the long line.

Attitude of the prophets to the cult.

What was the attitude of the great prophets to the sacrificial system? The greatest of them were certainly without enthusiasm for it, if they did not positively loathe it. Amos pours scorn upon the busy cult activities of Ephraim. He asks: 'Did ye bring unto me sacrifices and offerings in the wilderness forty years, O house of Israel?' (5^{25}), and evidently expects the answer 'No'. In other words he does not believe that sacrifice is part of the pure religion of Mosaic times. The almost vitriolic words of Isaiah 1 cannot be explained away by saying that he represents the combination of hypocrisy with sacrifice as loathsome to Yahweh. 'I delight not in the blood of bullocks', saith Yahweh. 'Your new moons and your appointed feasts my soul hateth; they are a trouble unto me; I am weary to bear them.' It is impossible to resist the conclusion that Isaiah did not believe that the scent of blood and the reek of scorching flesh were as incense to God.

What Amos puts as a question Jeremiah states as a fact. 'I spake not unto your fathers, nor commanded them in the day that I brought them out of the land of Egypt, concerning burnt offerings or sacrifices' (7^{22}). It is true that an opposite attitude appears in Jeremiah 17^{26}, 33^{18}, but these verses are almost certainly not Jeremiah's. The most striking statement of the point of view which regards sacrifice as displeasing to God is Micah 6^{6-8}:

Wherewith shall I come before Yahweh, and bow myself before the high God? shall I come before him with burnt offerings, with calves of a year old? Will Yahweh be pleased with thousands of rams, *or* with ten thousands of rivers of oil? shall I give my firstborn for my transgression, the fruit of my body for the sin of my soul? He hath shewed thee, O man, what is good. And what doth Yahweh require of thee, but to do justly, and to love mercy, and to walk humbly with thy God?

Nor is Deutero-Isaiah far removed from this position when he represents God as so highly exalted that all the wild beasts in the forest of Lebanon would be inadequate to furnish him a sacrifice, all its trees to furnish wood for its kindling (40^{16}). The same idea is

The Development of Prophecy

expressed again in the Psalms. Thus in Psalm 51^{16-17}: 'Thou delightest not in sacrifice; else would I give it: Thou hast no pleasure in burnt offering. The sacrifices of God are a broken spirit: A broken and a contrite heart, O God, thou wilt not despise.'

This doctrine was never widely accepted. And when the priest and prophet are combined in one person, as in Ezekiel, we cannot well expect it to be held. Indeed, it came to be regarded as a heresy, and some orthodox editor has corrected the false doctrine, as it seemed to him, of Psalm 51, by appending a short passage concluding, 'Then shalt thou delight in the sacrifices of righteousness, in burnt offering and whole burnt offering: then shall they offer bullocks upon thine altar', an absolute anticlimax.

Hebrew prophecy unique?

To what extent did prophecy as we find it in Israel derive from external sources? Eduard Meyer has laboured to show that there was something analogous in Egypt, but his instances have failed to impress. Other scholars have supposed that there was in Canaan a recognized prophetic formula of coming doom to be followed by felicity. But the only real piece of evidence for anything comparable to Hebrew prophecy is the existence of the Phoenician prophets of Baal, who certainly seem to be of the same type as the early *nabi'*. For the great prophets of Israel, whose words are still vibrant with the plea for justice and reverence, still able to reveal the holiness and loving-kindness of God, no parallel has yet been discovered. They remain unique in their majesty.

CHAPTER XII

THE WRITING PROPHETS

Amos.

THE earliest in time of Israel's writing prophets is Amos. If he had any predecessor, nothing has survived to show it. He seems to emerge suddenly, like some great crag standing out from a plain. Between him and the kind of prophet that flourished in Israel there seems to be little connexion, and, as we have seen, he deliberately rejects for himself the name of prophet. It is no accident that the time of his appearance immediately precedes the growth of Assyria's power to such a point that it becomes a menace to the kingdom of Palestine. Indeed, that menace is so evidently in his mind as to make the exact date of his utterances a problem. The date usually assigned to him ranges from 760 to 750 B.C. The title later added to his prophecy says that he was active during the reign of Jeroboam II, and this statement is amply confirmed by the one biographical section of the book, 7^{10-17}, and by its general tenor. The generally accepted chronology would not bring Jeroboam's reign down later than 745. On the other hand, it was not until 745 that Tiglath-pileser usurped the Assyrian throne, and it must have been two or three years later still before the danger from Assyria became really threatening. But so definitely is this threat stated by Amos—he even says that the people of the Northern Kingdom shall go into exile 'beyond Damascus', 5^{27}, which can mean only as the captives of Assyria—that some recent scholars have argued forcibly for bringing the date of Amos down to 741. The chronology of the kings is obscure and uncertain, and this new view may possibly be right.

The first of the great prophets, though a native of Tekoa in Judah, speaks his prophecies in Ephraim. The prevailing view of scholars is that he had no message at all for his own people. But while it is true that there is little reference to Judah in the book, there are one or two passages that suggest a wider application for his message than the limits of the Northern Kingdom. No stress can be laid upon the oracle on Judah, 2^{4-5}, because it is not certainly the work of Amos, and in any case is one of a series of oracles dealing with foreign peoples. But it is hard to believe that when Amos speaks to 'the whole family', which Yahweh brought up out of Egypt (3¹), he does not include Judah. 'Woe to them that are at ease in Zion' (6¹) is a clear reference to Jerusalem, and no plausible case for emending the passage has yet been presented. And in view of the unsatisfactory social condition of Judah it is almost incredible that a prophet with so lofty a social ideal should have addressed no word of remonstrance to his own people.

The dominant note in the teaching of Amos is the conception of God as being pre-eminently righteous, or, as we might more accurately put it, just. God is the embodiment of justice, and demands of his people that they too shall be just. Because they are so sadly removed from this condition it is inevitable that God must punish them, and the doom will be exile beyond Damascus at the hands of an Assyrian invader.

Amos has little teaching that is specifically theological. The sins he denounces are acts of inhumanity. In the opening oracles in which he gives examples of the sins of the surrounding nations, all the instances are of this kind. Cruelty in war, slave-raiding, desecration of a corpse—these are the things singled out. For the cult Amos makes no claim. We have seen that he denies its necessity (5²⁵), and elsewhere he treats the busy practice of it with scornful irony (4⁴ᶠ·, 5²¹⁻³). It is one of the reasons for suspecting the oracle on Judah not to be genuine that the crime instanced in that case is transgression in the matter of cult rather than inhumanity.

With scathing invective Amos denounces the wealthy who have built themselves luxurious houses of hewn stone and furnished them with ivory inlaid couches. They eat lambs and fattened calves, and anoint themselves with the most costly ointments. Sometimes the invective is almost coarse, as when Amos speaks of them as swilling wine by the bucket—the 'bowl' of 6⁶ is one of particularly large size—or calls the fine ladies of Samaria, 'kine of Bashan'. For this luxury is purchased with money obtained by oppression of the poor. No poor man can get justice, because if he goes to law the verdict is given to his rich oppressor who bribes the judges. The corn-merchants swindle their customers by giving short weight, overcharging, and selling inferior goods (8⁴⁻⁶).

In short, the luxury of the rich is founded on exploitation of the poor. The extension of the national boundaries and the increase of trade are no substitute for justice. The God for whom Amos speaks, who is Lord of nature, and Controller of the destinies of nations, for not only did he bring Israel out of Egypt, but he also transported the Philistines and Syrians from their places (9^7), pronounces the impending doom. The future is no Day of Yahweh according to the popular conception, no joyous triumph, but a day of impenetrable gloom. An invader shall surround the land, the palaces of luxury shall perish, the king shall die by the sword, the people shall be carried away captive. No fervent practice of the cult will dissuade God from his purpose. One thing only had he required, 'Let judgement roll down as waters, and justice as a perennial stream' (5^{24}). This demand has been ignored; therefore 'the end is come upon my people Israel' (8^2).

Later some one who could not be content with so stern a message as that which concludes the book of Amos—'the eyes of the Lord God are upon the sinful kingdom, and I will destroy it from off the face of the earth' (9^8)—attempted to modify it by attaching to these terrible words a 'happy ending'. This happy ending is for many reasons clearly not the work of Amos, not least because it speaks of a coming material prosperity while ignoring altogether those social values of justice by which the prophet set so great store.

Hosea.

We pass next to Hosea, because, though he was slightly later than Isaiah, his work followed that of Amos in the Northern Kingdom. His activity may be assigned mainly to the two decades after the fall of Jeroboam's dynasty, and it is possible that it continued to the fall of Samaria. When Amos uttered his denunciations in Bethel and Samaria, Ephraim was, at least on the surface, a prosperous country. It was Hosea's fortune to live through the most troubled period of Ephraim's history, when king succeeded king in rapid and violent succession, and a desperate policy sought now to this, now to that, nation for alliance to make possible a stand against the Assyrian menace, or maintained for a brief

The Writing Prophets

interval the attitude of obedient vassalage to that great empire. These vacillating policies are referred to by Hosea in contemptuous terms: 'Their kings are fallen. . . . Ephraim, he mixeth himself among the peoples; Ephraim is a cake not turned. . . . Ephraim is like a silly dove, without understanding: they call unto Egypt, they go to Assyria' (7^{7-11}).

This difference in the historical background accounts in some measure for a difference in emphasis between the messages of Amos and Hosea, but even more responsible for the development we find in Hosea is a difference in personality. Unlike Amos, who was a foreigner in Ephraim and could view its sufferings impartially, Hosea, as a native, was intimately involved in the ruin which wrong policy brought to his people, and bound to share with them the penalties he prophesied. It is wrong to represent Amos as unconcerned about the folk to whom his stern words were spoken, for even he was moved to the repeated plea for Ephraim's forgiveness—'O Lord God, forgive, I beseech thee, how shall Jacob stand? for he is small' (Amos 7^2, ^{5}). But every blow that falls upon Ephraim falls upon the sensitive heart of Hosea. It has been well said that Hosea was to Amos as Melanchthon to Luther, and certainly he possessed a sensitive spirit akin to that of Jeremiah.

In social standing the two prophets may not have been far apart. Amos was apparently a small-holder; Hosea may have belonged to a rather more prosperous family. But Hosea had been qualified for his work by a personal experience to which we find no parallel in Amos. The repeated attempts to show that the story of Hosea's marriage (1^{2-9}, 3^{1-3}, ? 2^{2-7}) is an allegory are unconvincing, and we must accept the story of that marriage as part of his actual experience. To summarize in bare form one of the most tenderly related incidents in literature, Hosea's wife, whom he dearly loved, betrayed him, and deserted him for her lover. She went from bad to worse, and became at last a slave, or possibly a temple-prostitute; but despite it all, Hosea loved her still, and bought her back from those who owned her.

In this tragedy of his own experience Hosea learned to interpret in a new way the relation between Yahweh and his people. Israel was the chosen bride of Yahweh, who gave her lavish gifts. But she deserted him for the Baals, from whom she supposed she might gain more. So Yahweh is bound to punish her, but he loves her still. And when at last she has learned her lesson he will 'allure her, and bring her into the wilderness, and speak comfortably unto her' (2^{14}). In other words, the felicity of the honeymoon days, when Yahweh and Israel were covenanted in the wilderness, shall be renewed in the same place. This was the deeper note in Hosea's message, the unchanging love of God. For Amos, God is essentially the God who 'does justly', for Hosea, the God who 'loves mercy'. In Hosea's eyes the essence of religion is love and loyalty. His most passionate indictments of his fellow countrymen are shot through with a tender sympathy.

Hosea does not close his eyes to the social evils of his day. God charges his people with guilt 'because there is no truth, nor mercy, nor knowledge of God in the land' (4^1). More than once the prophet speaks of the iniquity and wickedness of the country. But he is concerned more about the wrongness of their relationship to God, for he has realized that social wrongdoing springs from defective religion. Even when the people nominally worship Yahweh they treat him as just another Baal, having no real understanding of his character. They use idols, and copy the worst features of the licentious fertility-rites of Canaanitish cult. And Hosea takes to all the elaboration of the cult the attitude which we find in the greatest of the prophets. Sacrifice is, if not wrong, at least not the demand of God. 'For I desire mercy, and not sacrifice, and the knowledge of God more than burnt offerings' (6^6). Religion is inward, rather than outward. It is better to cry unto God with the heart than to make loud protestations (7^{14}).

But despite all their ingratitude Yahweh cannot give up his people. In another tender picture the prophet speaks of God as Israel's father, teaching his infant child to walk (11^{1-4}). Though the son may have become a prodigal the father's heart yearns for him still. When the prodigal acknowledges his offence, and seeks his father's face (5^{15}), he will find a welcome on his return. The motto prefixed to the book of Amos is:

Yahweh will roar from Zion, and thunder from Jerusalem;
And the pastures of the shepherds shall mourn, and the top of Carmel shall wither.

The Writing Prophets

If we are seeking a motto for the message of Hosea we might very well choose the words of Faber:

> For the love of God is broader than the measures of man's mind,
> And the heart of the Eternal is most wonderfully kind.

Isaiah.

Isaiah was a Judaean of Jerusalem, certainly of the upper class, and possibly of royal blood. He received his call to the prophetic office by means of the vision recorded in Isaiah 6. This is dated 'in the year that king Uzziah died', that is, *c.* 740 B.C. His ministry lasted at least until 701, and may possibly have extended into the reign of Manasseh. What has survived of his work is recorded mainly in cc. 1–11, 17–18, 20, 22, 28–32 of the book that bears his name.

The distinctive note of Isaiah's message is found in the vision of c. 6. The majesty and the holiness of Yahweh are imprinted for ever in his heart as he sees Yahweh seated on a throne and hears the antiphonal chant of the seraphim:

> Holy, holy, holy, is Yahweh of Hosts:
> The whole earth is full of his glory.

The 'Holy One of Israel' is his characteristic name for Yahweh. For Isaiah this holiness has an ethical content, for he feels that in contrast to the holiness of Yahweh he and his people are unclean. In the commission he receives the failure of his preaching is foretold; the fate of the people is to be utter destruction. Later he came to hold a belief that a righteous remnant would survive, as the nucleus of a restored people. This doctrine of 'the remnant' is expressed in 6^{13}, which is a later addition to the original vision, possibly from Isaiah's own hand.

Three outstanding events of the history are associated with Isaiah: the attack of the Syro-Ephraimite coalition on Judah, in 734; the fall of Samaria, which he foretold, in 722; and the invasion of Sennacherib, in 701. Throughout all the changes and chances of world history Isaiah held fast to his faith that Yahweh was the ruler of the universe, and used the nations as his tools. The dreaded Assyrian is but the instrument in Yahweh's hands, 'a razor that is hired', and will be cast aside when he has served his purpose. Therefore Isaiah consistently advocated a policy of implicit trust in Yahweh, and the avoidance of entangling alliances with other nations.

His first public utterance as a statesman was to Ahaz, when that prince and his people were trembling 'as the leaves of the forest are moved with the wind' for fear of Pekah and Rezon. He bids the king 'take heed and be quiet'. Yahweh will not suffer the attack on Jerusalem to succeed. But, as 7^9 has been felicitously rendered, 'If ye will not confide, ye shall not abide'. Unfortunately for Judah, Ahaz preferred to seek the help of Assyria rather than to trust in Yahweh. Similarly, when the danger from Sennacherib seemed to be inescapable, Isaiah maintained his confidence. He condemned the policy of seeking help from Egypt, and proclaimed the inviolability of Zion, forecasting the coming disaster which should wreck the strength of Assyria (c. 31).

Isaiah was concerned more with nations than with individuals, but he denounces the social wrongs of his country in vigorous terms. The city that was once the abode of justice has become the lodging-place of murderers! The series of 'Woes' in 5^{8-24} reminds us inevitably of the indictments spoken by Amos. The antipathy of Isaiah to the sacrificial cult, so strongly expressed in 1^{10-17}, has already been noted (see p. 180).

It is in Isaiah that we first encounter the type of prophecy that is called 'Messianic', that is, prophecy foretelling the coming of a Messiah who will be raised up by God to deliver His people once and for all. The sign which He offered to Ahaz (7^{10-16}) of the child to be called Immanuel does not come under this head, for it refers to a natural event, to happen in the immediate future; though some later hand has given it a Messianic interpretation by adding v. 15, which tells that the child shall eat butter and honey, which typify not poverty but divine food. The prophecy of the wonderful child who is to come, $9^{6f.}$, is a true Messianic prophecy, which may be Isaiah's. On the other hand, the prophecies of a coming golden age, such as 2^{2-4}, 11^{1-9}, 32^{1-5}; $^{15-20}$ are almost certainly of later date than Isaiah.

Isaiah has more points of contact with the *nabi'* than we found in Amos and Hosea. He does not disdain the title himself (see p. 177). He has ecstatic experiences, such as the vision of c. 6, and uses the technical term for describing them—'Yahweh spake thus

The Writing Prophets 189

to me with a strong hand' (8^{11}). He offers a sign to Ahaz 'either in the depth, or in the height', and has no doubt that he will be able to work whatever wonder may be required of him. Evidently Ahaz, who refused the offer, had no doubt on the matter either. It is as a wonder-worker that Isaiah is portrayed in c. 38, able to cause the shadow on the sun-dial to retrace its steps, or to heal the sick prince by means of a fig-plaster. But for religion Isaiah is remembered as the prophet who asserts regally the majesty and holiness of God, and who trusts Him with an utter and unshakable faith.

Micah.

Micah was contemporary with Isaiah, but lived in the countryside of Judah. In many ways he reminds us of Amos. No vision is recorded in his prophecy, though he seems to have regarded such phenomena as characteristic of the prophets ($3^{6f.}$). If 1^8 is not merely metaphorical it records a symbolic action like that of Isaiah (Isaiah 20^3). He inveighs repeatedly against those who robbed the poor of the land, with such vehemence as to suggest that he may have been himself a victim of this oppression. He has no respect for the venal prophets of the country (2^{11}, $3^{5f.}$) who speak fair words to those who pay them. Like Amos, he sees in Assyria the agent by whom the iniquity of the country is to be punished, but Assyria is to lay desolate not only Samaria (1^6) but also the house of Judah (1^{10-16}). Even Jerusalem and the temple will be involved in the catastrophe. Although his prophecy of doom is quoted by Jeremiah (Jeremiah 26^{18}) he contributes little to the development of religion and theology, for the genuine prophecies of Micah are confined to the first three chapters of the book. The superb indictment of the sacrificial system in c. 6 must be attributed to a later time.

Zephaniah.

Zephaniah's prophecy is uttered against the background of the Scythian raids, shortly after 630 B.C. It is unlikely that the Hezekiah to whom his ancestry is traced back is the king of that name, because, apart from chronological difficulties, some definite indication of such a fact would be looked for. The two chief features of his prophecy are his vivid portrayal of the Day of Yahweh as, contrary to popular expectation, a day of disaster (1^{14-18}), and his doctrine that a righteous remnant will survive it (2^{3-7}). Some verses, such as 2^{11}, 3^9, anticipate the universalism of Deutero-Isaiah, but the whole of c. 3 and c. 2^{8-11}, are later additions to the book.

Jeremiah.

Jeremiah began his work at the same time as Zephaniah, and prophesied in Jerusalem until the Kingdom of Judah came to its end. He came of a priestly family at Anathoth, just north of Jerusalem, and may have been a descendant of Moses. Certainly he was in the line of spiritual descent from his great forerunner. He was a man of culture, well versed in the national traditions, and influenced by the work of Hosea. A man of property ($32^{6ff.}$), he had many influential friends in Jerusalem, to which he migrated early in his career, and it was due to these friends that the constant persecution to which, because of his outspoken criticisms of the national policy, he was subjected did not cost him his life.

Some six years after the beginning of his prophetic activity the great Deuteronomic reform took place. He does not mention it directly—nor, somewhat surprisingly, does the account of the reform in Kings refer to Jeremiah. We might naturally have supposed that advice would be sought from him rather than from the otherwise unknown prophetess Huldah, who is named in Kings. But he must have taken up some definite attitude to the reform. Did he support it, or not? To this question very different answers have been given. Most probably he did lend it his countenance, though later he came to realize that something more drastic than a reform of the cult was necessary for the salvation of the country. The ethical and humanitarian elements in the Code must have made a strong appeal to him, and in $22^{15f.}$ he pays a very high tribute to the character of Josiah. But in view of his definite repudiation of the sacrificial cult (6^{20}, 7^{21-6}) he cannot have been rapturously enthusiastic over the Code, though he must have welcomed its attempts to extinguish the pagan forms of worship at the local shrines, against which he so often inveighs.

More than any other of the prophets he admits us to the inmost recesses of his heart. He was of a sensitive and shrinking nature, moved with deepest sympathy for the sorrows of his people. 'Oh

The Writing Prophets

that my head were waters, and mine eyes a fountain of tears, that I might weep day and night for the slain of the daughter of my people!' (9^1) is a vivid expression of the grief which was ever his companion. He found, like all true prophets, the people to whom he spoke unwilling to listen and resentful of his words; none opposed him more insistently than the priests and prophets. His prophetic mission was undertaken against his own desires. But when he would fain remain silent he cannot, for, he says, 'there is in mine heart ... a burning fire shut up in my bones, and I am weary with forbearing, and I cannot *contain*' (20^9). Sometimes he is so self-distrustful that he fears Yahweh has deceived him (20^7), and in words reminiscent of Job he curses the day of his birth ($20^{14f.}$).

The great advance in religious thought which we find in Jeremiah is his doctrine that religion is a matter of the heart rather than of outward observances, and because this is so religion becomes a matter between the individual soul and God. Perhaps his greatest utterance is the famous passage concerning the new covenant, 31^{31-4}:

Behold, the days come, saith Yahweh, that I will make a new covenant with the house of Israel, and with the house of Judah: not according to the covenant that I made with their fathers in the day that I took them by the hand to bring them out of the land of Egypt. ... But this is the covenant that I will make with the house of Israel after those days, saith Yahweh. I will put my law in their inward parts, and in their heart will I write it; and I will be their God, and they shall be my people ... they shall all know me, from the least of them unto the greatest of them, saith Yahweh.

When the law is written, not upon tables of stone, or even on priestly scrolls, but in the heart, a man must be directly responsible to the God who writes it there. The old conception of religion as a thing between the nation and God with whom it had made a covenant was becoming every day more impossible to Jeremiah, as he watched the swift descent of the nation to ruin. A new nation must be created by Yahweh, in which every man shall answer for his own sins ($31^{29f.}$).

Like Isaiah, Jeremiah advocated reliance upon Yahweh rather than trust in foreign allies. His policy was always that of passivity for Judah. When the Babylonians were besieging the city he advocated non-resistance. Possibly because of this policy Jeremiah was left behind when most of the notable persons were deported to Babylon, as the conquerors would regard him as likely to exercise a tranquillizing influence on the people who remained. Though he was offered the alternative of going to Babylon with prospects of comfort (40⁴) he elected to stay in Judah. As he had bidden the exiles of the earlier deportation to dwell quietly in Babylon, so now he exerted his influence to persuade the inhabitants who remained to accept the Babylonian rule without fear. Had he and Gedaliah been permitted to guide the destinies of Judah at this time, Jeremiah might have seen some approach to the ideal of a true people of Yahweh which was in his mind. But the assassination of Gedaliah, and the subsequent flight to Egypt, in which Jeremiah was compelled by force to join, prevented him from seeing of the travail of his soul. He passes into the shadow, the bravest and tenderest of the goodly fellowship of the prophets.

Nahum and Habakkuk.

Two prophets, Nahum and Habakkuk, who were contemporaneous with Jeremiah, may be mentioned briefly, for they contribute little to the development of the religion. Nahum obviously writes just before the fall of Nineveh, 612. His great invective against the 'bloody city' is a splendid piece of rhetoric, but contains hardly anything that is definitely religious. Assyria is not regarded as an instrument in the hand of God, and there is no assertion of the idea that reform within the Judaean kingdom must precede deliverance and triumph. The tone of the book is so intensely nationalist that there is much to be said for the view that Nahum really represents the popular type of prophet whom Jeremiah denounces. An attempt has been made to redeem the book by giving it an eschatological interpretation, so that it becomes 'not a mere product of national hatred, or even of a just desire for vengeance, but a hymn to that Nemesis, at once ethical and divine, which inexorably realizes itself in history' (Sellin); but this is an artificial view.

It seems clear that Habakkuk 1^{2-11} derives from the reign of

The Writing Prophets

Jehoiakim, but the rest of the book suggests a later origin, not earlier than the end of the Exile. Its most striking feature is its reference to the problem of suffering, 1^{13}. Why does God permit the righteous to suffer? the wicked man to flourish? This problem was insistent in the later periods of the history, as it was bound to become once religion had been recognized to be a matter between the individual and God, rather than between the community and God. It is probable that the reference to this problem is one of the later additions to the original nucleus of Habakkuk, and we may leave it for discussion where it is raised more definitely in other books. Habakkuk has no solution to offer save patient fidelity (2^{2-4}).

Ezekiel.

The great importance of Ezekiel lies in the fact that he represents the transition stage from the old Yahweh religion to the Judaism which was a substitute for the old national ideal. He was a priest who was deported to Babylon with the exiles of 597 B.C. There he was allowed considerable liberty, and the elders of the exiled community in which he dwelt resorted to him for oracles. His early predictions are almost exclusively utterances of doom, and he was not regarded very seriously until the later capture and destruction of Jerusalem and the temple justified his ominous words.

More than any other of the writing prophets Ezekiel was subject to trance and ecstasy, and gifted with clairvoyance. He made large use of symbolic action to enforce his message. One great difficulty raised by his book is that he seems to be able to see all that goes on in Jerusalem, and that many of the prophecies, though uttered in Babylonia, seem to be addressed to an audience in Palestine. Recently the usually accepted view of the book has been challenged on two sides. Torrey has sought to show that it is really a production of the third century B.C. But while he has stated excellently the difficulties in the orthodox position his own solution is even more open to question. J. Smith, on the other hand, has attempted to mitigate the difficulties by supposing that much of the prophecy was uttered in Palestine before Ezekiel was exiled, a view which has a good deal in its favour. That, as this scholar believes, Ezekiel's prophetic activity commenced *c*. 722, either in Ephraim or among the exiles deported by Assyria, is less plausible.

Ezekiel conceives of God as spiritual, powerful, and especially as 'holy'. The sin of the nation which makes its punishment inevitable is a long-continued course of conduct which has profaned the holiness of God. This punishment is the destruction of the state. But here, again, a problem arises. In the eyes of all orientals a god and his people were so closely bound together that one could hardly exist without the other, and destruction of a state was tantamount to the defeat of its god. The destruction of Judah, then, would seem to be an admission of the impotence of Yahweh. This difficulty Ezekiel meets in two ways. First he lays emphasis on the fact that the nations who brought about Judah's fall were merely instruments in the hand of Yahweh, and therefore had achieved no victory over him. Secondly, he proclaims that Yahweh will create for himself a new people, after cleansing the nation. The nucleus of the restored people will be drawn from the exiles, whom Ezekiel, like Jeremiah, regards as the true heirs of the spiritual tradition, rather than those who remained in Palestine after the deportations.

This idea resulted further in a development of the position that religion was a matter for the individual. When once the state had been definitely broken up the new nation could be formed only by the gathering together of cleansed individuals. The individualism of Ezekiel's teaching is set forth in detail in c. 18. Each man has his own standing before God. He will not be condemned because his ancestors sinned, or saved through their virtues. If he repent he will not be condemned for his own past guilt. The individual is judged by his present standing in the sight of God. The whole argument proceeds on the assumption that suffering is the penalty of sin. Later, in the book of Job, this assumption is challenged, but Ezekiel does not seem to be conscious of its moral difficulties.

With Ezekiel, who was himself a priest, we have a definite change in emphasis, from the prophetic religion of grace to the priestly religion of ritual. For him, in contrast with Jeremiah, righteousness means above all complete obedience to the ordi-

The Writing Prophets 195

nances which express the will of Yahweh. He draws no sharp line between correct cult and correct conduct; rite and right are almost synonymous. He has a keen appreciation of the importance of morality, but it would hardly be unfair to say that for him ritual is quite as important as righteousness. Certainly he would have regarded the great prophets who had earlier attacked the sacrificial cult as heretics.

Ezekiel emphasizes very strongly the transcendence of God. This is brought out very clearly in the splendidly bizarre vision of c. 1. The deity is half revealed but half concealed in the vision. The very brightness and colour that surround him hide him. And when Ezekiel is driven in the end to use the anthropomorphic symbol which is inescapable for the human mind he does not say that he saw God in the form of a man, but, more vaguely, 'a likeness as the appearance of a man' (1[26]). This remoteness of God from man causes the prophet to think of intermediary beings filling the gulf between the two. It is 'spirit' that sets him upon his feet when he is prostrate after the vision. The six macebearers and the recorder of c. 9 are angelic beings. The cherubim of the chariot in c. 1, and even its wheels, must be regarded as supernatural beings, because the very wheels have eyes. In later Judaism we find an order of angels definitely called 'Wheels'.

Ezekiel has much to say of a coming judgement, a Day of Yahweh, in which Yahweh will pour out his fury upon his sinful people. Sword, pestilence, and famine will be the instruments he employs. Storm, darkness, cloud will furnish the natural setting for these dread judgements. Yahweh will himself be the ruler of the people, but his rule will be stern and merciless until he has purged the transgressors from his people. Sometimes, however, the prophet speaks as if the king of the latter days will be a descendant of David, who shall be as a shepherd to his people, though at the same time he may utter an oracle in which God himself is the shepherd (c. 34). Although in these eschatological pictures Ezekiel is using largely the material of his predecessors he introduces new features, and his figure of the shepherd is very probably the source to which the twenty-third Psalm and the utterances of Jesus about the 'Good Shepherd' may be traced. While we may feel that in some ways Ezekiel as a spiritual teacher is on a definitely lower plane than Isaiah, Jeremiah, or Hosea, we must recognize that in his teaching on the subject of forgiveness and cleansing he strikes out a new path.

In one other respect Ezekiel is a pioneer, for he is the earliest of the prophets to develop apocalyptic ideas about the future. The pre-exilic prophets thought of the future as being shaped by God through the use of human agents. God might employ the surrounding nations to punish Israel, or Israel might become cleansed and strong, enabled to work out her own salvation under his guidance. If the Golden Age should return, it would be through the agency of a new David, seated on the throne, or by means of a Messiah, who, though standing in a special relation to God, was yet a man. In short, the future destiny of Israel would be determined by events that were within the bounds of national statesmanship. After the destruction of the nation as a state such conceptions were hard to hold. Accordingly there was developed a teaching that the salvation of Israel and the bringing in of the Golden Age would be the result of the direct intervention of Yahweh himself, in a supernatural way. Such teaching is apocalyptic, as distinguished from normal prophecy.

The apocalyptic teaching of Ezekiel is contained in cc. 38 f. Yahweh reveals to the prophet that after many days the nations hostile to his people will descend upon the land to ravage and spoil it. They are led by a mysterious ruler called Gog. But when their armies are assembled for the attack Yahweh will annihilate them with torrents of hail, fire, and brimstone showered from heaven. The corpses of the slain enemy will be so numerous that the burying-parties sent out by the Jews to cleanse the land of their defiling presence, and to burn the wood of the discarded weapons, are occupied seven months in the former task and seven years in the latter. This final triumph will establish for ever the people of God in the earth: the exiles shall be gathered to their own land, and the spirit of God will be poured out upon the house of Israel. The description is gruesome and bizarre, yet not without a certain majesty. It shows, at any rate, how great a change has come over the conceptions of the future held by important religious leaders. A noteworthy feature of Ezekiel's teaching is his belief that the happy days to come will be shared by the descendants of the northern tribes (37^{15-28}), a view shared by others of the later prophets. For the Northern Kingdom Ezekiel has a very kindly feeling.

Deutero-Isaiah.

Out of the darkness of the Exile comes another voice, from an anonymous poet whose religion is much more tender and deep than was Ezekiel's. Because his poems were added to the prophecies of Isaiah by later editors, and now form cc. 40–55 of Isaiah, he is generally known as 'Second' or 'Deutero-' Isaiah. He writes while Cyrus is marching from victory to victory, but before the fall of Babylon, and may be dated about 540 B.C. Even his dwelling-place is a matter of controversy, but it is most likely that he lived in Babylon.

Although he knows full well the faults of his people, and at times will call them senseless, deaf, and blind, his heart is filled with a sublime pity for them. Whereas Ezekiel had denounced them unsparingly and prophesied chiefly of disasters to come upon them, Deutero-Isaiah speaks words of heartening consolation, for in his view his country's sufferings have more than atoned for her sins. 'Her iniquity is pardoned: for she hath received of the Lord's hand double for all her sins.' In the triumph of Cyrus, who is a servant of Yahweh destroying the tyranny under which the Jews have been crushed, he sees the dawn of a new hope. The exiles shall return to Palestine, crossing the wilderness upon a miraculous road which shall be built through the desert. God himself will lead them, as a shepherd leads his flock. The wonder of this new Exodus will so far exceed the wonder of the Exodus from Egypt that the latter—hitherto the signal mark of God's favour in the national history—will be remembered no more.

No writer of the Old Testament expresses more clearly than Deutero-Isaiah the idea of absolute monotheism. God is the sole creator of the universe, the absolute ruler of its destinies. He shapes the history of the nations. None can thwart his power. So surely does he control the issues of history that he has been able long beforehand to tell his prophets of the coming of Cyrus, and the event has proved not only his foresight but his absolute power. With withering scorn he pours contempt on idols and their worshippers. Images that must be propped up to save them from falling—how can they sustain their worshippers! Gods that are carried off as spoil by victorious armies, mere burdens for the backs of weary beasts—how powerless are they, and how foolish those who worship them!

But though Yahweh is the embodiment of power and majesty, he is infinitely tender of heart. He will care for his people with the patient solicitude of a shepherd. And he has other sheep that are not of David's fold. All the peoples of the earth are the sheep of his pasture, though they have wandered and strayed. In good time they, too, will return home, and it is part of Israel's glory that she is to be the instrument by which this happy end shall be accomplished. When the nations see the happiness of Israel, restored in her own territory, and blessed by her God, they will come humbly entreating to be numbered among the worshippers of so kind and powerful a god. In some passages the nations are thought of as becoming tributary to Israel, but in others the thought rises almost to a pure universalism, in which the idea of Israel's pre-eminence fades out of sight. It is not merely to the God of Israel, but to the God of the universe, who has been revealed to them by his dealings with Israel, that the nations come.

The highest note of all is touched in the so-called 'Servant-Songs' (Isaiah 42^{1-4}, 49^{1-6}, 50^{4-9}, 52^{13}–53). These have been the subject of much controversy. They are separable from their context and have been regarded by many as later insertions. There is no cogent reason for denying them to Deutero-Isaiah, and even if he did not write them they are in exact accord with his religious ideas. The most hotly contested point is whether the Servant of the poems represents Israel, or some individual martyr. To either of these theories there are grave objections. If either has to be accepted absolutely the former is the less open to criticism, and undoubtedly accords with the language of Deutero-Isaiah elsewhere, for he definitely refers to Israel as Yahweh's servant. But recent discussion is tending to reconcile the opposing views. In Hebrew psychology the individual does not distinguish himself so sharply from the nation of which he forms a part as we do. He can pass in thought from the individual to the nation without feeling that he has changed the object of his thought. And it may

The Writing Prophets

well be that in his descriptions of the Servant Deutero-Isaiah, while thinking of Israel primarily, thinks sometimes of Israel as embodied in some great spiritual sufferer, such as Jeremiah, or even himself. In this way it may be possible to reconcile the fact that, while it seems most natural to interpret the Servant as meaning Israel, there are passages concerning him which would be regarded as more naturally spoken of an individual.

But the vital importance of the Servant-Songs is a new note in religion that is struck by them, the possibility of vicarious suffering. Deutero-Isaiah asserts that Israel had received of Yahweh's hand double for all her sins. Surely a God who is a tender Shepherd cannot have inflicted unmerited penalty! How, then, is that unwarranted suffering to be explained? It can be nothing other than suffering endured for the sake of others. Most explicitly is this taught in the last of the Servant-Songs. The nations say 'Surely he hath borne our griefs and carried our sorrows; ... he was wounded for our transgressions, bruised for our iniquities; the chastisement of our peace was upon him, and by his stripes we are healed.' And if the view be preferred that individuals are speaking here of a martyr the doctrine of vicarious suffering is expressed just as truly. How lofty is this conception, seeing that Christians of all ages have felt the words to apply with such force to the life and death of Jesus himself!

Haggai and Zechariah.

We have seen that the course of the history in the period after the Exile is difficult to follow because our sources of information are so scanty. In some measure the same thing is true of the religious development, though on this side we have more material.

Haggai and Zechariah are important chiefly because of their work towards the rebuilding of the temple in Jerusalem. It has been conjectured from Haggai 2^{10-13} that the prophet was opposing the participation of the Samaritans in the building, but the inference is precarious. Zechariah, whose prophecies are confined to the first eight chapters of the book that bears his name, gives his message largely in the form of visions. These are often described as apocalyptic, though it is doubtful whether they are so in the full sense of the term. Some of them are bizarre enough for apocalypse, but in view of the fact that Zechariah looked for a Messiah—or rather, a unique feature in Old Testament prophecy, for two Messiahs, in the persons of Zerubbabel and Joshua—the strange pictures of the visions may be regarded as grotesque symbol more than true apocalypse. Zechariah has a very much developed conception of angels.

But with all Zechariah's emphasis on temple and cult he inherits the old prophetic doctrine that righteousness alone exalteth a nation, and his little summary of ethical duties in 8[16-17] is not unworthy of Amos. His picture of the idyllic future Jerusalem, its men and women living to a peaceful old age, its boys and girls playing in the streets of the city, is one of the most beautiful forms this forecast assumes.

Trito-Isaiah.

The concluding chapters of Isaiah, 56–66, often referred to as 'Trito-Isaiah', though they are probably not the composition of one author, reflect the conditions in Jerusalem perhaps two generations later than the activities of Haggai and Zechariah; but 63[7]–64 may well be earlier than those prophets, for the passage is from a time when the temple is still in ruins. In some parts of Trito-Isaiah we have expressions of spiritual religion that are in true descent from the great prophets before the exile. The rebuilding of the temple as a dwelling-place for Yahweh rouses no enthusiasm. 'Heaven is my throne, and the earth is my footstool: what manner of house will ye build unto me?' (66[1]). God is 'One that inhabiteth eternity', dwelling also with him that 'is of a contrite and humble spirit' (57[15]). The fasts are useless, because those who fast are evil-minded. The fast that finds favour in the eyes of Yahweh is 'to loose the bonds of wickedness . . . to let the oppressed go free . . . to deal bread to the hungry', and to cover the naked (58[6-7]). When we find in Trito-Isaiah passages of a very different kind, exalting the cult and the temple, sacrifices and sabbath-keeping, we can hardly avoid the inference that Trito-Isaiah gives us, not the message of a single teacher, but reproductions of diverse religious tendencies that in those days, as in earlier times, were contending for the mastery.

Isaiah 34 and 35 may well have been written by a poet of the

Trito-Isaiah period. The first of these prophecies is a terrible portrayal of the fate in store for Edom. The second paints in beautiful colours the miraculous highway through the desert, and the transformation of the desert itself into wondrous fertility: its language seems to echo the earlier prophecy of Deutero-Isaiah. A number of isolated prophecies inserted into the rolls of the earlier prophets, for example, Isaiah 15 and 16, and the concluding verses of Amos, may be assigned to the same time.

Malachi.

Contemporary, too, with Trito-Isaiah are the utterances of an anonymous prophet whom we call Malachi. This name is simply the Hebrew for 'my messenger', and has been taken from Malachi 3^1 as the name of the unknown author. This writer, apart from his vindictive hatred of the Edomites, has a lofty spiritual outlook. The scandalous laxity of the people in respect of the cult moves him to indignation, but he is equally severe in condemning their moral laxity. His hatred of Edom is balanced by his assurance that the Day of Yahweh will purge Jerusalem as with fire. It is from him that there comes the wonderful passage which can hardly be construed as less than universalistic: 'For from the rising of the sun even unto the going down of the same my name is great among the Gentiles; and in every place incense is offered unto my name, and a pure offering: for my name is great among the Gentiles, saith the Lord of hosts' (1^{11}).

Joel.

The earlier part of Joel may be assigned to a date soon after 400 B.C. This deals with the desolation wrought by a plague of locusts, and the gracious response of Yahweh to the solemn prayers of the people in a day of humiliation, restoring the fertility of the land. Joel is devoted to the cult, yet it is from him that we have the classic expression of protest against a religion that is exclusively concerned with ceremony—'Rend your heart, and not your garments'. The later parts of the book, which are strongly apocalyptic, probably come from a later hand.

CHAPTER XIII
THE LATER LITERATURE

THE great stream of prophecy began to diminish during the Exile, and by the end of the fifth century had become almost a trickle, losing itself, as some would say, in the sands of institutional religion. But such a statement, with its implication that the religion of the post-exilic period is dry and lifeless, by no means does justice to the facts, for this period, after all, produced the wisdom literature and the psalm book. It would seem that when the stream of prophecy ebbed away those members of the community whose temperaments found the institutional religion uncongenial, or who were, perhaps, through their remoteness from Jerusalem shut out from active participation in it, turned to meditation on religion. For we must remember that the 'wisdom' of the Jews is allied more closely to religion than to philosophy. 'Folly' for the Jew is always moral obliquity rather than intellectual stupidity. The fool is not the ignorant man, but the perverse man, and the fear of Yahweh, that is, reverent religion, is the beginning of wisdom. And when, as in the book of Proverbs, the precepts of the wise seem to us to be concerned with purely mundane affairs, the real truth is that the religion of the Jew embraces the smallest detail of his daily life, and such precepts are the application of that religion.

Proverbs.

The book of Proverbs may be dated from about 400 B.C., and no doubt received supplements later. It evidently consists of several collections of proverbs, and this is confirmed by the fact that the Greek Bible varies considerably in the order of the contents of Proverbs. The name of Solomon is attached to the book merely because it was the custom of the times to borrow the name of some famous man in the past to lend distinction to a new compilation.

The book condemns in pithy sentences various forms of evil. Anger, idleness, lustfulness, misuse of the tongue, violent or fraudulent ways of attaining wealth, are held up to reprobation. But the dominant note of the book is insistence on wisdom. Wisdom is regarded as a divine attribute, is personified in vivid fashion, and becomes almost a manifestation of God himself. The motto of the book is 'Trust in God and do the right'. Its view is confined within the limits of this life's horizons. It reaches a lofty ethical standard, and is deeply suffused with a reverent fear of God. A few years ago it was discovered that some of the material in Proverbs appears in almost identical form in the Egyptian book of wisdom called the 'Teaching of Amen-em-ope'. The likeness is so close that either the one has borrowed from the other, or both have made use of common material. It is generally thought, though this is not demonstrated, that Proverbs is directly dependent on the Egyptian model.

Ecclesiastes.

Some two centuries later comes the book of Ecclesiastes, which is sceptical to the point of pessimism, and only with difficulty secured a place in the Hebrew canon. It has some affinities with Proverbs, but the simple faith of the latter has given place to a pathetic distrust of life. God is looked upon as the divinity that shapes man's ends, but not to his comfort. A man's fate is predestined, and he is helpless to change it. He must submit to the inevitable, and make the most of such opportunities of happiness as come his way. Nor will the injustice of this life be compensated for in a future life, for all men, good and bad alike, pass to the shadowy afterworld, where there is neither work, nor device, nor knowledge, nor wisdom (9^{10}).

Job.

The supreme literary achievement of the Old Testament is the book of Job, written about 400 B.C. Its anonymous author has taken an old folk-tale, telling of the sufferings, and subsequent compensation, of an ancient worthy called Job, and used it as a framework for his own contribution. The first part of the folk-tale, which he seems to have rewritten to some extent, introducing the episodes dealing with the Satan and the three friends, he has used as a prologue. The rest of the folk-tale forms the epilogue to his work. Since the epilogue has no reference to the Satan it appears to be in its old folk-tale form. Probably the author rewrote that also, but the love of a happy ending caused a later generation to substitute for his revised version the original form of the end of the story. The present writer, at all events, finds it impossible to believe that the poet allowed his book to conclude with a section in which the compensation of the suffering hero is entirely material.

Between the two sections of the folk-tale the poet has inserted a series of dialogues between Job and his three friends. The friends hold the orthodox Jewish doctrine that all suffering is punishment for sin, and become increasingly indignant with Job for refusing to acknowledge it. Job vehemently asserts that he has not merited the suffering which has been inflicted upon him, and maintains his rectitude against man and God with a passionate utterance that comes near to profanity. The author gives no answer to the age-long question 'Why do the righteous suffer?' though he refutes the orthodox Jewish view. Perhaps, indeed, the real problem he has set himself is not so much to solve an intellectual puzzle as to show what is the proper bearing of a good man in affliction. In all his trouble Job has the fundamental belief that God is his friend, and must do him justice, even though his bitter agony causes him to charge God with torturing him malignantly, as a cat plays with a mouse. Every now and again Job seems to be lifted above the plane of his suffering, and to apprehend, however vaguely, that in the communion of the soul with God is the solution of problems too hard for thought to deal with.

It is generally agreed that the chapter on the Praise of Wisdom, the speeches of Elihu, and the descriptions of behemoth and leviathan (40^{15}–41^{34}) are later additions to the book. The present writer would add to these the speeches of Yahweh, though most scholars take a contrary view.

Daniel.

Daniel is one of the most puzzling books in the Old Testament. It is written partly in Aramaic, partly in Hebrew. The earlier chapters, 1–6, contain stories about Daniel and his three friends. The rest of the book consists of visions seen and described by Daniel. The author of the book is not named, but the traditional view, both Jewish and Christian, is that he was Daniel, a seer of the Exile period, or even earlier. The almost unanimous conclusion of modern scholars is that the book was written during the Maccabean struggle. The argument for this later date is based on a number of weighty considerations, and has not been weakened by the recent attempts of one or two scholars to defend the traditional view.

The purpose of the book is clear. It seeks to strengthen the faith of a people undergoing persecution, by showing that others in times past have suffered in like circumstances, but, remaining true to their faith, have triumphed in the end. Chapter 11 very accurately depicts, in vision form, the history of the persecutor Antiochus Epiphanes. The author hopes by showing that the sufferings of the Jews under Antiochus had been foreseen by a seer of long ago, who predicted a victorious issue for the people of God, to enforce the lesson that all is happening under divine providence, and that the end is under divine control. If only they believe this the victims of persecution will be loyal to their faith.

The work is apocalyptic rather than prophetic in the earlier sense, and is marked by advanced theological conceptions. It has a highly developed doctrine of angels, and a doctrine of resurrection. The date of its publication is clearly round about 166 B.C.

Psalms.

The book of Psalms has often been described as the hymn-book of the Jewish community. While this description is in general true, it must be regarded as subject to some modification. Not only does the book contain psalms—for example 119—which are obviously suited rather to meditation than to song, as is indeed the case with some modern hymn-books, but it seems clear that the song-service of the temple was mainly sustained by the priestly choirs of which we read so much, the part of the congregation being restricted probably to the 'amens' and refrains.

The critical fashion of the last generation was to regard the Psalms as being nearly all of post-exilic origin, and to suppose that very many were actually composed during the Maccabean period. More recently scholars have reacted from this view: Gressmann, indeed, has gone so far as to say that there are 'no

Maccabean psalms whatever in the Davidic Psalter'. This reaction seems to be justified on every ground. Babylonian and Egyptian temples had their psalms long before the time of David, and it is inconceivable that the temple at Jerusalem and the great shrines of other Israelite cities should have lacked this universal accompaniment of worship. It is impossible that the so-called 'royal psalms' can have arisen after the fall of the kingdom, for the attempts to explain references to the king as applying to the Messianic king are quite unsuccessful. Psalm 45 is obviously written by a court poet to celebrate the nuptials of a Hebrew king, who may very well have been Ahab or Jehu. We may well believe that many of the Psalms are pre-exilic, even if none of them is actually composed by David.

The book as it stands in our Bible is divided into five sections, each of which closes with a doxology. This is a comparatively late arrangement, modelled upon the division of the Pentateuch into five books. Behind these five books of the Psalms lie earlier and smaller collections. Some individual psalms are presumably adaptations of Babylonian or Egyptian temple hymns for use in the worship of Yahweh. Occasional sentences such as Psalm 72[8] betray this foreign origin. Psalm 104 is so very much like the famous hymn of Akhenaten to the Sun in subject-matter and form that there can be no reasonable doubt that there is a literary connexion between the two.

The oldest psalms are probably those which are closely related to the ceremonial of the temples, the so-called 'cult-psalms'. Psalm 24, for example, seems to be connected with a solemn procession of the ark, and others are related to the sacrificial ceremonies (cf. 118[27]). We have also parallels to the 'penitential' psalms of Babylonia, used by the individual suppliant.

Containing, as the book does, psalms of very different ages, it represents different and even conflicting religious ideas. Some psalms express thorough-going devotion to the cult, while others, for example, 50, 51, express rather the spiritual religion of the great prophets in whose eyes the cult was empty if not loathsome. The concluding verses of Psalm 51 read very much like the correction of some devotee of the cult who could not accept the doctrine that 'the sacrifices of God are a broken spirit'.

Since, like modern hymnals, the Psalms represent very diverse types of religious thought, we cannot set forth a 'theology of the Psalms'. The doctrine of God is, on the whole, a very lofty one. Many of the Psalms insist on the unique power of Israel's God, and his worth in contrast with the vanity of idols. His providential care for his people is a note struck again and again. Sometimes this is emphasized so as to make Yahweh almost a nationalistic God, but elsewhere the heights of monotheism are reached. The righteousness of God is emphasized, and the necessity of righteousness for the man who hopes to please him. Prevailingly the idea of death as the final end of human existence in any real sense is accepted, but once or twice, like the poet of Job, the author of a Psalm seems almost to grasp the idea of life eternal. And when one has allowed for all crudities of thought the fact remains that in the Psalms we have the finest expression of the inner life of religion to be found in the Old Testament. In all lands, to-day, Christian people turn naturally to the Psalms for the language in which they express their deepest spiritual feelings.

CHAPTER XIV

ISRAEL'S DEBT TO OTHER NATIONS

WE have already seen that the religion of the Hebrews contained many elements that are the common property of primitive religion. Our increased knowledge of the religion and civilization of neighbouring peoples has made it clear that the Old Testament contains besides this common inheritance many things that are closely paralleled elsewhere. The parallels, particularly those from Babylonia, have lighted up some dark pages in the Old Testament, and many of them are so striking that a widespread opinion exists that the religious traditions of the Hebrews have little originality. This opinion is as extreme as the opposite view which refuses to admit the reality of Hebrew indebtedness to other nations. Let us summarize the facts upon which a judgement must be based.

Israel's debt to Babylon.

Attention has already been called (see p. 167) to the importance of the Code of Hammurabi for comparison with Old Testament legislation, and in particular with the Book of the Covenant. The code is inscribed on a black diorite stela which was dug up at Susa in the winter of 1901–2 by French excavators. It stands about eight feet high, and although it was broken into three pieces, very little of the inscription is damaged. A few lines have been lost where the stone had been polished smooth, probably in order to provide for an inscription in honour of some Elamite king who captured it and removed it from Babylon as a war-trophy, though the intention was never carried out.

At the top of the stela is a bas-relief, representing a deity extending his hand towards another figure who stands in the attitude of a worshipper. It is generally agreed that these figures portray Shamash, the sun-god, who was regarded in Babylonia as the patron of law, and Hammurabi, the famous king of that empire, who reigned during the last years of the third millennium B.C. A translation of its contents runs to about eight thousand words.

In the prologue Hammurabi recounts the glories of his reign, and enlarges on his care that justice should prevail in his land.

THE STELA OF HAMMURABI

After the laws comes an epilogue in which the king asserts that he has protected the weak, the orphan, and the widow. That no man may suffer injustice through ignorance of the law, the king has caused this stela to be set up, wherein the oppressed may find what are his rights. The stela which was actually found stood originally at Sippar, but presumably replicas of the monument were set up in all the important cities. Fragments of one such replica have been discovered.

The regulations of the code cover a wide range. A few regulations dealing with legal procedure are followed by about 120 sections dealing with the laws of property and about 150 sections relating to persons. A study of the laws enables us to create a picture of Babylonian civilization very full of detail. Agriculture is prominent, for 24 of the 282 sections into which scholars have divided the code are concerned with field, orchard, or garden. An interesting little group of four sections contains the 'licensing laws'. For infractions of these the wine-seller—who appears always to be a woman—is put to death. The elaboration of the economic system is evident from the numerous regulations for the conduct of trades and arts. Several laws are concerned with boats and boatmen, to which Hebrew legislation offers no parallel, as the Hebrews had no navigable rivers and were not a seafaring people. Rates of pay for tradesmen, and of hire for implements, are fixed.

One interesting fact shown by the laws is that society was organized on a class basis. People are divided into gentlemen, plebeians, and slaves. Penalties for breaking the law vary according to the status of the injured party, and a doctor's fees increase with the social rank of his patient. Sometimes we are struck by the ingenuity with which the penalty is made to 'fit the crime'. For example, a man who is detected stealing property when pretending to assist in putting out a fire is to be thrown into the fire. Another ingenious scheme regulates the pay of the gardener, who was paid no wages for the first four years of his service, but entitled to half the produce of the garden in the fifth year. This method ensured the good cultivation of the garden, and was made more effective by a further regulation that any barren part of the garden must be reckoned in the gardener's half.

Israel's Debt to other Nations

A great part of the law is based on the principle of the *lex talionis*—eye for eye, tooth for tooth, life for life. This is elaborated very carefully in the case of the builder who builds a house so badly that it collapses after he has sold it. If the purchaser is killed by the fall of the house the builder must be killed. If the purchaser's son is killed the builder's son forfeits his life. Any slave who is killed must be replaced by the builder, and so, too, any property that is destroyed. And on top of all the builder must rebuild the house. This would be difficult if he had already been killed, but as a matter of practice the family of the owner would agree to accept some form of compensation as a substitute for the life that had become forfeit. Such regulations must have acted as an admirable deterrent to the jerry-builder!

That there is a likeness between the Code of Hammurabi and Hebrew legislation, and especially the Book of the Covenant, is obvious. One instance has been cited earlier (see p. 167), and many others might be added. General principles are much the same in both cases. Not a few examples of almost coincident phraseology may be quoted. It is not, perhaps, surprising that some scholars have asserted that the Book of the Covenant is directly dependent upon the Code of Hammurabi. Yet we should do well to hesitate before accepting this view. The code itself is no new composition, but a codification of laws that existed earlier. Very close parallels to some of its regulations are to be found in Sumerian, Hittite, and Assyrian codes. The more scientific explanation of all these resemblances is that all over the Nearer East—in Palestine as well as Babylonia—the different peoples acknowledged common customs in matters of law. The same problems would arise, and since many of the cases belong to elementary stages of human life the solutions offered for them would tend to be expressed in similar formulae. In all these codes we have a body of very much older legal custom, developed and modified according to the several different economic structures. The resemblances between the Code of Hammurabi and the Book of the Covenant are most readily explained, then, by supposing that each adapts to the social economy of its people this primitive form of law.

Many creation stories were told among the Babylonians. Of these the most famous is that known—from its opening words—

as *enuma elish*, and sometimes as *The Babylonian Epic of Creation*. This is a highly composite liturgical poem, dating in its original form from at least as far back as 2000 B.C., though it continued in use at the great Babylonian New Year Festival celebrated in the temple of Marduk, the national deity, almost down to the Christian era. It is much too long to be summarized in the space at our command, and we can but call attention to certain features in it which seem to be definitely related to the creation story with which Genesis opens.

One striking feature possessed by both stories in common is that in the beginning was a watery chaos out of which everything is developed. And there is no doubt that the 'Deep' of Genesis 1^2, which is in the Hebrew original a proper name, Tᵉhôm, is to be identified with Tiamat, the primeval power who in *enuma elish* is vanquished by Marduk. It is clear, too, that the description of the way in which Marduk dealt with Tiamat when he had slain her is echoed in the language of Genesis 1 where the making of the firmament is described. Marduk

> Divided the monster, devising cunning things.
> He split her up into two parts like a shellfish.
> Half of her he set up, and made the heavens as a covering.
> He slid the bolt and caused watchmen to be stationed;
> He directed them not to let her waters come forth.

Scholars who find a Babylonian origin for everything possible have asserted that the writer of Genesis 1 simply took the Babylonian story and purged it of its grosser elements. But whatever points of resemblance exist they are few in comparison with the points of difference. In the most striking case, the identity of Tᵉhôm and Tiamat, the Old Testament has, as a matter of fact, the older form of the name. Certainly no pious Jew of the exilic period or later, the time to which we must assign the writing of Genesis 1, would have taken a Babylonian story as a basis upon which to construct his own narrative of the creation. The few common features are accounted for by the fact that in Genesis 1, which contains elements from Hebrew tradition much older than the time at which it was composed, things survive in fossil form that had belonged to more general early speculation about the origin of the universe. Nor should certain points of external

A Babylonian relief, possibly representing the combat of Marduk with Tiamat.

resemblance blind us to the fact that the majestic idea of God found in Genesis 1 is infinitely removed from the gross polytheism of *enuma elish*. Certainly nothing of religious value was borrowed by its author from Babylonian sources.

To the Garden of Eden story no close and complete parallel has yet been discovered in Babylonian literature, though there are scattered parallels to individual features in the story.

On the other hand, Babylonia has provided us with some interesting parallels to the list of antediluvian patriarchs given in Genesis 5. In that list we have a genealogy of ten names, beginning with Adam and ending with Noah, thus bridging the space from the creation to the deluge. The striking feature of the list is the great length of life assigned to each of the patriarchs. Methuselah is credited with 969 years, and, save Enoch, who has a mere 365, the others lived at least 777 years. A tradition, preserved by Berossos, a Babylonian priest who wrote at Babylon *c.* 300 B.C., giving a list of *kings* who reigned before the flood has long been familiar. This agrees in the number of names, and in the detail that the last name given is that of the hero of the flood story. The years assigned to each king are even more beyond the normal span than those of the patriarchs. Three of the kings are credited with reigns of 64,800 years, and the shortest reign is 10,800. Ingenious attempts have been made to connect the names in the two lists, and in one or two cases with plausible success.

In recent years further material has come to light. In the Weld-Blundell collection at the Ashmolean Museum Langdon found a prism containing lists of kings of Sumer and Akkad (see p. 20). The date of the prism he puts at *c.* 2089 B.C. This list gives eight names, the last of them being that of the father of the deluge hero, whose name is not mentioned. The lengths of reign assigned vary from 19,600 to 43,200 years. A tablet in the same collection gives a list of ten antediluvian kings, two of the names being undecipherable. In this case the last name is that of the deluge hero. The reigns vary in length from 21,000 to 72,000 years. Connexions have been established between some of the names in these lists and corresponding names in the list of Berossos.

Israel's Debt to other Nations

It would be idle to deny that these Babylonian lists of antediluvian kings and the lists of patriarchs in Genesis 5 are variants of a very ancient tradition to the effect that world history is divided into two epochs by the occurrence of a great flood, before which there reigned ten kings who enjoyed great longevity, and the last of whom survived the flood. But once again the differences between the Biblical and the Babylonian lists make it improbable that the former is directly derived from Babylonian sources.

A considerable number of Babylonian documents preserve traditions about a great deluge. Most of them are fragmentary, but two are of considerable length. The accounts do not agree in detail, which is not surprising when we remember that the account in Genesis is compiled from two distinct and irreconcilable documents. Of the longer Babylonian accounts the version recorded by Berossos presents several points of close contact with the Biblical tradition. The other, which is found on the eleventh tablet of the twelve which contain the Epic of Gilgamesh, is even more important for comparison with Genesis. A summary will easily make this clear.

The city Shuruppak, on the Euphrates, was very old, and the gods, instigated by Ellil, determined to send a deluge. Ea (a god who is more than once represented as friendly to men), desiring to save Utnapishtim, advised him of the impending disaster, told him to build a ship, and put aboard it specimens of all living creatures. Utnapishtim promises Ea that he will carry out the instructions, but asks how he shall explain his strange conduct to his fellow citizens. Ea tells him to say that, having incurred the wrath of the god Ellil, he is going on an ocean voyage to dwell with Ea, and that Ellil will send a plenteous rain, with catches of birds and fish for the city. [A lacuna in the text is followed by a description of the ship Utnapishtim built.] It was 120 cubits high on each side, in six stories, with numerous subdivisions, and caulked with bitumen within and without. The workmen who fashion it are encouraged by daily feasts of lambs and bullocks, at which beer and wine flow like water. The ship is loaded with gold and silver, cattle, the family of the Utnapishtim, specimens of wild beasts, and craftsmen of every kind. Shamash, the sun-god, appoints a time when Utnapishtim is to enter the ship and close the door. Among the craftsmen aboard was Puzur-Amurru, a sailor, to whom, very sensibly, Utnapishtim makes over the charge of the voyage. The gods send terrible storms of thunder, lightning, and rain. The deluge covers the mountains, and the gods themselves ascend into the highest heaven of Anu, where they cower like dogs. The goddess Ishtar cries 'like a woman in travail', and regrets that in the divine assembly she had counselled this evil. The gods huddle together in abject terror for six days and six nights. On the seventh day the storm ceases, and the surface of the water is calm. Mankind has been turned into clay, floating on the surface of the water. On the twelfth day an island emerges, and the ship grounds upon Mt. Nisir, which holds it fast. On the seventh day after the grounding Utnapishtim sends forth first a dove and then a swallow, each of which finds no resting place and so returns. Then a raven is sent forth, and wades, croaking, in the mud left by the receding water. Utnapishtim offers a libation upon the mountain peak, setting out the sacrificial vessels in sevens. The gods, smelling the sweet savour, 'gather like flies round the sacrifice'. Ishtar says that Ellil, who 'took not counsel and sent the deluge', shall not come to the offering. When Ellil approaches and sees the ship he is enraged, suspecting that some of the gods have treacherously connived at the escape of Utnapishtim. Another god, Ninib, hints that probably Ea knows something about the matter. Ea defends himself by asserting that an undiscriminating deluge was unfair. By all means let sinful men be punished; but wild beasts, famine, or pestilence, might have been used for that purpose. Ea goes into the ship, brings out Utnapishtim and his wife, makes them kneel face to face, stands between them and blesses them. 'Formerly Utnapishtim was a man; now let Utnapishtim and his wife be like the gods, even us. Let Utnapishtim dwell afar off at the mouth of the rivers.'

In the case of the deluge stories we have so many points of resemblance that no unbiased reader will deny a real connexion between Genesis and the Babylonian parallels. The details as to the taking on board of specimen animals, the sending forth of the birds, and the offering of sacrifice when the voyage is ended, are sufficient to establish the relation. When the Babylonian stories were first brought to light it was thought that they were bizarre variants of the story in Genesis. But the fact that they are much older than the time of Moses makes this view untenable. Naturally the theory was then reversed, and it was held that the Biblical account is a revised version of the Babylonian, although the idea that there is direct literary dependence is not now so widely

Israel's Debt to other Nations

entertained. In view of the widespread occurrences of deluge stories in various forms in other parts of the world it is wise not to be dogmatic as to the exact nature of the relation.

However this may be, the account in Genesis is far superior to the Babylonian parallels in matters that affect religion. The account we have summarized is grossly polytheistic, and presents the gods in a most unfavourable light. They are subject to panic, and reduced to a humiliating impotence by the unforeseen consequences of their blundering design. They are divided in the heavenly council, and intrigue one against another. How far removed is all this from the majestic picture in Genesis of the one God who rules the universe!

We have noticed earlier (see p. 140) that the Sheol of the Old Testament has a close parallel in the Arallu of the Babylonians, and that the Hebrew Sabbath, though its name is etymologically the same as the Babylonian *shabattu*, was probably not derived directly from Babylonia (see p. 145).

There are some literary parallels which ought to be briefly mentioned. There can be no doubt that the author of Ecclesiastes 9[7-10], when he writes

> Go thy way, eat thy bread with joy,
> And drink thy wine with a merry heart;
> For God hath already accepted thy works.
> Let thy garments be always white;
> And let not thy head lack ointment.
> Live joyfully with the wife whom thou lovest.
>
> . . . .
>
> For that is thy portion in life.
>
> . . . .
>
> For there is no work, nor device, nor knowledge, nor wisdom,
> In Sheol, whither thou goest.

is echoing the advice given by the goddess Sabitu to Gilgamesh in the Epic:

> Gilgamesh, whither runnest thou?
> The life that thou seekest thou wilt never find.
> When the gods created mankind
> They assigned death as the fate of mankind;
> Life they retained as their own prerogative.

> As for thee, Gilgamesh, fill thy belly,
> Rejoice day and night,
> Every day make a feast,
> Day and night be joyful and content.
> Let thy garments be clean.
> Let thy head be washed, wash thee with water.
> Look upon the little child that clings to thy hand.
> Be happy with the wife of thy bosom.

It is probable, too, that the author of Job was acquainted with the well-known Psalm of Innocence, but the coincidences in idea and expression are far from showing, as has been sometimes asserted, that his work is an imitation of a Babylonian original. And while study of the Psalms used in Babylonian worship has revealed that they are in many ways similar to the Old Testament Psalms, often illuminating them, it is not demonstrated that Babylonia exercised any direct influence upon the Hebrew Psalter.

Israel's debt to Egypt.

In our discussion of the Decalogue (see p. 143) we noted that probably there existed in Egypt lists of commandments much more elaborate and extensive than those of the Ten Words, but the likelihood (see p. 144) that Babylonia possessed similar codes prevents us from regarding the commandments as a direct legacy from Egypt. Probably, just as a common basis of legal custom was developed among the Hebrews into the Book of the Covenant, and among the Babylonians into the Code of Hammurabi, and into yet other codes among the Sumerians, the Hittites, and the Assyrians, a generally recognized body of ethical practice assumed different forms in different lands. But in any case the commandments which deal with the duty of worshipping one God and with the prohibition of idols cannot be paralleled. It is true that some scholars would derive the monotheism of Israel from the teaching of Akhenaten, but this view we have already set aside (see p. 150).

The ark may very well have been copied from Egyptian models. But considering how close Egypt is to Palestine, it is remarkable how small are the traces of Egyptian influence on Hebrew

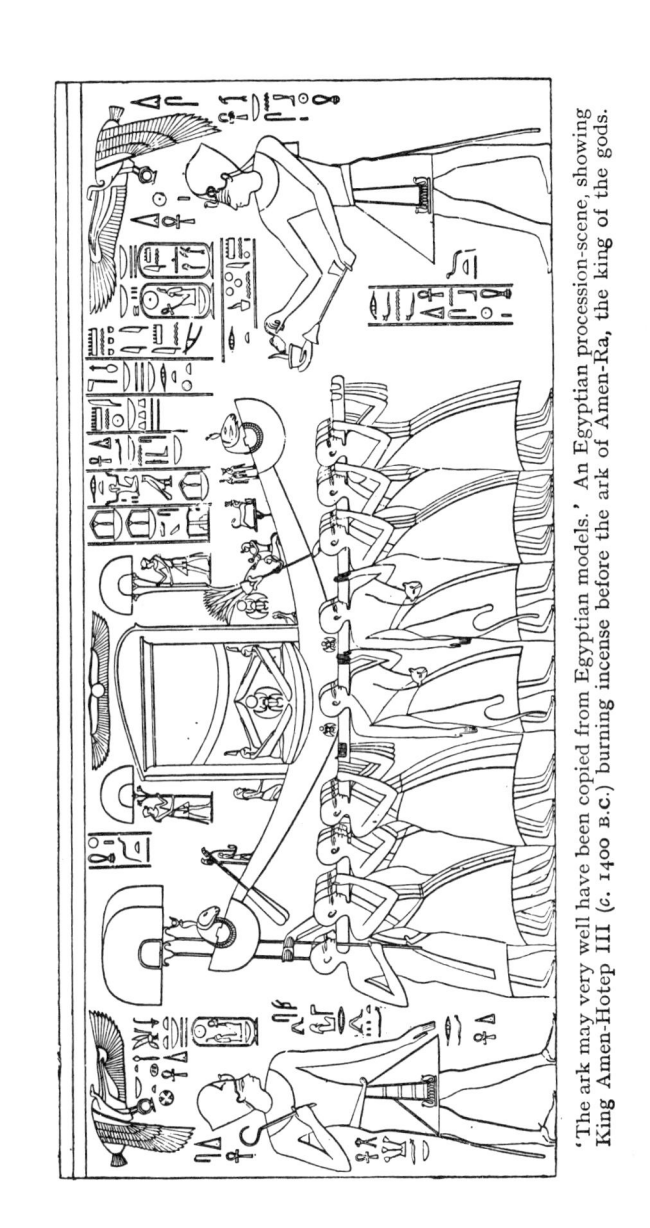

'The ark may very well have been copied from Egyptian models.' An Egyptian procession-scene, showing King Amen-Hotep III (c. 1400 B.C.) burning incense before the ark of Amen-Ra, the king of the gods.

religion. Of the very elaborate Egyptian beliefs about the future life hardly anything can be found among the Hebrews.

On the other hand, Egypt may have exercised some real influence on the poetry of the Old Testament. Psalm 104 bears so much resemblance to Akhenaten's famous hymn in praise of the sun-god, Aten, that, though some scholars think the parallels to be quite fortuitous, it is hard to resist the conclusion that the Psalmist is imitating the Egyptian hymn. In the Wisdom literature the evidence of Egyptian influence is more patent. We have noted in Babylonian literature a close parallel to Ecclesiastes 9^{7-10}. From Egypt the so-called *Song of the Harper* presents more than one parallel to utterances of Ecclesiastes. In most cases these may not be more than examples of similar thought finding similar expression, though occurring independently to different minds. But the passage

> So long as thou livest
> Put myrrh on thy head and clothe thyself in fine linen.
> . . . . . .
> Follow thy heart and thy inclination,
> Do thy business on earth and be not anxious (?)
> Till the day of lamentation comes to thee.
> . . . . . .
> For to none is it granted to take his goods with him;
> And none who has departed thither has returned.

suggests that the author of Ecclesiastes may have been acquainted with similar philosophical writings of Egyptian origin.

The clearest case of Egyptian influence on Old Testament literature is found in the realm of proverbial utterance. Here examples might be quoted from several Egyptian works, such as *The Instruction of Ptahhotep, The Wisdom of Ani,* and *The Admonitions of a Sage.* But in these cases the coincidences may be dismissed as accidental. In the case of *The Teaching of Amen-em-ope* we have something much more convincing. Budge, who discovered this work, would date it roughly about 1500 B.C., but other scholars, with greater probability, would bring it down to 700 or even 600 B.C. It contains thirty chapters of pithy sayings interspersed with more consecutive passages. Like the book of

Israel's Debt to other Nations

Proverbs, it has a profoundly religious background to its philosophy of life. For its author, too, the fear of God is the beginning of wisdom.

We must be content to quote as examples one or two of the passages which are parallel to Old Testament utterances:

> Better is poverty in the hand of God
> Than wealth in the storehouse.
> Better is bread with a happy heart
> Than wealth with trouble. (Cf. Proverbs 15$^{16f.}$; Psalms 37^{16})

> Move not the scales, and falsify not the weights,
> And diminish not the parts of the corn-measure.
>   (Cf. Proverbs 20$^{10, 23}$; Amos 8^5)

> A scribe who is skilful in his office
> Findeth himself worthy to be a courtier. (Cf. Proverbs 22^{29})

> Speak not to a man in falsehood
> —The abomination of God—
> Sever not thy heart from thy tongue
> That all thy ways may be successful. (Cf. Proverbs 12^{22}, 11^{20})

If we hesitate to find in numerous resemblances such as these evidence of direct influence our hesitation is removed when we find that a section of Proverbs—22^{17} to 24^{34}—which is generally agreed to be a block inserted into its context, has over a large part of its content parallels in Amen-em-ope. The convincing proof is found, however, in Proverbs 22^{20}, where the Hebrew word rendered *excellent things*—a pure guess!—has long defied explanation. Its consonants would permit of the translation *thirty*, but that seemed to be without meaning. Turning to a parallel passage in Amen-em-ope—*consider these thirty chapters*—we see the solution. *Thirty* is right, but the noun, whether *proverbs* or *chapters*, has been accidentally lost.

The probable conclusion from a study of Amen-em-ope seems to be that the work was very familiar to writers of the Old Testament, who used it as a model, and quoted from it, as most scholars hold, though it is not impossible that Oesterley may be right in his view that the authors of the Egyptian book and of Proverbs made use of common Wisdom material.

Israel's debt to Persia.

In Persia a religion which has many likenesses to the religion of the Old Testament was founded by Zoroaster, or as he is more correctly called, Zarathushtra. Of all religions this approaches most nearly to the pure monotheism of the loftier Hebrew thought. But, seeing that Israel came into touch with this religion only after the monotheistic ideas had been developed in Israel, in this respect we must rule borrowing out of account.

In spheres of less importance it seems highly probable that some Persian influence may be traced. In the later writings we find the Old Testament beginning to develop a doctrine of angels. Early Hebrew tradition knows of angels who act as intermediaries between God and man. This may be illustrated from the story of Jacob's ladder in Genesis 28. These angels are, however, different from those of our stained-glass windows, for they have no wings, but go up and down the ladder. The word rendered by *angel* would more accurately be translated by *agent*. A figure often encountered in the older stories is that of the 'Angel of the Lord'; this angel, again, is a representative of Yahweh, and in some cases before the story ends we find that the angel has been identified with Yahweh himself. The doctrine of angels which begins to develop from the time of Ezekiel, and is found in more elaborate forms in Zechariah and Daniel, is generally agreed to owe much to Persian models. Zoroastrianism represented the good god Ahura Mazda as surrounded by a host of angels, all of whom had their special functions. That the Jews recognized their debt in the matter of this doctrine is clear from a saying in the Jerusalem Talmud, to the effect that 'the names of the angels came with them from Babylon'. In the apocryphal writings the conception of hierarchies of angels is developed to a fantastic degree.

Possibly Persian influence may be traced also in the Old Testament references to the Satan, and the one or two late passages which speak of resurrection. Most authorities hold that in this field the contribution of Persia was rather the stimulation of ideas already existing among the Jews than the transmission of new ones. But here, as in the case of the angels, it is certain that

Israel's Debt to other Nations

later developments of the themes in post-biblical literature borrow many details from Zoroastrianism.

A particular case of Persian influence has often been seen in Ezekiel 8[17], where the holding of the branch to the nose has been interpreted as illustrating a feature of Persian ritual, the holding of a branch of twigs before the face. But this explanation seems to rest on a false understanding both of Ezekiel's words and of the Persian custom.

Our debt to Israel.

A study of the religion of Israel in comparison with other ancient religions is apt to lead, more or less unconsciously, to a depreciation of that which is peculiar to its genius. Interesting as such a study may be, and valuable as may be the light thrown by it on many passages of the sacred writings, a sober review will show that it is wrong to suppose that Israel was a wholesale borrower from other nations. Admittedly the religion of Israel inherited much from primitive religious belief, as of necessity all religions of that age must have done. But this legacy was confined almost entirely to matters of cult, much of which had become obsolete long before the close of the Old Testament era. The indebtedness of Israel to Babylon, Egypt, and Persia has been absurdly exaggerated. In so far as it may be substantiated it affects law, cult, and myth, rather than the more important matters of religion.

Had the religion of Israel consisted of an amalgamation of primitive beliefs with ideas borrowed from the religions of the surrounding peoples it would have perished as those religions have perished. Indeed, we may go further, and say that if the religion of Israel had been no more than the popular religion as professed by the greater part of the nation before the latter days of the kingdom of Judah it would have vanished with the cults of Chemosh or Milcom. What is unique and vital in Old Testament religion is the noble doctrine of ethical monotheism taught by the great prophets. The idea of God which they developed is the splendid legacy of Israel to the present age. When all has been said the fact remains, and can be explained away by no study of parallels in other faiths, that the best elements of the Hebrew religion are to-day treasured possessions of three great religions, Judaism, Mohammedanism, and Christianity. Hebrew religion must have possessed something imperishable which the dead religions lacked. That unique treasure, as we have urged before, is the ethical monotheism of the great prophets. To this no real parallel from ancient times has yet been adduced. It was borrowed from no foreign source. Indeed, is there any explanation of it other than the belief that it was revealed by the Spirit of God to men of old time?

INDEX

Aaron, 158, 174.
Abdi-ashura, 18.
Abdihiba, 17, 19.
Abdon, 51.
Abiathar, 64, 68, 70, 71, 157.
Abigail, 65.
Abijah, 94, 96.
Abijam, 96.
Abimelech, 50, 51.
Abishag, 70.
Abner, 62, 66.
Abraham, 30, 32, 33.
Absalom, 67, 68.
Achan, 135, 136.
Achish, 64, 65.
Adad-idri, 81.
Adad-nirari III, 90.
Adam, 214.
Adonijah, 68, 70, 71.
Adullam, 64.
Agade, 20.
Ahab, 79–82, 84, 87, 97, 160, 161, 176–9, 206.
Ahaz, 100, 188, 189.
Ahaziah, 84–6, 97, 161.
Ahijah, 78, 148.
Ahimelech, 63.
Ahi-yahu, 148.
Ahura Mazda, 222.
Ai, 136.
'Ain Kderat, 38.
'Ain Kdes, 37.
'Ain Kus, 38.
Akaba, 6, 34–6, 73, 84, 99.
Akhenaten, 18, 19, 31, 150, 151, 206, 218.
Akkad, 20, 23, 214.
Akkadians, 20.
Alexander, 23.
Amalekites, 38, 47, 65.
Amaziah, 98, 99.
Amaziah (priest), 132, 179.
Amel-Marduk, 115.
Amen, 150.
Amenemhet I, 17.
Amen-em-ope, 203, 220, 221.
Amenhotep III, 24, 25, 219.
Amenhotep IV, 25, 150.
Amen-Ra, 219.
Amman, 9.
Ammizaduga, 23.
Ammonites, 14, 16, 47, 51, 57, 114.

Amon, 104, 105.
Amorites, 16.
Amos, 8, 91, 93, 141, 177, 179, 180, 182–6.
Amosis I, 17.
Amraphel, 22, 30.
Amrith, 139.
Amurru, 16.
Anathoth, 70, 190.
Ani, 220.
Antiochus Epiphanes, 205.
Anu, 216.
Aphek, 81.
Arabah, 91.
Arabia, 4, 20, 22, 73, 115.
Arabs, 10, 14, 135.
Arallu, 140.
Arameans, 14, 108.
Ark, 55, 134, 157, 158, 219.
Artaxerxes, 118, 120, 121.
Artaxerxes I, 120–2.
Artaxerxes II, 120, 122, 125.
Artaxerxes III, 120.
Arzawa, 25.
Asa, 78, 96.
Ashdod, 5, 44, 102.
Asher, 41, 43, 49.
Asherah, 130, 153, 160.
Ashur, 107.
Ashur-banipal, 103–6.
Ashurdan I, 28.
Ashur-etil-ilani, 106.
Ashur-nasir-pal, 81, 131.
Ashur-uballit (Amarna period), 25, 28.
Ashur-uballit (c. 610 B.C.), 107.
Asia Minor, 44.
Askelon, 5, 12, 102.
Assyria, 2, 4, 10, 16, 26, 28, 77, 88–93, 100–7, 160, 182, 188, 194.
Assyrians, 14, 218.
Aten, 150, 229.
Athaliah, 80, 97, 98, 161.
Attharates, 121.
Attharias, 121.
Azariah, 99.
Az-ri-ya-hu, 99.
Baal, 153, 158–62, 176, 181, 186.
Baal of Judah, 67.
Baalis, 111.
Baasha, 78, 96.
Babylon, 2, 4, 10, 16, 22,

24–6, 28, 30, 66, 77, 91, 101–4, 106–8, 110, 115–19, 124, 136–8, 146, 148, 179, 185, 192.
Babylonia, 18, 20, 22, 112, 113, 118, 140, 144, 146, 158, 193, 206, 208, 211, 214, 223.
Babylonians, 14, 18, 218.
Barak, 45, 46, 48, 54.
Bashan, 8, 183.
Bathsheba, 68, 70.
Bedaween, Bedouins, 19, 37, 64, 65.
Beersheba, 56.
Belgium, 4.
Benaiah, 68, 70.
Benhadad, 78, 96.
Benhadad II, 80–2, 90.
Benjamin, 49.
Ben-Tabeel, 100.
Berodach-baladan, 101.
Berossos, 214.
Bethel, 41, 77, 130.
Bethlehem, 61.
Bethshan, 17, 19.
Bethshemesh, 55–9.
Betsani, 17.
Boghaz-keui, 26.
Book of the Dead, 143–5.
Breasted, 14, 44, 47.
Budde, 42.
Budge, 220.
Burraburriash, 25, 28.
Byblus, 16.
Cairo, 16, 18.
Caleb, 40, 46, 128.
Canaan, 2, 14, 15, 25, 31 37, 38, 43, 44, 46, 156, 162, 168, 181.
Canaanites, 25, 41–3, 48, 50, 53, 74, 152–4, 167.
Caphtor, 43.
Cappadocia, 44.
Carchemish, 116.
Carians, 44.
Carmania, 116.
Carmel, 5, 10, 17, 176, 186.
Carter, 25.
Charu, 13.
Chemosh, 51, 84, 127, 155, 223.
Chronicler, The, 116, 118, 119, 124, 125.
Clay, 22, 31.
Clough, 136.

2546.17 Q

Index

Crete, 22, 43, 44.
Croesus, 115.
Cromwell, 50.
Cush, 97.
Cushan, 35.
Cushan-rishathaim, 46.
Cyaxares, 107.
Cyprus, 22, 104.
Cyrus, 115, 116, 118, 119, 197.
Dagon, 44, 158.
Damascus, 74, 77, 78, 80, 81, 88, 90, 98, 100, 102, 153.
Dan, 41, 43, 49, 52, 56, 77.
Danes, 43.
Daniel, 174, 204, 205, 222.
Darius, 119.
David, 11, 41, 44, 54, 59–70, 72–6, 79, 80, 82, 94, 126, 134, 152, 156, 157, 176, 195, 196, 198, 206.
Dead Sea, 8, 10, 11.
Debir, 40.
Deborah, 45–8, 54, 55.
Decalogue, 142–4, 146, 150, 158, 165–7, 218.
Delta, 43.
Deluge, 154.
Deutero-Isaiah, 141, 180, 190, 197–9, 201.
Diban, 82.
Dodona, 129.
Druzes, 8.
Ea, 215, 216.
Ecclesiastes, 203, 220.
Edom, 34, 35, 47, 67, 73, 74, 90, 98, 99, 102, 110, 140, 141, 201.
Edomites, 14, 16, 115, 201.
Eglon, 47.
Egypt, 2, 4, 10, 16–19, 22, 24–6, 29, 32, 33, 36, 37, 43, 44, 72–4, 77, 92, 94–6, 101, 104–8, 110–12, 136, 144, 147, 180–5, 188, 191, 192, 197, 218, 220, 223.
Ehud, 47.
Einstein, 142.
Ekron, 5, 102.
El Shaddai, 147.
Elah, 78, 79.
Elam, 23, 101, 105, 115.
Elamites, 20.
Elath, 34, 99.
Elephantine, 114, 122, 130.
Eldad, 176.

Elhanan, 62.
Eli, 54, 55.
Eliakim, 107.
Eliashib, 121, 124.
Elihu, 204.
Elijah, 93, 161, 163, 176.
Elisha, 84, 85, 93, 175–7.
Ellil, 215, 216.
Eltekeh, 102.
Ely, 23.
En-Mishpat, 132.
Enoch, 214.
Enosh, 147.
Ephraim, 7, 41, 42, 49, 55, 88, 161, 179, 182, 184, 185, 194.
Esarhaddon, 103–5.
Esdraelon, 5, 41, 42, 48.
Ethiopia, 97.
Euphrates, 1, 4, 20, 21, 27.
Evil-Merodach, 115.
Ezekiel, 8, 110, 139, 171–3, 177, 178, 181, 193–5, 197, 222, 223.
Ezion-geber, 34, 74, 97.
Ezra, 120–2, 125, 126, 173.
Fotheringham, 23.
France, 4.
Gad, 30, 40, 49.
Galilee, 5, 6, 10, 15, 74.
Garstang, 12.
Gath, 5, 64, 65, 90, 98.
Gaza, 3, 73, 101.
Geba, 96.
Gebal, 16, 18, 19.
Gedaliah, 111, 114, 192.
Gentiles, 201.
Gerar, 3.
Germany, 90.
Gezer, 12, 16, 71, 72, 130.
Gibbethon, 78.
Gibeonites, 40.
Gideon, 45, 49, 50, 52, 130, 152, 153, 157.
Gilboa, 59, 65.
Gilead, 49.
Gilgal, 13.
Gilgamesh, 52, 215, 217, 218.
Gobryas, 116.
Gog, 196.
Goliath, 44, 61, 62, 64, 69.
Gomorrah, 103.
Habakkuk, 192, 193.
Habiru, 19, 31.
Hadad, 74.
Haggai, 118, 119, 134, 199.
Hamath, 91, 100, 148.
Hammurabi, 22, 23, 30,

31, 165, 167–9, 208, 209, 211, 218.
Hanani, 124.
Hananiah, 124, 178.
Haran, 30.
Harran, 107.
Hathor, 16.
Hauran, 6, 8.
Hazael, 85, 88, 90, 98.
Hebron, 6, 10, 40, 66, 67.
Henry of Navarre, 87.
Hercules, 52.
Hereward, 23.
Hermon, 6, 88.
Herodotus, 2, 106.
Hiram, 67, 72–4.
Hittites, 18, 19, 23, 26, 218.
Hophra, 110.
Horeb, 36.
Horites, 13, 156.
Hosea, 8, 88, 92, 93, 159, 184–8, 190, 196.
Hoshea, 92.
Huldah, 190.
Huleh, 6.
Humbaba, 137.
Hyksos, 17, 32.
Ibzan, 51.
Iluma-ilum, 23.
Immanuel, 188.
India, 13.
Isaac, 147, 155, 178.
Isaiah, 8, 177, 187, 188, 191, 196, 200.
Ishbaal, 65, 66.
Ishbosheth, 60, 65.
Ishmael, 111.
Ishtar, 117, 216.
Islam, 173.
Issachar, 49.
Jabbok, 8.
Jabesh, 57, 66.
Jabin, 48.
Jacob, 32, 33, 130, 147, 178, 222.
Jael, 49.
Jaffa, 5.
Jair, 51.
Jebusites, 41, 67.
Jehoahaz, 90, 97, 107.
Jehoash, 90, 91, 98, 99.
Jehohanan, 121, 122.
Jehoiachin, 108.
Jehoiada, 98.
Jehoiakim, 107, 108.
Jehonadab, 87, 162.
Jehoram (of Judah), 80, 97, 161.
Jehoram (of Ephraim) 84–6, 97, 155.

Index

Jehoshaphat, 80, 82, 84, 97.
Jehosheba, 98.
Jehu, 84–8, 90, 98, 161–3, 176, 206.
Jephthah, 51, 154, 155.
Jeremiah, 56, 106–8, 110, 111, 114, 129, 154, 166, 171, 178–80, 185, 190–2, 194, 196, 199.
Jericho, 7, 12, 40, 136, 152, 158.
Jeroboam I, 74, 76–8, 94.
Jeroboam II, 90, 91, 99, 182.
Jerusalem, 6, 13, 17, 31, 41, 56, 66–8, 73, 79, 90, 94, 95, 98–103, 105, 110, 118–25, 154, 158, 160, 161, 171, 183, 186, 187, 189, 193, 199, 200.
Jethro, 36, 149.
Jezebel, 79, 86, 97, 160, 161.
Jezreel, 85–7.
Joab, 66, 68, 70, 71, 74.
Joash (king), 98.
Joash, 152.
Joel, 201.
Job, 139, 191, 194, 203, 204, 207.
Johanan (High Priest), 121.
Johanan, 111.
Jonah, 126.
Jonathan, 58, 59, 63.
Jonathan (High Priest), 121.
Joppa, 5.
Joram (= Jehoram of Judah), 80.
Jordan, 5–7, 10, 13, 16, 40, 42, 47, 49, 65, 88, 92, 111.
Joseph, 32, 139.
Josephus, 10.
Joshua, 31, 32, 40, 41, 45, 136.
Joshua (priest) 118–20, 200.
Jotham, 99, 100.
Judaea, 122.
Judah, 4, 6, 65.
Kadesh, 27, 28, 32.
Kadesh (Orontes), 81.
Karnaim, 91.
Karnak, 94, 95.
Kassites, 24.
Keilah, 64.
Kenizzites, 40, 42.
Khattusil, 26.
Kirjath-jearim, 55.
2546.17

Kishon, 48.
Kittel, 16.
Kugler, 23.
Laban, 156.
Labashi-Marduk, 115.
Lachish, 12, 99.
Lahmi, 62.
Lebanon, 5, 8, 10, 18, 180.
Levites, 170–3.
Libnah, 97.
Lo-debar, 91.
Luther, 185.
Lycians, 44.
Lydia, 115.
Maccabees, 126.
Macalister, 12.
Machir, 49.
Mahanaim, 66.
Malachi, 201.
Mamre, 129.
Manasseh, 40–2, 49, 50.
Manasseh (king), 104.
Marah, 38.
Marduk, 212, 213.
Mattan, 98.
Mattaniah, 110.
Mecca, 135.
Medad, 176.
Medes, 106, 107.
Medinet Habu, 60.
Mediterranean Sea, 2, 5, 7, 72, 73, 81, 105.
Megiddo, 12, 18, 86, 107, 130.
Melanchthon, 185.
Menahem, 91, 92.
Merenptah, 19, 33.
Meribah, 38.
Merodach-baladan, 101, 102.
Mesha, 82, 84, 100, 154.
Mesopotamia, 14, 22, 26, 30, 46, 47, 146.
Messiah, 196.
Methuselah, 214.
Meyer, Eduard, 181.
Micah, 189.
Micaiah, 178.
Michal, 156.
Midian, 35, 36, 54.
Milcom, 223.
Miriam, 37.
Mizpah, 56, 58, 96, 111.
Moab, 8, 40, 47, 51, 54, 72, 80, 82, 84, 101, 102, 110, 140, 141, 155.
Moabites, 14, 16, 51, 108, 115, 127.
Moreh, 129.
Moses, 32, 33, 36, 38, 40,

Q 2

134, 135, 141–5, 147–52, 160, 165, 166, 172–4, 176, 190, 216.
Nabal, 65.
Nabonidus, 115, 116.
Nabopolassar, 106, 107.
Naboth, 82.
Nabunaid, 115.
Nadab, 78, 96.
Nahash, 57.
Nahum, 107, 192.
Naphtali, 41, 43, 49.
Napoleon, 23.
Nathan, 67, 68.
Nazirites, 162.
Nebuchadnezzar, = Nebuchadrezzar II, 108, 110, 111, 114, 115, 117, 118, 119.
Nebuzaradan, 111.
Necho, 104, 107, 108, 110.
Nehemiah, 114, 120–2, 124, 125.
Neriglissar, 115.
Newton, 142.
Nile, 1.
Nineveh, 83, 103, 107, 109, 192.
Ninib, 216.
Noah, 14, 154, 214.
North Africa, 13.
Nubia, 26.
Oesterley, 221.
Omri, 12, 79, 80–2, 88, 91, 97.
Ophir, 73.
Ophrah, 50, 130, 152, 157.
Opis, 116.
Oreb, 49.
Osiris, 143.
Osorkon I, 96.
Othniel, 46.
Padi, 102.
Palestine, 2–7, 10, 12, 13, 16–18, 22, 25, 26, 30, 31, 38, 40, 43, 44, 54, 59, 72, 73, 88, 90–2, 94, 103, 136, 141, 149, 182, 218.
Paris, 87.
Pazuzu, 137.
Pekah, 92, 100, 188.
Pekahiah, 92.
Peleset, 43.
Pelethites, 44.
Pepy I, 16, 17.
Persia, 115, 120, 124, 223.
Persian Gulf, 23, 101.
Petrie, 12, 44.
Philistia, 5, 55, 59, 67, 90, 101, 106.

Index

Philistines, 2, 5, 43, 44, 51–7, 60, 63–5, 97, 115, 158, 184.
Phoenicia, 26, 92, 141.
Phoenician ports, 4.
Polonius, 2.
Psammetichus, 105, 106.
Ptahhotep, 220.
Pul, 91.
Pulesati, 43.
Puzur-Amurru, 215.
Pyramid, The Great, 174.
Rachel, 156.
Rahab, 136.
Ramah, 96.
Ramoth-Gilead, 82, 84, 85.
Ramses II, 19, 33.
Ramses III, 19, 43, 60.
Rechabites, 87, 149, 162, 163.
Red Sea, 34, 36.
Rehoboam, 76–8, 94.
Reuben, 40, 49.
Reuel, 36.
Rezon, 74, 92, 100, 188.
Rib-addi, 18, 19.
Riblah, 107, 111.
Rim-sin, 23.
Rome, 66.
Sabbath, 143, 145, 146, 172, 217.
Sabitu, 217.
Samaria, 12, 79, 80, 82, 85–7, 93, 101, 104, 114, 122, 124, 135, 162, 183, 184, 187, 189.
Samaritans, 173, 199.
Samson, 51, 52, 162.
Samsu-ditana, 24.
Samsu-iluma, 23.
Samuel, 45, 54, 56–61, 157, 175.
Sanballat, 114, 122, 124.
Sanir, Mt., 88.
Sargon of Agade, 20, 22.
Sargon, 93, 101, 148.
Satan, 203, 222.
Saul, 11, 54, 56–66, 69, 156, 174–6.
Schumacher, 12.
Scotland, 11.
Scythians, 105.
Second Isaiah, 116.
Seir, 35.
Sekmem, 17.
Sellin, 12, 148, 192.
Sennacherib, 101–4, 187, 188.
Sesostris I, 17.
Sesostris III, 17.

Sety I, 19.
Shabattu, 145, 217.
Shallum, 91.
Shalmaneser I, 26.
Shalmaneser III, 81, 88–90.
Shalmaneser V, 92, 93.
Shamash, 165, 208.
Shamgar, 47.
Shamsi-adad V, 90.
Sharon, 5.
Sheba, 68.
Shechem, 17, 50, 59, 76.
Shem, 14.
Sheol, 139, 217.
Shephelah, 5.
Sheshbazzar, 118.
Shiloh, 55, 56.
Shishak, 94–6.
Shurpu, 144.
Shurruppak, 215.
Shushan, 122.
Shuwardata, 19.
Sidon, 72, 90, 110.
Siloam, 104.
Simeon, 40, 42, 49, 55, 120.
Sin, 115.
Sinai, 34–6, 134, 158.
Sin-shar-ishkun, 106, 107.
Sin-shum-lishir, 106.
Sisera, 45, 49, 53.
Smith, J., 193.
Smith, Robertson, 132.
Smith, Sidney, 156.
Snefru, 16.
Sodom, 103.
Solomon, 11, 41, 54, 68–76, 80, 94, 152, 160, 167, 202.
Spain, 153.
Stonehenge, 13.
Sumer, 20, 22, 23, 214.
Sumerians, 20, 218.
Sumu-abu, 22.
Syria, 14, 18, 20, 22, 44, 73, 75, 81, 84, 88, 90, 92.
Syrians, 14, 82, 133, 178, 184.
Taanach, 12, 130, 148.
Tarhundaraba, 25.
Teima, 115.
Tekoa, 182.
Tell Jemmeh, 3.
Tell-el-Amarna, 4, 17, 18, 26.
Tell-el-Hesy, 12.
Thapsacus, 73.
Thothmes I, 18.
Thummim, 157.

Tiamat, 212, 213.
Tibni, 79.
Tiglath-Pileser III, 79, 91–3, 99, 100, 182.
Tigris, 1, 4, 20, 116.
Tirzah, 78, 79, 96.
Tobiah, 124.
Tola, 51.
Torrey, 193.
Trans-Jordania, 6, 9, 59, 82.
Trito-Isaiah, 200, 201.
Trumbull, 37, 38.
Tutankhamen, 25.
Tukulti-ninib I, 28.
Tutulki-ninurta II, 81.
Tyre, 5, 67, 72–4, 79, 90, 102, 110, 160.
Ur, 22, 30.
Uriah, 108.
Urim, 157.
Usher, 1.
Utnapishtim, 215, 216.
Uzza, 134.
Uzziah, 99.
Victoria, 1.
Wadi Arabah, 6.
Wady el-Arish, 5.
Weni, 16, 17.
Winckler, 22.
Woolley, 22.
Yah, 148.
Yahu, 148, 149.
Yahweh, 147.
Ya'qobhar, 33.
Yarmuk, 6.
Ya-u-bi'-di, 148.
Ya'udi, 99.
Ya-ve, 148.
Zadok, 70.
Zalmunna, 49.
Zarathushtra, 222.
Zebah, 49.
Zebulon, 41, 43, 49.
Zechariah (prophet), 118, 119, 199, 200, 222.
Zechariah (king), 91.
Zedekiah (prophet), 178.
Zedekiah (king), 110, 111.
Zeeb, 49.
Zephaniah, 106, 189, 190.
Zerah, 96, 97.
Zerubbabel, 114, 118–20, 200.
Zeus, 129.
Ziklag, 65.
Zimri, 78, 79, 86.
Zion, 183, 186, 188.
Zoroaster, 222.
Zoroastrianism, 223.

THE OLD TESTAMENT
CHRONOLOGICALLY ARRANGED
by EVELYN W. HIPPISLEY, S.Th.

Licensed Teacher in Theology, Tutor to Women Theological Students, King's College, London.

N.B.—The dates of the Kings of Israel and Judah are taken from the article 'Chronology of the Old Testament' in the *Encyclopaedia Biblica*; and the articles in Peake's commentary and in Hastings' *Dictionary of the Bible* on the separate books have been consulted. Other books which have been used are the *International Critical Commentary*, the *Westminster Commentaries*, the *Expositors' Bible*, the *Century Bible*, Dr. Driver's *Introduction to the Literature of the Old Testament*, Dr. Oesterley's *Books of the Apocrypha*, and Dr. Charles' *Apocrypha and Pseudepigrapha*.

Principal Foreign Power = the principal foreign power with which Israel was in contact at the time.

Inscriptions = inscriptions, chiefly on Babylonian and Assyrian monuments which refer to events in the history of Israel. These are mostly translated in the Appendix to Dr. Foakes-Jackson's *Biblical History of the Hebrews*. The Code of Ḥammurabi, Selections from the Tell el-Amarna letters, and the Babylonian Flood Stories are published by S.P.C.K. (1s., 4d., and 6d. each).

The Book of Genesis, divided into sources by Dr. T. H. Robinson, is published by the National Adult School Union (1s.).

Book.	Contents.	Origin.
The Hexateuch	Genesis to Joshua—contains four strands of narrative: (i) Jahvistic, Judaean in origin, *circ.* 850 B.C.; (ii) Elohistic, Ephraimitic in origin, *circ.* 750 B.C., both written from a prophetic standpoint; (JE combined *circ.* 650 B.C.). (iii) D Deuteronomic revision, 7th century B.C.; (JED combined early in Exile). (iv) P Priestly author and editor, 5th century B.C.; (JEDP combined and re-edited before 3rd century B.C.).	

N.B.—*No analysis of sources is given, but large portions belonging to the Priestly writer are indicated, as it is important to recognize the later standpoint.*

Book.	Contents.	Origin.
Genesis	i–xi. Prehistoric Narratives. xii–xlix. Stories of the Patriarchs.	JEP.
Exodus	The Exodus and Wanderings.	JEP (xxv–xxxi, xxxv–xl P).
Numbers	The Story of Wanderings.	JEDP (i–x. 28, xvii–xix, xxvi–xxxi, xxxiii–xxxvi P).
Joshua	The Conquest of Canaan.	JEDP (xv–xix P).
Judges	The Conquest of Canaan and Settlement of Tribes.	Compiled from old material (perhaps JE) by a Deuteronomic editor, 6th century B.C.
1 and 2 Samuel	History of Establishment of Monarchy, and Early Kings.	Two strands of narrative of 9th and 8th centuries B.C. woven together by a Deuteronomic editor, 6th century B.C.
1 and 2 Kings	History of Kings of Israel and Judah from Solomon to Fall of Jerusalem.	Compiled from Court and Temple records and biographies of prophets by a Deuteronomic editor, and re-edited during the Exile.

(3)

Important Events.	Date B.C.	Principal Foreign Power.	Inscriptions.
Ḥammurabi's Code of Laws, based on an older Sumerian Code.	circ. 1950	First Babylonian Empire, 2050–732 B.C.	Code of Ḥammurabi.
	circ. 1230	Egypt.	Tell el-Amarna Letters (1450–1370). Stele of Raamses (Rameses) II (1300–1234) found at Beth-shan, showing that Semites had built city of Raamses. Stele of Merneptah (1234–1225 B.C.).
Crossing of Jordan.	circ. 1196		
Philistines settling in Canaan, circ. 1200 B.C.			
SAUL	1025		
DAVID	1000		
SOLOMON	970		
Division of Kingdom.	933		
Kings of Judah. Kings of Israel. REHOBOAM JEROBOAM ABIJAM ASA NADAB BAASHA	933 916 914 912 911		

Book.	Contents.	Origin.
Amos	Warning to Israel by a Judaean.	Prophecies delivered in the reign of Jeroboam II (2 Kings xiv. 23-9), 760-746 B.C.
Hosea	Warning to Israel by an Israelite.	Prophecies delivered in reign of Jeroboam II, and later (2 Kings xiv. 23-xv), 746-734 B.C.
Micah	Denunciations of Israel and Judah by a Man of the People.	Chapters i-iii—prophecies delivered in reigns of Jotham, Ahaz, and Hezekiah (2 Kings xv. 32, xvi, xviii-xx)—739-693 B.C. Chapters iv-vi anonymous prophecies, added later.
Isaiah i-xxxix	The Statesman - Prophet's Warnings to Jerusalem.	Prophecies delivered in reigns of Uzziah, Jotham, Ahaz, and Hezekiah (2 Kings xix. 20, xx), 739-701 B.C. (omit xiii-xiv. 23; xxi, xxiv-xxvii, xxxiv, xxxv, and possibly other passages which are post-exilic).

(5)

Important Events.	Date B.C.	Principal Foreign Power.	Inscriptions.
Kings of Judah. Kings of Israel.			
ELAH	888		
ZIMRI	887		
OMRI	887		
AHAB	876		
JEHOSHAPHAT	873	Assyria	
Battle of Ḳarḳar	853	(Shalmaneser	Moabite Stone.
AHAZIAH	853	III. 859).	Ḳarḳar Inscription.
JORAM	853		
Completion of Jahvistic narrative.	850		
JEHORAM	849		
AHAZIAH	842		
ATHALIAH JEHU	841		
Jehu pays tribute to Shalmaneser.	841		Black Obelisk of
JOASH	835		Shalmaneser.
JEHOAHAZ	814		
JOASH	797		
*AMAZIAH	795		
AZARIAH or UZZIAH	789		
JEROBOAM II.	782		
JOTHAM (regent)			
Compilation of Elohistic narrative	750		Tiglath-Pileser III
ZECHARIAH	743		reduces Hamath.
SHALLUM	743		
MENAHEM	743		
JOTHAM	739		
Menahem pays tribute to Tiglath-Pileser III.	738		Tribute of Menahem.
PEKAHIAH	736		
AHAZ PEKAH	735		
Ahaz pays tribute to Tiglath-Pileser III.	734		
HOSHEA	730		Hoshea placed on throne by Tiglath-Pileser III.

* The Biblical Chronology here obviously needs reconstruction. The dates given here are those of Marti in *Encycl. Biblica* ; cf. Steuernagel, *Einleitung*, and Box, *Isaiah*.

(6)

Book.	Contents.	Origin.
Jeremiah	Warnings and Pleadings to Jerusalem.	Prophecies uttered in reigns of Josiah, Jehoiakim, Jehoiachin, and Zedekiah (2 Kings xxii–xxv). Earlier prophecies written down by Baruch; later prophecies, especially xlvi–li, added by a compiler during or after the Exile—626-500 B.C.
Zephaniah	Doom of Wicked Nations.	Prophecy uttered *circ.* 626 B.C., when the Scythians were threatening Jerusalem, and edited in post-exilic times.
Deuteronomy	The Law-Book (with additions) found in the Temple, on which Josiah based his reform.	A revision of the earlier laws, compiled *circ.* 640 B.C.
Nahum	Doom of Nineveh.	Chapters ii and iii written *circ.* 612 B.C.; chapter i a post-exilic acrostic poem.
Habakkuk	Moral Problem raised by God's use of Chaldaeans.	Chapters i and ii written *circ.* 600-550 B.C., when Chaldaea, i.e. New Babylon, was becoming powerful; chapter iii a lyric ode of post-exilic date.
Ezekiel i–xxxii	Prophecies of Doom, and Denunciations of Jerusalem and foreign nations.	Written in Babylon before the Fall of Jerusalem by an exile banished in 596 B.C.
Ezekiel xxxiii–xxxix	Picture of the Restitution of Israel.	Written in Babylon after the Fall of Jerusalem—584-572 B.C.

(7)

Important Events.	Date B.C.	Principal Foreign Power.	Inscriptions.
Kings of Judah. Kings of Israel. Fall of Samaria End of Kingdom of Israel	721		Capture of Samaria by Sargon II.
*HEZEKIAH Invasion of Sennacherib MANASSEH AMON JOSIAH	{ 720? { 715? 700 692 638 637		Siloam Inscription. Invasion of Sennacherib.
	625	New Babylonian Empire founded by Nabopolassar.	
Finding of Law-Book (2 Kings xxii) Reform of Josiah Fall of Nineveh Battle of Megiddo JEHOAHAZ JEHOIAKIM Battle of Carchemish JEHOIACHIN First deportation to Babylon ZEDEKIAH	621 621 612 608 608 607 605 597 596 596	Nebuchadrezzar King of Babylon 604–561.	
Fall of Jerusalem Exile.	586		

* See Dr. Robinson's note, p. 232.   If the view is accepted that Hezekiah was associated with Ahaz for a time, this would dispose of part of the discrepancy.

Book.	Contents.	Origin.
Ezekiel xl–xlviii	A Vision of the Ideal Theocracy.	Written after 572 B.C.
Lamentations	A Book of Dirges.	These poems, arranged as acrostics (except ch. v), are of exilic date.
Isaiah xl–lv	The Promise of Return.	Prophecies delivered by an unknown author at the close of the Exile, probably between 549 and 538 B.C. The Servant-Songs are possibly later.
Obadiah	Doom of Edom.	Verses 1–14 belong to an exilic prophecy; the rest is probably post-exilic.
Leviticus xvii–xxvi	The Law of Holiness.	Old Laws of Priestly character grouped together towards the close of the Exile.
Haggai *Zechariah* i–viii	Call to rebuild the Temple.	Prophecies delivered 520 B.C. (Ezra v, vi). Prophecies delivered 520, 518 B.C.
Isaiah lvi–lxvi	The Restored Community: its Faults and its Blessings.	Prophecies delivered by an unknown author in Palestine *circ.* 450 B.C.
Malachi	Rebuke of the Moral and Religious Condition of the Jews.	Probably delivered *circ.* 450 B.C.
Ruth	A Pastoral Idyll.	Probably used as a Tract for the Times about Foreign Marriages in Nehemiah's day.
Job	A Wisdom-Book, treating of the Problem of the Innocent Sufferer.	Probably based on an older story by a post-exilic author.
Leviticus	The Priestly Code of Laws.	Compiled during the Exile, and possibly published by Ezra.
Joel	The Day of the Lord.	The date is probably early in the fourth century B.C.

Important Events.	Date B.C.	Principal Foreign Power.	Inscriptions.
Cyrus overthrows the Medes.	549	Persian Empire.	
Capture of Babylon by Cyrus.	538		
Edict of Cyrus.	538		
The Return.			
Return of Zerubbabel and Joshua (Ezra i, ii).	537		
Building of Temple.	520–516		
Dedication of Second Temple (Ezra vi. 16).	516		
		Artaxerxes I.	
Return of Nehemiah (Neh. ii).	445		
Nehemiah's second visit (Neh. xiii. 7).	433	Artaxerxes II.	
Ezra's Return.	? 397		
		Artaxerxes III. (Ochus).	
Jaddua, High Priest (Neh. xii. 11).	351		
Samaritan Schism.	335		

Book.	Contents.	Origin.
Zechariah ix–xiv	An Apocalyptic Vision.	The work of a post-exilic prophet or prophets, *circ.* 320 B.C. or later.
Jonah	An Evangelical Allegory.	Written *circ.* 300 B.C., and probably based on an old tradition.
1 and 2 Chronicles	History re-edited from an ecclesiastical standpoint.	Compiled, with additions, from previously existing sources by a Temple Levite, *circ.* 300–250 B.C.
Ezra *Nehemiah*	Narrative of the Return and Rebuilding of the Temple.	Compiled by the Chronicler, *circ.* 300 B.C., from City and Temple records, Aramaic documents, and memoirs.
Proverbs	One of the Wisdom-Books of the Hebrews, containing Moral Maxims.	Several collections of Proverbs of various dates combined by an editor, *circ.* 250 B.C.
Song of Songs	A Marriage Drama, showing the triumph of faithful love.	Probably written in Jerusalem during the Greek period.
Esther	A Didactic Romance.	Written, perhaps on an historical basis, *circ.* third century B.C., to defend the keeping of the Feast of Purim.
Ecclesiastes	A Wisdom-Book, containing the Meditations of an Unsatisfied Man.	Written *circ.* 200 B.C.
Psalms	The Hymns Ancient and Modern of the Second Temple.	Five books of gradual growth, containing 'Praise-Songs' dating probably from the time of David to the second century B.C.
Daniel	An Apocalypse of Encouragement.	Probably founded on an older story, and written *circ.* 168 B.C. to encourage the Maccabaean party.

Important Events.	Date B.C.	Principal Foreign Power.	Inscriptions.
Alexander the Great becomes ruler of the world.	331	Macedonian Empire.	
Conquest of Palestine by Alexander.	331		
Death of Alexander and division of his Empire.	323		
		Ptolemaic and Seleucid Empires.	
Palestine under the Ptolemies of Egypt.	311		
Antiochus III conquers Palestine.	198		
Persecution of Jews by Antiochus IV (Epiphanes).	169		
Maccabaean Revolt against Antiochus Epiphanes.	167		

A list, chronological as far as possible, is appended of the principal
in the Alexandrian Canon (the Septuagint), but not in the
were never included in either Canon, but are important as greatly

Book.		Contents.	Origin.
APOCRYPHA.	APOCALYPTIC.		
Ecclesiasticus (Wisdom of Jesus, son of Sirach.)		A Wisdom-Book, containing counsels for daily life.	Written in Hebrew, probably *circ.* 180 B.C., and translated into Greek by the author's grandson, *circ.* 130 B.C.
Tobit		An Idyll of Home-Life.	Written probably in Aramaic, *circ.* 190–175 B.C.
	Book of Enoch	A series of Apocalyptic Visions.	Written in Palestine by several Hebrew authors belonging to the party of the Ḥasidim, between 170 and 64 B.C.
Prayer of Azariah			An addition to the Greek text of Daniel, probably written in Hebrew, *circ.* 170 B.C.
Song of the Three Children.		The Thanksgiving of the Three for Deliverance (*Benedicite*).	Dating from the Maccabaean triumph, *circ.* 165 B.C.
1 Esdras		History of the Jews from the reign of Josiah to the Proclamation of the Law (639–? 400 B.C.).	Written probably at Alexandria between 170 and 100 B.C.
Rest of Esther		Contains additional details as to Esther, probably imaginary.	A Greek interpolation in the Hebrew text, *circ.* 150 to 100 B.C.
Judith		A story of the Deliverance of Israel from Assyria by a Jewess.	Written *circ.* 150 B.C. and edited *circ.* 60 B.C.
Baruch		A work in four divisions, containing prayers of Exiles and messages to Exiles.	Written by three authors, probably between 2nd century B.C. and 2nd century A.D.
	Testaments of the XII Patriarchs.	The Dying Commands of Jacob's Twelve Sons.	Written, probably in Hebrew, by Ḥasidim, *circ.* 130–10 B.C. (contains later Christian interpolations).
2 Maccabees		History from the reign of Seleucus IV to the death of Nicator (176–161 B.C.). (Parallel with part of 1 Maccabees, but not so trustworthy.)	Probably abridged *circ.* 40 A.D. from a larger work by an Alexandrian Jew, written *circ.* 120 B.C.

Apocryphal and Apocalyptic Books. The *Apocrypha* were included Palestinian Canon (Massoretic Text). The *Apocalyptic* writings influencing New Testament thought and phraseology.

Important Events.	Date B.C.	Principal Foreign Power.	Inscriptions.
		Seleucid Empire.	
Maccabaean Revolt.	167		
Re-dedication of Temple.	165		
Death of Judas Maccabaeus.	160		
Jonathan, High-Priest.	160		
Simon, High-Priest, and Ethnarch.	142		
Independence of the Jews.	142		
John Hyrcanus.	135		
Rise of Pharisees and Sadducees.			
JOHN HYRCANUS, King of Judaea (Hasmonean Dynasty).	107		

Book.		Contents.	Origin.
APOCRYPHA.	APOCALYPTIC.		
1 Maccabees		History of the Jews from the accession of Antiochus Epiphanes to the death of Simon (175–135 B.C.).	Compiled from existing sources in Hebrew by a devout Jew, between 100 and 90 B.C.
Story of Susanna		A Story in praise of the wisdom of Daniel.	Probably written to support new laws as to witnesses, *circ.* 100 B.C. An addition to the Greek text of Daniel.
Story of Bel and the Dragon			Perhaps written originally in Aramaic; an addition to the Greek text of Daniel, *circ.* 100 B.C.
Wisdom of Solomon		A Wisdom-Book inculcating the beauty of Divine Wisdom.	Written by an orthodox Alexandrian Jew, *circ.* 100–50 B.C.
Prayer of Manasses.		A Jewish Penitential Psalm.	Perhaps written in Greek—date uncertain.
	Psalms of Solomon or *Psalms of the Pharisees.*	Eighteen Psalms, containing important Messianic teaching.	Written in Hebrew by a Pharisee, 70–40 B.C., probably for use in synagogues.
	Book of Jubilees	The narrative of Genesis, rewritten from a later standpoint.	Written in Hebrew by a Palestinian Jew, *circ.* 40–10 B.C. or later.
	Secrets of Enoch	An Account of the Creation.	Written in Greek by an orthodox Alexandrian Jew between 30 B.C. and 50 A.D.
2 Esdras		An Apocalypse, containing Visions of Ezra at Babylon.	A Jewish work, probably belonging to 1st century A.D., with later Christian interpolations.

Important Events.	Date B.C.	Principal Foreign Power.	Inscriptions.
ARISTOBULUS I.	105		
ALEXANDER JANNAEUS.	104		
ALEXANDRA.	78		
HYRCANUS II and ARISTOBULUS II dispute the throne.	69		
Rise of the House of Antipater.		Roman Empire.	
Pompey enters Syria and conquers Jerusalem.	65		
Judaea divided into five districts.	57		
Antipater becomes Procurator of Judaea.	47		
HEROD, King of Judaea.	37		
Herod marries Mariamne, the last of the Hasmoneans.	35		
Herod's Temple begun.	20		
Death of Herod.	4		

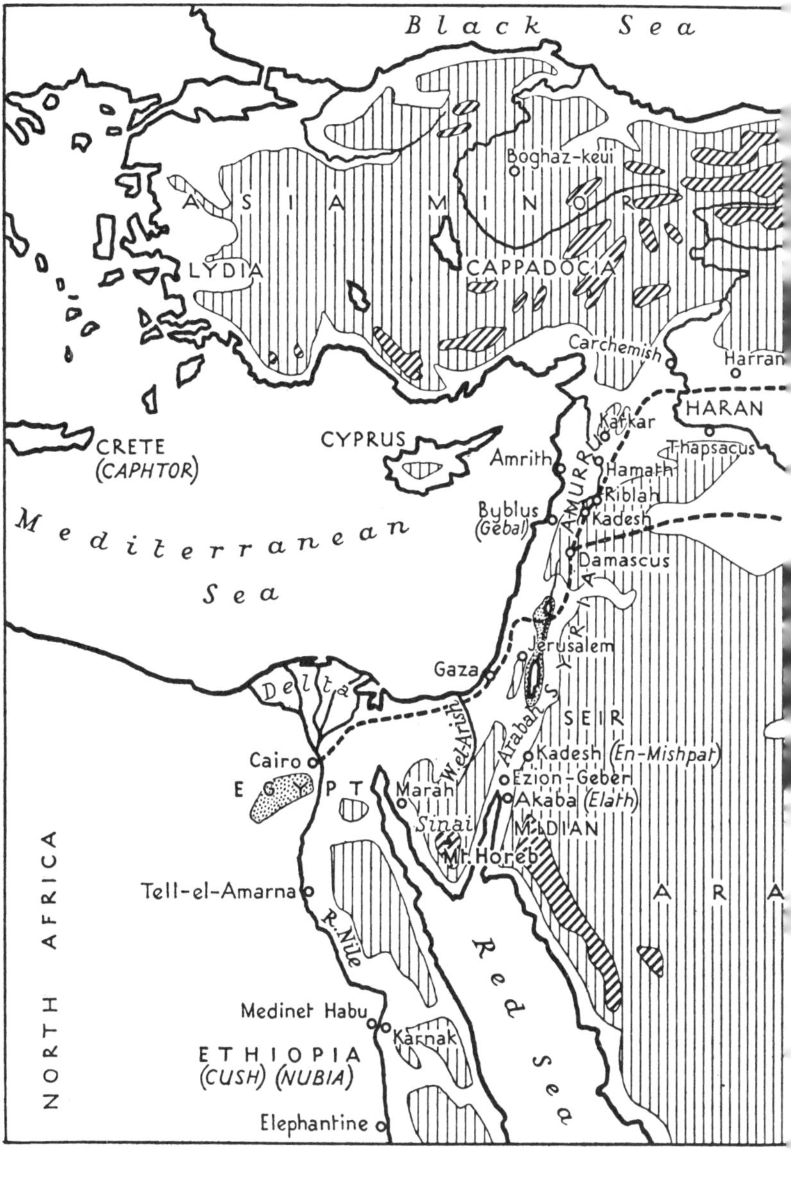

Black Sea
A S I A M I N O R
Boghaz-keui
LYDIA
CAPPADOCIA
Carchemish
Harran
HARAN
Karkar
Thapsacus
CRETE
(CAPHTOR)
CYPRUS
Amrith
AMURRU
Hamath
Riblah
Byblus
(Gebal)
Kadesh
Damascus
Mediterranean
Sea
SYRIA
Jerusalem
Gaza
Delta
Arabah
SEIR
W. el-Arish
Kadesh (En-Mishpat)
Cairo
Ezion-Geber
E G Y P T
Marah
Akaba (Elath)
Sinai
MIDIAN
Mt. Horeb
NORTH AFRICA
Tell-el-Amarna
A R A
R. Nile
Red Sea
Medinet Habu
Karnak
ETHIOPIA
(CUSH) (NUBIA)
Elephantine